U.S. Direct Investment in China

U.S. Direct Investment in China

K. C. Fung
Lawrence J. Lau
Joseph S. Lee

The AEI Press

Publisher for the American Enterprise Institute

WASHINGTON, D.C.

Available in the United States from the AEI Press, c/o Client Distribution Services, 193 Edwards Drive, Jackson, TN 38301. To order, call toll free: 1-800-343-4499. Distributed outside the United States by arrangement with Eurospan, 3 Henrietta Street, London WC2E 8LU, England.

Library of Congress Cataloging-in-Publication Data

Fung, K. C. (Kwok Chiu)
    U.S. direct investment in China/K.C. Fung, Lawrence J. Lau, Joseph
S. Lee.
        p. cm.
Includes bibliographical references and index.
    ISBN 0-8447-4106-X
    1. Investments, American—China. 2. United States—Foreign economic
relations—China. 3. China—Foreign economic relations—United States.
I. Title: United States direct investment in China. II. Lau, Lawrence
J., 1944– III. Li, Cheng, 1939– IV. Title.

    HG5782.F86 2004
    332.67'373051—dc22

                                                        2003058251

10 09 08 07 06 05 04   1 2 3 4 5 6 7

Printed in the United States of America

Contents

Illustrations

FIGURES

Foreword

I remember distinctly my first meeting with Deng Xiaoping, who at that time was China's supreme leader and great innovator. He was in many respects the bluntest and most direct foreign leader I had ever met.

At our meeting in late January 1983, we both had clear agendas. Deng Xiaoping wanted to be sure that I understood his priorities and his goals. He wanted economic development for China as rapidly as possible. And he said that meant China had a stake in forming and maintaining peaceful relationships with its neighbors. He feared the Soviet Union as he observed its menacing presence along the Chinese border and its influence in Afghanistan, in Vietnam, and in India. He viewed the United States as an important counterweight to the Soviet threat.

But he focused on economic development. He told me that although China was lagging economically, its people were enterprising and energetic. His job was to enable those instincts to assert themselves. He told me that he started with agriculture and small enterprises and that the process of development was moving forward rapidly. Most importantly, particularly in the light of materials presented in this book, he emphasized what he called China's two openings. Deng said that one opening was within China itself, and that was important, but it was not enough. China also had to open itself to the outside world, particularly to the United States. The reason, he said, was that China was backward and needed the knowledge, the technology, and the markets that the rest of the world in general and the United States in particular had to offer. He spoke bluntly and, as events since that time show, prophetically.

China's economy has expanded remarkably since that time and so have foreign trade and foreign direct investment in China. China's real GDP per capita has more than quadrupled in the two decades between

1979 and 1999. The United States has now become China's second largest trading partner and second largest direct investor. With China's entrance into the World Trade Organization, yet another major element in Deng Xiaoping's second opening is in place.

China's foreign trade has risen dramatically. Today the value of its exports of goods and services ranks tenth in the world. If China and Hong Kong are combined, the rank is fourth. China's size and increasing presence in the world mean that students of China and potential investors in or traders with China have a stake in understanding what is taking place in its economy. This book is welcome and timely, as it represents a major effort to describe and analyze direct investment from the United States in China. The authors present us with the first such comprehensive and systematic study, having used their best professional judgment to examine the reasons, the nature, and the impact of U.S. direct investment in China on both China and the United States. They base their analyses on official statistics of both the United States and China, as well as on survey data collected by private and public organizations of both countries. They have also provided comparisons of U.S. direct investment with other foreign direct investment in China, and, in a more limited way, with U.S. direct investment elsewhere.

The relationship between the United States and China is multifaceted and exceedingly complex, with elements that are as full of promise as they are of tension. Although the relationship is by no means limited to trade and investment, these economic matters are of critical importance. The following book presents a wealth of carefully assembled information on foreign and, in particular, U.S. direct investment in China. Anyone interested in this subject will find it an important reference, full of facts that can illuminate thinking about the present and the future of China's presence in the world and the implications of that presence for both the United States and China.

GEORGE P. SHULTZ
Stanford, California

Acknowledgments

We would like to thank Harry Rowen, Stephen Parker, Nancy Justin, Claude Barfield, Samuel Thernstrom, Hitomi Iizaka, June Sieh, Robert Baldwin, researchers at the Chung-Hua Institution for Economic Research and at the Hong Kong Institute of Economics and Business Strategy, and many others for their kind help and encouragement during the writing and research for this book. This research project is partially supported by funding from the American Enterprise Institute; from the Asia-Pacific Research Center of Stanford University; by a grant from the University Grants Committee of the Hong Kong Special Administrative Region, China (Project No. AoE/H-05/99); and by a research grant from the Japan Foundation Center for Global Partnership (CGP).

1

Introduction

The relationship between the United States and China is a complex one with many areas of cooperation and potential disagreement. In recent years, at least five developments have helped shape the bilateral relationships. First, since the horrific terrorist attacks of September 11, 2001, the two nations have been cooperating to combat global terrorism jointly. Second, confronted with the nuclear threats from North Korea, China has now taken the lead role to host multilateral talks to attempt to diffuse tension in the region. Both of these events have contributed to a more constructive relationship between the two nations. Third, with Taiwan seemingly going to hold a referendum on issues related to China, the cross-straits political tension will continue to be a potential obstacle to a smooth relationship between China and the United States. Fourth, in the upcoming U.S. presidential election in 2004, jobs and outsourcing to developing countries such as India, Mexico, Russia, the nations of Eastern Europe, and China will likely remain a key contentious issue. Rhetoric in the campaign can fuel negative feelings toward these economies, including China. The last event is primarily economic—China's entry into the World Trade Organization (WTO). In November 1999, the United States and China reached a landmark bilateral agreement for Chinese entrance into the WTO, with wide-ranging implications for U.S.-China trade and for U.S. direct investment in China. On May 24, 2000, the U.S. Congress passed legislation granting China permanent-normal-trade-relations (PNTR) status, a necessary condition for both the United States and China to benefit from the WTO agreement. On December 11, 2001, China officially joined the WTO and became its 143rd member.

Cooperation on global terrorism and on North Korea helps keep the two countries politically engaged. Economically, the bilateral WTO agreement substantially mended their relationship, even though many real and perceived problems still face the United States and China. This book focuses on only one important issue: the direct investment relations between the two countries.

The status of direct investment between the United States and China is important for several reasons. First, the relationship affects the economic interests of the United States. China, with a population of 1.28 billion as of year-end 2002,[1] is the largest and fastest growing emerging market. Direct investment is critical so that U.S. firms can serve and gain better access to that market. Most products produced by U.S. firms in China are sold in the Chinese market. Moreover, under the WTO agreement between the United States and China, the scope for U.S. direct investment in the service industries in China has expanded considerably.[2]

Thanks to its economic reform begun in 1979, China has become one of the fastest growing economies. Despite cycles of boom and bust, China's real gross domestic product has grown almost 10 percent annually over the 1979–2003 period. For the coastal provinces of China—from Guangdong in the south up through Fujian, Jiangsu, and Zhejiang to Shandong in the north—the average annual rates of real economic growth have been even higher, in excess of 12 percent. In 2003, Chinese GDP reached $1.34 trillion (at the market exchange rate). According to the purchasing-power-parity (PPP) exchange rates estimated by the World Bank, China is the third largest economy, after the United States and Japan. However, Chinese per-capita income has remained low, at approximately $1,047 in 2003. But with the enormous population, if even a small fraction of people can afford to purchase high-quality consumer goods, China will be a significant consumer market for both domestic and foreign firms, including U.S. multinational corporations. Moreover, the rapid economic growth, coupled with a domestic savings rate on the order of 40 percent, generates tremendous demand for fixed investment, which in turn means a large and growing demand for imported capital equipment and technology. Given that the United States is the most technologically advanced country in the world, China's increasing need of capital goods and technology transfer provides ample opportunities for U.S. firms. Compared to two decades ago, many U.S. multinationals are now doing successful business in China.[3] According to industry experts, the profit margins of

General Motors (GM) are at least twice as high on cars it makes in China as on similar models made in the United States. China is the largest cell phone market in the world. Chinese consumers also buy more photographic film than the Japanese. They also purchase as many vehicles as the Germans. According to Motorola executives in China, China has become the single most important market for mobile phone handsets and equipment, generating billions of dollars of annual revenue.

Many multinationals have shifted their focus to the Chinese *domestic* market. China is no longer just a low-cost manufacturing base for exports. Domestic retail sales indicate the potential size of the Chinese market. Retail sales in China have grown more than twenty-seven-fold since 1979. That year, the first year of China's new open door policy, total retail sales of consumer goods in China were 147.6 billion yuan or renminbi (the Chinese currency); by 2002, total retail sales of consumer goods reached 4,091 billion yuan, or $500 billion. One year after China joined the WTO, many multinational corporations were bullish about their performance in the Chinese market. According to a recent study by the International Monetary Fund (IMF), companies with operations in China earned returns of 13–14 percent on invested capital during the mid- to late 1990s.[4] Today, almost all involved companies have reaffirmed their need to stay in China. Investing in China is increasingly profitable and is a long-term strategy to gain a foothold in the large emerging market. If a company wants to be an Asia-Pacific or even a global player, it simply cannot afford *not* to be in China.

In the initial stage of Chinese economic reform, almost all foreign direct investment came from Hong Kong; most investment involved material processing and assembly. A foreign firm would subcontract part of the production process to a Chinese entity. The investment primarily intended to take advantage of China's low labor costs. Classification as processing and assembly requires that all equipment and raw materials be imported and all outputs exported. However, with the continued growth of domestic Chinese demand, and with foreign exchange availability no longer a constraint because of continuing large surpluses in current accounts, a significant proportion of foreign direct investment (FDI) in China, especially by multinational corporations, has shifted toward sales in the Chinese *domestic* market.

The East Asian currency crisis of 1997–1998 seemed to dim the growth prospects of many emerging markets, including China. But China, with its large foreign exchange reserves (more than $286.4 billion at year-end 2002) and relatively small proportion of short-term—and hence withdrawable—foreign capital, is much less vulnerable than other East Asian economies, which were severely affected by the sudden withdrawal of foreign capital from their countries. More than 95 percent of China's foreign capital inflows is in the form of foreign direct investment, which is generally more long-term in nature, rather than portfolio investment, and cannot be easily withdrawn. Short-term loans constitute no more than 32 percent of total Chinese external debt. As mentioned, much foreign direct investment from the industrialized countries is aimed at the domestic Chinese market. Thus, the East Asian currency crisis per se has not significantly affected China's attraction for long-term direct investment by industrialized countries. In fact, with China in the World Trade Organization, in the eyes of many executives, it has become the most attractive place to invest.

And although China's growth rate slowed since 1997, it remained at a high level—7.8 percent in 1998 and 7.1 percent in 1999—thanks to the increased government investment in the infrastructure. In the current year and the next several years, China will spend more than $1.2 trillion on the infrastructure to develop the western and central regions of China and stimulate the domestic consumer demand. With the recovery of other East Asian economies in 1999, Chinese economic growth also picked up—it grew 8 percent in 2000, 7.3 percent in 2001, and in 2003, it grew by 9.1 percent. China should be able to continue to grow 7–8 percent annually in the foreseeable future. Although the Chinese economy continues to face many internal problems of economic reform, its medium- and long-term prospects remain positive.

The characteristics of such foreign investment have strong implications for the bilateral trade relationship. The link between foreign investment and trade is not unique to China, but the depth of the linkage is extraordinary (a point raised by various authors; see Lardy 1994; Fung 1998). Over time foreign investment has diversified to encompass different forms of joint ventures and even wholly foreign-owned enterprises. Figure 1-1 presents the value of exports by foreign-invested enterprises (FIEs) in

FIGURE 1-1

TOTAL FIE EXPORTS, NON-FIE "PROCESSING AND ASSEMBLY" EXPORTS, AND TOTAL EXPORTS OF GOODS TO THE WORLD

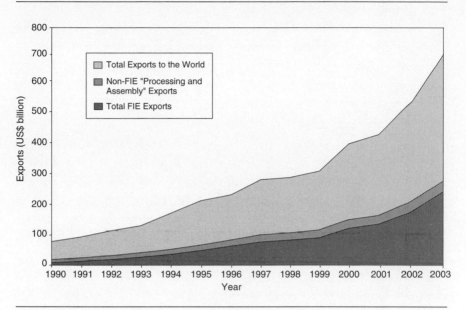

SOURCE: PRC, General Administration of Customs, Economic Information and Agency 1990–2003.

China, non-FIE processing and assembly Chinese exports, and total Chinese exports (we have estimated total processing and assembly exports for 1990–92, and for such exports from foreign-invested enterprises for 1990–94). The importance of foreign direct investment for Chinese exports is apparent. The bulk of the increase in total Chinese exports since 1990 can be attributed to the phenomenal increase in exports by foreign-invested enterprises in China. In 2003, foreign-invested enterprises in China were responsible for $240.3 billion in exports, of total Chinese exports of $438 billion. Non-FIE processing and assembly exports were responsible for another $33.3 billion. If FIE and processing and assembly exports are excluded, the average annual growth rate of Chinese exports between 1990 and 2003 would have been reduced significantly, from 16.7 percent to 11.7 percent.

Another link may exist—between a country's foreign direct investment in China and its exports of capital and intermediate goods to China.

For example, U.S.-invested enterprises that produce personal computers import critical components such as microprocessors from the United States. Foreign-invested enterprises commonly import equipment, components, and parts from parent corporations in the home countries.

Foreign direct investment and foreign subcontracting fuel trade in both directions; U.S. direct investment and subcontracting will have significant implications for U.S.-China trade and the bilateral U.S.-China trade balance. (For an analysis of the trade imbalance, see Fung and Lau 2001.) Foreign firms in China, including U.S. firms, play an important role in China's exports and imports.

Partly because of the activities of U.S. and other foreign firms, in 2003 China became the fourth largest global exporter of goods and services combined (see table 1-1).[5] Foreign direct investment helps make China a player in the world market. At the same time, the importance of foreign investment and subcontracting in China's trade raises the issue of how much economic welfare Chinese nationals can derive from its exports.[6] It will be useful to have an idea of how foreign direct investment affects the distribution of the economic benefits of exports. Since foreign firms own partly or wholly the produced output, at least a fraction of the benefits from Chinese exports will accrue to non-Chinese residents, including U.S. entrepreneurs and shareholders. For exports associated with processing and assembly, foreign firms will likely receive the bulk of the economic benefits (measured in terms of value added or employment); even if the activities are subcontracted to a wholly Chinese entity, the value added by the Chinese enterprise will be relatively small. As a rule of thumb, the processing fee earned by a local subcontractor is only 10–20 percent of the value of the exports.

Despite frequent allegations that Chinese imports, especially those exported back by U.S. firms in China, cost American jobs, empirical survey data show that the bulk of the output of U.S.-invested firms in China is sold in the Chinese domestic market. In the aggregate less than 10 percent of the output of firms with U.S. investment is exported back to the U.S. home market.

Foreign direct investment is good for China. FDI can raise China's gross domestic product and its growth rate directly by contributing to capital formation as well as adding higher quality of machinery and

TABLE 1-1
RANKING BY TOTAL OF EXPORTS OF GOODS AND SERVICES, 2003

Rank	Exporter	Commercial Services Value (US$ billion)	Merchandise Trade Value (US$ billion)	Total Value (US$ billion)	Share of World Exports (percent)
1	United States	724.0	282.5	1,006.5	10.9
2	Germany	748.4	111.7	860.0	9.3
3	Japan	471.9	70.2	542.2	5.9
4	China	438.4	44.5	482.9	5.2
5	France	384.7	98.0	482.6	5.2
6	United Kingdom	303.9	129.5	433.4	4.7
7	Italy	290.2	72.8	363.0	3.9
8	Netherlands	293.4	64.1	357.6	3.9
9	Canada	272.1	39.2	311.3	3.4
10	Belgium	254.6	41.7	296.3	3.2
11	Hong Kong, China	224.0	43.2	267.3	2.9
12	Spain	151.9	76.4	228.3	2.5
13	Korea, Republic of	194.3	31.2	225.5	2.4
14	Mexico	165.3	12.5	177.8	1.9
15	Singapore	144.1	30.4	174.6	1.9
16	Taipei, Chinese	150.6	23.0	173.6	1.9
17	Russian Federation	135.2	15.9	151.1	1.6
18	Austria	96.2	41.4	137.5	1.5
19	Switzerland	100.6	32.7	133.3	1.4
20	Sweden	100.9	31.0	131.9	1.4

SOURCE: World Trade Organization 2003.

equipment. Although foreign direct investment is a significant part of the Chinese economy, it is by no means an overwhelmingly important part. In 2002, foreign direct investment accounted for about 4 percent of China's gross industrial output, approximately 10.4 percent of gross fixed capital formation, and 10.4 percent of gross capital formation (see

FIGURE 1-2

THE SHARE OF FOREIGN DIRECT INVESTMENT IN CHINA (percent)

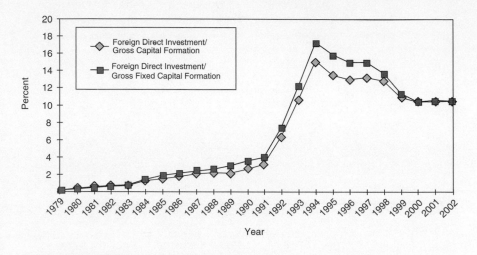

SOURCE: PRC, National Bureau of Statistics 2003.

figure 1-2). Quantitatively, foreign direct investment is not critical to China, where the high level of savings finances most domestic investment.

The potential contribution of FDI to a country such as China far exceeds its apparent quantitative importance. First, a foreign firm makes a direct investment in China and competes in an uncertain and unfamiliar environment against firms with a home-court advantage only if it has a unique competitive edge in the form of technology, trade secrets, know-how, brand name, market, or organization. That firm can do something that firms in China cannot do on their own and add more value than Chinese firms in the same line of business. Moreover, the presence of firms with foreign investment can help a country transform itself to a market economy in other ways—for example, by accelerating the process of institution building. Contacts with foreign firms and foreign markets encourage domestic producers to play by the rules of the market, not the rules of a command economy. Enterprises must meet deadlines to deliver products, pay attention to product quality, and honor signed commercial contracts. The need to compete in both the domestic and the world market will continue to be the key to raising China's productivity and economic efficiency. And foreign firms can aid in China's economic development through the transfer of technology. The United States, the most technologically advanced nation, is also one of the largest foreign direct investors in China. In 2002, according to official Chinese statistics, the United States was the second largest foreign direct investor there (excluding the Virgin Islands). As China slowly improves its capability to absorb foreign technology, it will move up the technology ladder, and the United States will become increasingly important as a potential source of technology transfer.

In the bilateral WTO agreement, China has committed itself to reducing its industrial tariffs to an average rate of 9.4 percent by 2005. In information technology, tariffs on products including computers, semiconductors, and all Internet-related equipment will drop to zero by the year 2005. For major agricultural products (beef, grapes, wine, cheese, poultry, and pork), tariffs dropped from an average level of 31.5 percent to 14.5 percent in January 2004. Moreover, China will prohibit the use of export subsidies in agriculture and will for the first time allow trade between private parties in agriculture. For the first time, foreign firms will be granted direct trading rights in industrial goods—the right to import and export directly without a Chinese state-owned trading firm as the middleman. The lowering of tariffs will encourage more U.S. exports and may reduce the incentive for some U.S. firms to locate in China simply to avoid paying the high tariff rates. Chinese accession to the WTO will also boost investors' confidence in the Chinese economy and market and may increase foreign, including U.S., direct investment. In fact, for the year 2003, realized foreign direct investment in China reached $53.51 billion.

U.S. firms will receive full rights to engage in distribution in China, including wholesale, retail, and after-sale service, repair, maintenance, and transport. They will be able to control their own distribution networks in China. The Chinese concessions to the United States open opportunities for direct investment. China is committed to opening its telecommunication sector to foreign investment. Before its entry into the WTO, China did not allow foreign investment in telecommunication services. Under the WTO accession agreement for value-added and paging services, China allowed 49 percent ownership in selective cities starting December 2002. Ownership rose to 50 percent with no geographic restriction in December 2003.

Under the WTO agreement, foreign life insurance companies can own up to 50 percent of joint ventures in China starting December 2001. Foreign life insurance companies will be able to choose their own joint-venture partners. For non–life insurance companies, China permitted 51 percent foreign ownership beginning in December 2003. Foreign insurance companies will be allowed to expand the scope of their activities to include group, health, and pension. In banking, China has allowed foreign banks to conduct local currency business with local enterprises since December 2003. Foreign banks will have the same rights as Chinese banks; China is committed to full market access for foreign and U.S. banks by 2006. With China's entry into the WTO in 2001, nonbank financial institutions can now offer automobile financing. The government will allow minority foreign-owned joint ventures to engage in fund management under the same conditions as domestic firms. As the scope of business expands for domestic firms, foreign joint-venture securities companies will be allowed the same expansion. Furthermore, one-third of the security joint ventures will be permitted to underwrite domestic equity issues and trade in international equities and all corporate and government debt issues.

The government has agreed to implement the WTO agreement on trade-related investment measures. For example, trade and foreign exchange balancing requirements and local content requirements imposed on some foreign direct investors will no longer be valid. Laws related to the transfer of technology will meet the WTO agreement on the protection of intellectual property rights.

As a part of the original WTO treaty, U.S. import quotas on Chinese textiles in the Multi-Fiber Agreement are to be completely phased out by the end of 2004. The elimination of the import quotas may stimulate more foreign textile firms to locate in China, since by that time China will have much freer market access to the United States. (China conversely has agreed to a special mechanism that permits the United States to increase tariffs— not limited to textiles—temporarily to stabilize Chinese imports in general into the United States whenever a sudden disruptive increase—a surge— threatens the welfare of the domestic U.S. producers. The safeguard measure is product specific and addresses solely imports from China. The provision will remain in effect until 2013, twelve years after China joined the WTO.)

Chinese membership in the WTO, coupled with the passage by the U.S. Congress of the permanent-normal-trade-relations status for China, will increase not only trade between the two countries, but also U.S. and other foreign direct investment through Chinese commitment to opening new sectors for potential investment.

But China's foreign sector plays a rather different role in the development of its economy than the foreign sectors in the Four Little Dragons, Hong Kong, South Korea, Singapore, and Taiwan.[7] Exports have primarily fed the growth of those economies. In contrast, China, as a large continental economy, cannot rely on exports as its main source of growth because no foreign markets large enough for the Big Dragon exist (Lau 1994; Fung 1997). China's economic growth will likely be more similar to that of the United States in the nineteenth century. Imported capital and technology combined with improvements in internal infrastructure (such as canals and railroads) and the growth of the domestic market nourished the growth of the U.S. economy. Exports were important but never as dominant as they have been for the four East Asian dragons or even Japan. From the standpoint of China's economic development, foreign direct investment, particularly from the United States, can play a similar role as it did in the earlier economic development of the United States.

2

Reasons for
U.S. Direct Investment in China

U.S. firms have made direct investments in China for several complementary reasons. In 1990 the U.S.-China Business Council surveyed 125 operating U.S.-invested enterprises in China and found that their primary goal was to penetrate the Chinese market. Other objectives were to integrate a venture in China into a company's global operations, to establish a low-cost production base to access Asian markets, and to obtain access to raw materials or natural resources (U.S.-China Business Council 1990). In another 1990 survey of 500 major U.S. corporations that invested in developing economies, favorable taxation, guaranteed remittance of earnings, projected market growth, and market size were the most important factors in selecting a country for direct investment (Wallace 1990).

Beginning in 1992, another series of surveys, conducted for the Chung-Hua Institution for Economic Research (CIER), Taipei, by the National Bureau of Statistics of the People's Republic of China, asked U.S.- and other foreign-invested firms in China for the three most important reasons for investing there. Table 2-1 summarizes their responses. The two separate surveys conducted in 1993 and 1994 (for 1992 and 1993, respectively) did not yield significantly different results. For U.S.-invested firms as well as all foreign-invested firms, an "abundant labor supply" was the most cited reason. The second reason for U.S.-invested firms was the size of the Chinese market, while the category of all foreign-invested firms considered preferential tax treatment second most important. Tax incentive programs ranked third as a reason for U.S. direct investment in China. "Cheap industrial supplies" was the fourth most important reason for U.S.-invested firms but only the sixth for all foreign-invested firms. "Low land price or rent" and "similarity in language/dialect" were relatively unimportant for U.S.-invested firms. By far the most important factors for U.S.-invested as well as foreign-invested firms were "abundant labor supply," "market size," and "tax incentive programs."

The 1993 CIER asked U.S.- and foreign-invested firms for the determining factors for the geographical location of their direct investment. U.S.-invested firms listed, in order of importance, preferential tax treatment and infrastructure (the most important factors), the quality of labor, transportation cost savings, and the availability of natural resources, including land.[1] In a complementary econometric study using data for U.S. direct investment in various regions of China from 1990 to 1999, Fung, Iizaka, Lin, and Siu (2002) found that the size of the local market, the quality of labor, and tax incentives in the Economic and Technological Development Zones (ETDZs) are the top three most important factors in determining the geographic choices of U.S. investment within China.

In 1999 the Ministry of Economy, Trade and Industry (METI) of the Japanese government conducted a survey of the motives of 1,835 Japanese manufacturing firms investing in China.[2] According to the survey, the top motive for investing in China is "to take advantage of lower costs" or "to lower their costs." The second most common motive is to expand their market shares in China, while the third most common reason to invest in China is to provide parts to firms that are already in China.[3]

Finally, in 2002, A. T. Kearny conducted a survey of the largest one thousand companies and found that China has overtaken the United States as the most favored place for foreign investors for the next few years. Furthermore, A. T. Kearny constructed a Foreign Direct Investment Confidence Index based on the survey. China had the highest score of 1.99 in 2002, with the United States having a score of 1.89, Britain 1.51, and Hong Kong 0.95. Several factors contributed to China's number one position, including its large market, continued economic growth, stable political situation, sound investment environment, membership in the World Trade Organization, and China's successful bid for the Olympics.[4] More concretely, several U.S. companies are now publicly acknowledging the importance of the *domestic* Chinese market as a source of revenue and profits. For Motorola, China has become the most important market for mobile phone handsets and equipment. While Lucent Technologies and Nortel suffer enormously in the world

TABLE 2-1

THREE MOST IMPORTANT REASONS FOR INVESTING IN CHINA, 1992 AND 1993
(percent of firms citing specified reason)

Factors	United States 1992	1993	Hong Kong 1992	1993	Japan 1992	1993
Abundant labor supply	77.1	70.1	81.9	77.6	78.2	80
Tax incentive programs	60.6	52.6	˙57.6	52.8	72.7	61.4
Market size	68.9	56.7	50.3	48.9	56.4	65.7
Low land price or rent	18.1	24.7	33.3	31.8	30.9	22.9
Similarity in language or dialect	14.8	9.3	25.2	24	7.3	14.3
Cheap industrial supplies	32.8	26.8	24.2	23.1	23.6	35.7
Customers moved to China	6.6	7.2	9.1	8.2	9.1	10
Industrial peace	1.6	5.2	4.1	4.8	5.5	4.3
Tariff and quota jumping	4.9	3.1	2.1	2.1	1.8	4.3
Low pollution abatement costs	1.6	0	2.5	2.5	0	1.4
Other	6.6	5.2	4.2	3.9	7.3	7.1
Number of cases	61	97	648	896	55	70

SOURCE: Chung-Hua Institution for Economic Research 1993, 1994.

market, they benefit from having big Chinese contracts, including a $1 billion order in 2002. According to AES, a power company based in Virginia, China is now the top cash generator for the whole corporation.[5]

Those surveys, reports, and studies highlight several commonly cited reasons why U.S. firms decide to invest in China. They also give us an impression of the relative importance of these motives. Whatever the motives of the U.S. investors, it should be noted that in order to be successful, U.S. or other foreign investors must bring something to the table. Simply having money is not enough in China. An investor must have a competitive advantage—for example, technology, market know-how, or a brand name—an advantage over both Chinese and other foreign firms.

Based on the 1990 U.S.-China Business Council survey, the 1993 and 1994 CIER surveys, and academic research on U.S. foreign direct investment

Singapore		Taiwan		Others		All	
1992	1993	1992	1993	1992	1993	1992	1993
76.2	75.9	86.5	77.7	75.8	73.4	81.9	76.9
28.6	31	49.3	41.8	56.1	49.5	56.2	50.1
71.4	72.4	45.1	43.6	60.6	55.1	32	36.3
23.8	17.2	33	28.7	25.8	22.9	31.6	29.4
38.1	31	37.2	32.7	18.2	15.6	25.9	24.1
28.6	27.6	20.9	22.4	25.8	27.5	24.2	24.1
9.5	6.9	5.6	5.4	4.5	2.8	7.9	7.2
0	0	5.6	5.4	3	5.5	4	4.8
0	0	3.7	2.3	3	1.8	2.5	2.2
0	0	2.8	2.3	0	0.9	2.2	2.1
2	6.9	6	6.3	15.2	11	5.6	5.2
21	29	215	349	66	109	1,066	1,550

in general, we discuss here the four major reasons why U.S. firms make direct investments in China: (1) preferential tax and import duty treatments given to foreign firms; (2) increasing importance of the domestic market; (3) low labor costs; and (4) availability of natural resources.

In recent years China has been trying hard to lure foreign investors and has initiated many tax and customs duty reductions and exemptions for foreign direct investors. As chapter 3 details, while the general profit tax rate in China is 33 percent, U.S.- and other foreign-invested firms located in special economic zones, open coastal cities, economic and technology districts, open economic cities, and open economic areas can receive substantial reductions and/or exemptions. (See chapter 3 for definitions of those terms.) For example, within the special economic zones, foreign-invested firms are taxed at a 15 percent rate instead of the general 33 percent rate.

Firms with a contract term of more than ten years pay no taxes the first two years in which they make a profit. For the subsequent three years, the tax rate is reduced by half, to 7.5 percent (Chung-Hua Institution for Economic Research 1996; Cheng 1995; Ouyang 1997). The tax reduction and exemption of profit are not confined to foreign-invested firms located in special economic zones; the same rule applies to foreign-invested firms located in open coastal cities and economic and technology districts. Between 1994 and 1996, U.S.- and other foreign-invested firms in those regions could have received value-added tax (VAT) rebates of 17 percent and might have paid no import duties on machinery and equipment and raw materials and parts. With China's joining the WTO, however, it is expected that eventually national treatment will prevail; that is, China will have to apply the same tax rates toward domestic and foreign firms.

The preferential tax treatment given to foreign investors by China provides the incentives to locate in China as opposed to other countries. According to the CIER surveys, 87 percent of the U.S. firms in China received an exemption of the profit tax, 44.3 percent of the U.S. firms surveyed received an exemption or a reduction of customs duties, and 37.7 percent received an exemption of the local tax. Not only U.S. and other foreign firms take advantage of the favorable treatments; some Chinese capital is also transferred to Hong Kong and elsewhere illegally and recycled into China. The *round-tripping* allows the capital to be designated foreign so that the investment, though originally Chinese, can take advantage of the preferential treatment accorded to foreign-invested enterprises (Fung and Lau 1996; Fung 1996).

In April 1996 the exemptions and reductions concerning the VAT and import duties on machinery and equipment were eliminated. Smaller projects with contracts signed between October 1, 1995, and December 31, 1997, enjoyed a grace period and continued to receive the VAT and import duty exemptions. The policy shift partly reflected China's desire to implement international norms and standards in its treatment of foreign investors and to move closer toward the application of the principle of national treatment—that is, offering the same treatment to both domestic and foreign investors. Facing a spreading global financial crisis in 1998 and a slowdown in foreign direct investment from other East Asian countries, the Chinese government reinstated the exemptions, reductions, and

TABLE 2-2

PER-CAPITA GROSS DOMESTIC PRODUCT IN CHINA BY PROVINCE, MUNICIPALITY, AND AUTONOMOUS REGION, SELECTED YEARS (US$)

Location	1995	1996	1997	1998	2000	2001	2002
Shanghai	2,255 (1)	2,684 (1)	3,102 (1)	3,412 (1)	4,162 (1)	4,504 (1)	4,907 (1)
Beijing	1,556 (2)	1,813 (2)	2,016 (2)	2,232 (2)	2,706 (2)	3,075 (2)	3,351 (2)
Tianjin	1,227 (3)	1,478 (3)	1,662 (3)	1,788 (3)	2,168 (3)	2,428 (3)	2,265 (3)
Zhejiang	961 (4)	1,139 (5)	1,267 (4)	1,358 (4)	1,622 (4)	1,766 (4)	2,001 (4)
Guangdong	949 (5)	1,146 (4)	1,256 (5)	1,345 (5)	1,552 (5)	1,654 (5)	1,800 (5)
Jiangsu	869 (6)	1,018 (6)	1,126 (6)	1,210 (7)	1,418 (6)	1,557 (6)	1,739 (6)
Fujian	829 (7)	980 (7)	1,115 (7)	1,252 (6)	1,398 (7)	1,489 (7)	1,632 (7)
Liaoning	819 (8)	931 (8)	1,027 (8)	1,127 (8)	1,353 (8)	1,451 (8)	1,570 (8)
Shandong	685 (9)	823 (9)	914 (9)	981 (9)	1,151 (9)	1,261 (9)	1,406 (9)
Heilongjiang	651 (10)	779 (10)	873 (10)	911 (10)	1,032 (10)	1,126 (10)	1,236 (10)
National average	578	672	729	762	853	909	960

SOURCE: PRC, National Bureau of Statistics 1996b, 1997, 1998, 1999, 2001, 2002, 2003; Asian Development Bank 1996, 1997, 1999, 2001, 2002, 2003.

NOTE: The figures in parentheses are the respective rankings by per-capita gross domestic product for that year. Average annual official exchange rates were used to convert yuan to US$: For 1998, 2000, 2001, and 2002, we used US$1 = 8.28 yuan; for 1997 and 1996, we used US$1 = 8.3 yuan; for 1995, US$1 = 8.4 yuan.

rebates but extended its application to domestic enterprises as well to spur more investment, both foreign and domestic, in China. There have been recent reports that the separate tax systems applied to both domestic and foreign firms will be unified by the year 2005.

Second, U.S. firms invest in China to gain access to the rapidly growing Chinese domestic market. Although the per-capita income of China is still low ($1,047 in 2003), total retail sales of consumer goods have risen more than twenty-seven-fold between 1978 and 2002 and reached an aggregate value of $500 billion. But looking at the national per-capita income and retail sales alone is likely to be misleading because different regions in China have grown at different rates. Table 2-2 highlights the ten provinces, municipalities, and autonomous regions with the highest per-capita gross domestic product in selected years.

As the table indicates, the regional differentials are large. The average per-capita income of Shanghai ($4,907) in 2002 is more than five times that of China's average ($960); the average per-capita income of Beijing ($3,351) is more than three times the national average. Those high-income urbanized regions are of most interest to U.S. firms. Another indicator of the relative importance of different regions as markets for consumer goods is the total retail sales of the goods in each region. Table 2-3 documents the size and the rank of various regional consumer markets.

The regions with the highest retail sales of consumer goods coincide with those with the highest rates of growth of real GDP since the adoption of the open door policy in 1978. In terms of the effective size of the markets, the regions are the most likely ones where U.S. and other foreign consumer goods can be sold. Table 2-3 indicates that in 2002 Guangdong was the top region in terms of retail sales of consumer products. The coastal provinces of Jiangsu, Shandong, and Zhejiang were the second, third, and fourth largest consumer markets, respectively. The top-ranked regions seemed constant. Guangdong, Jiangsu, Shandong, and Zhejiang have been the top four largest consumer markets in China since 1995.

Certain industries hold particular promise for U.S. firms. China is projected to be the world's largest semiconductor market in ten to fifteen years (Howell, Nuechterlein, and Hester 1995). In fact, according to estimates by the American Electronics Association (AeA), China is already the third largest semiconductor market in the world. It is expected to become the second largest market by 2010 (AeA 2001). The semiconductor industry is a highly cyclical industry. Since 2003 it has recovered from the global slump induced by the East Asian currency crisis of 1997 and the burst of the technology bubble in the United States since 2000. The upward trend for longer-term growth is clear. The size of the semiconductor market in

TABLE 2-3

TOTAL RETAIL SALES OF CONSUMER GOODS BY PROVINCE, MUNICIPALITY, AND AUTONOMOUS REGION, SELECTED YEARS (US$ billion)

Location	1995	1997	1998	2000	2001	2002
Guangdong	27.4	35.2	39.2	49.1	54.4	60.6
	(1)	(1)	(1)	(1)	(1)	(1)
Jiangsu	19.6	25.5	27.0	31.4	34.6	38.8
	(2)	(2)	(2)	(2)	(2)	(2)
Shandong	17.2	23.1	25.7	30.7	34.2	38.4
	(3)	(3)	(3)	(3)	(3)	(3)
Zhejiang	16.6	21.2	23.1	27.7	30.8	34.8
	(4)	(4)	(4)	(4)	(4)	(4)
Liaoning	13.4	17.5	18.9	22.3	24.5	27.3
	(6)	(5)	(5)	(5)	(5)	(5)
Hubei	11.1	16.2	17.9	21.6	23.8	26.6
	(8)	(7)	(7)	(6)	(7)	(6)
Henan	10.8	16.4	18.1	21.5	23.9	26.4
	(9)	(6)	(6)	(7)	(6)	(7)
Shanghai	11.5	16.0	17.8	20.8	22.4	24.6
	(7)	(8)	(8)	(8)	(8)	(8)
Hebei	10.1	14.4	16.1	19.4	21.4	23.8
	(10)	(10)	(9)	(9)	(9)	(9)
Sichuan	15.5	14.6	15.7	18.4	20.2	22.3
	(5)	(9)	(10)	(10)	(10)	(10)

SOURCE: PRC, National Bureau of Statistics 1996b, 1998, 1999, 2001, 2002, 2003; Asian Development Bank 1996, 1997, 1999, 2001, 2002, 2003.

NOTE: Figures in parentheses are the ranks of each region by total sales of consumer goods for each respective year. Yuan are converted into US$ with the average annual official exchange rate for that year.

China in 1994 was estimated at $2–3 billion. The rate of growth of the market increased 10–20 percent until the onset of the East Asian currency crisis. Domestic semiconductor manufacturers supply approximately 20 percent of the Chinese market, primarily in standardized commodity chips or semiconductors at the low end of the quality spectrum. All high-quality semiconductors come from foreign firms. In the intermediate to long term the semiconductor market represents an excellent opportunity for increased sales by U.S. companies.

Another industry with a large market for U.S. firms is the commercial aircraft and aerospace goods industry. During the visit of Chinese President Jiang Zemin to Washington in October 1997, China signed a contract with Boeing to purchase fifty aircraft at a cost of $3 billion. In the year 2000, the aerospace industry had a trade surplus of $1.7 billion with China. As of July 2001, Chinese airlines operated 548 jet aircraft, 357 of which were made by U.S. manufacturers. Over the next twenty years, the Aerospace Industries Association (AIA) of America forecasts that China (including Hong Kong and Macau) will need 1,764 jetliners, worth a total of $144 billion. In the same period, AIA believes that China will become the second largest market for airplanes in the world (AIA 2001).

Foreign direct investment is one way to gain access to the Chinese market, but exporting from factories in the United States to China is another. Why do some U.S. firms locate their production facilities in China to sell in China? One reason is the so-called tariff-jumping motive. Some firms located in China to avoid paying the high duties imposed on imports into China. Before October 1997 the average tariff rate in China was 23 percent; beginning October 1, 1997, import tax rates on 4,800 commodities were reduced and lowered the average tariff rate to 17 percent (Ouyang 1997). Under the U.S.-China bilateral WTO agreement, tariffs will be further reduced to average levels of 9.4 percent and 17.5 percent for industrial products and agricultural products, respectively. With China's joining the WTO in December 2001, average tariff rates for industrial products actually were cut to 8.9 percent, while average tariff rates for agricultural products were cut to 15 percent. Most tariff reductions will be completed by 2004, and the final tariff cuts must be in place no later than 2010 (WTO 2003). While the reduction makes the average tariff rate more tolerable, the tariff still represents an additional cost to U.S. exporters. Table 2-1 indicates that "tariff and quota jumping" was near the bottom of reasons for direct investment in China, even though it was more important for U.S. firms compared with other foreign firms.

Another reason indicated in the surveys is to achieve lower transportation costs. As a rule of thumb, transportation costs (including insurance) represent 10 percent of the value of the goods exported. Ever since China joined the WTO, a good reason for U.S. firms to locate in China is to save, on average, 18.9 percent on the costs of exporting industrial products to China (average tariff rate plus the average transportation margin) and 25 percent on agricultural products. Nevertheless, the tariff-jumping motive for investing in China is becoming far less important.

A third factor influencing decisions to invest in China is its abundant supply of cheap labor. China represents an "unlimited" supply of labor (particularly low-wage, low-skilled labor) to U.S. multinationals. (China is also a potential source of low-cost engineering and scientific manpower.) With its low wages China can be an important part of a U.S. company's global production network strategy and can increase its profits. Products produced in China can be sold in China, exported to other Asian countries, or even exported to the United States. The average annual wage for staff and workers in China in 2002 was approximately $1,500, or $125 per month. In regions with rapid economic growth and strong consumer demand, the average labor costs can be higher. Table 2-4 highlights the average monthly wage rates of staff and workers in the ten regions with the highest average monthly wage rates.

In 2002, Tibet had the highest labor costs in China, followed by Shanghai, Beijing, Zhejiang, and Guangdong. The high wage rate of Tibet is attributable to the high cost of living: Its unique geographical location causes most daily necessities to carry high transport costs. However, even if we take the average monthly wage rate of Shanghai, the highest wage region in China in 2000, that $186.10 is still low compared with rates in other developing economies. The average hourly wage rate in Mexico in 2000 was four to five dollars. A standard forty-hour workweek would work out to $160–200 per week, or an average monthly wage of $640–800, a figure much higher than the 2000 wage rate of $186.10 in even a high-wage region such as Shanghai. Aside from Tibet, the five regions with the highest monthly wage rates in 2002 happen to be the five regions with the highest gross domestic product per capita in 1995–2002 (see table 2-2).

In 2002 the top five destinations of U.S. direct investment in China were (in order of the amount of contracted direct investment) Jiangsu, Shandong, Liaoning, Guangdong, and Shanghai (see chapter 5). Those top destinations are among the top nine regions in China in terms of per-capita GDP (see table 2-2) and include four of the top five regions in terms of total retail sales of consumer goods (see table 2-3). They also

TABLE 2-4
**AVERAGE MONTHLY WAGE OF STAFF AND WORKERS
BY REGION, SELECTED YEARS** (US$)

Location	1995	1996	1998	2000	2001	2002
Tibet	73.2	111.3	110.6	150.4	192.2	249.3
	(4)	(1)	(4)	(3)	(3)	(1)
Shanghai	92.1	107.1	136.7	186.1	218.7	241.1
	(1)	(2)	(1)	(1)	(1)	(2)
Beijing	80.8	96.2	125.3	164.2	192.3	220.0
	(3)	(3)	(2)	(2)	(2)	(3)
Zhejiang	65.7	74.4	98.2	131.3	164.5	189.1
	(5)	(6)	(6)	(5)	(4)	(4)
Guangdong	81.8	91.6	111.0	138.8	157.4	179.3
	(2)	(4)	(3)	(4)	(5)	(5)
Tianjin	64.5	76.7	100.1	125.3	143.7	163.6
	(6)	(5)	(5)	(6)	(6)	(6)
Qinghai	57.1	65.4	80.6	100.9	129.6	145.7
	(9)	(9)	(9)	(9)	(7)	(7)
Jiangsu	59.0	66.3	83.1	103.4	118.9	136.0
	(7)	(8)	(8)	(8)	(9)	(8)
Fujian	58.1	67.1	85.9	106.3	120.6	133.9
	(8)	(7)	(7)	(7)	(8)	(9)
Yunnan	51.1	62.6	77.2	92.7	105.8	120.6
	(14)	(10)	(10)	(10)	(10)	(10)

SOURCE: PRC, National Bureau of Statistics 1996b, 1997, 1999, 2001, 2002, 2003; Asian Development Bank 1996, 2001, 2002, 2003.

NOTE: Figures in parentheses represent the rank by wages by regions for that year. To convert yuan into US$, we used the average annual official exchange rate for that year.

include three of the top eight regions with the highest wage rates (see table 2-4). Low wage rates may not be as strong a location factor as proximity to potential markets for U.S. firms.

Moreover, although labor costs in China may be low, the cost of sending expatriate professionals to China can be high. A typical compensation package for an expatriate in China was reported to be $250,000–350,000 per year. The need for expatriates has been increasing. According to a 1995 survey of 138 companies, China was the emerging overseas destination to which employees were most often sent (Melvin and Sylvester 1997). Despite the high cost of expatriates, using local Chinese staff, especially at the senior management level, is not considered practical. But the low cost of labor in China must be enough to offset the high cost of expatriates, as U.S. and other foreign firms continue to invest in China.

As a final reason, U.S. firms invest in China to exploit untapped natural resources, including petroleum. U.S. firms have invested a fairly large amount in that type of activity. In 2001 and 2002, U.S. firms invested $1.774 billion and $2.059 billion, respectively, in the mining and utilities industry in China, or 15.6 percent and 20 percent of the total U.S. direct investment. Because China is still a developing economy, its vast amounts of natural resources and minerals have yet to be fully exploited. As chapter 3 details, investment in mining and utilities often takes the form of joint development in which the foreign firm and the Chinese government or firm jointly make arrangements to explore and extract these resources.

3

Institutional and Legal Framework of FDI in China

Since the adoption of the "open door" policy as part of its economic reform in 1979, China has accepted and welcomed foreign direct investment. In 1980 China established the four special economic zones (SEZs)—Shantou, Shenzhen, Xiamen, and Zhuhai—on its southern coast as locations for FDI. China has since enacted an elaborate web of laws governing the operation of foreign direct investment in the country. In 1986 China issued the Provisions of the State Council of the People's Republic of China for the Encouragement of Foreign Investment. The law offers privileges to foreign enterprises that export or introduce advanced technology to China. However, with China in the WTO, the different tax systems facing foreign and domestic firms will have to be harmonized. It is reported that the tax harmonization will be implemented by 2005. By the end of 2002 the government had signed more than 420,000 FDI contracts. Hong Kong is still by far the largest foreign direct investor, both by the value of foreign direct investment (contracted and realized) and by the number of foreign direct investment contracts. Investment is overwhelmingly concentrated in the coastal provinces and municipalities in eastern and southern China.

Types of FDI

Under current Chinese laws, five types of foreign direct investment are allowed: Sino-foreign equity joint venture (EJV), Sino-foreign contractual (or cooperative) joint venture (CJV), wholly foreign-owned enterprise

(WFO), joint development (JD), and, since 1995, foreign-funded joint-stock limited company.

Sino-Foreign Equity Joint Venture. A Sino-foreign equity joint venture is a limited-liability company incorporated in China, in which foreign and Chinese investors each hold equities. Many laws and regulations govern the EJV (as well as other modes of FDI). More than five hundred laws and regulations at all levels of government pertain to the operations of FDI in China. Among the more important are the Law on Joint Ventures Using Chinese and Foreign Investment (adopted July 1, 1979, and amended April 4, 1990), the Foreign Economic Contract Law of 1985, Provisions for Encouragement of Foreign Investment (the Twenty-Two Articles) of 1986, and the 2001 revised Law of the People's Republic of China on Chinese-Foreign-Equity Joint Ventures.

Numerous other regulations concern land use rights, customs tariffs, labor management, and technology transfers. The special economic zones and open coastal cities have issued their own laws that at times appear to contradict national laws. A later section discusses how the *implementation* of those laws can differ significantly in various locations and in different contexts.

The Sino-foreign equity joint venture usually has a term of fifty years, but the term can be extended. An EJV in some favored industries may enjoy an unlimited period of operation. Profits derived from the joint venture are shared according to the proportion of capital contributions. The equity joint venture may be terminated only by agreement of the investors as well as the approval of the original investment approval authority. Investors are typically restricted from withdrawing their registered capital during the life of the contract. A minimum of 25 percent of the original capital must be provided by the foreign partner.

Sino-Foreign Contractual Joint Venture. This form of joint venture is also called Sino-foreign cooperative joint venture. As the name suggests, the terms of specific contracts primarily define the Sino-foreign contractual joint venture. Unlike the Sino-foreign equity joint venture, sharing profits as well as risks need not be related to the share of capital contributed by each partner. No requirement details how much the foreign partner must contribute. The organization of the firm, the management, and the handling of the assets are flexible. Each partner can contribute capital as well as other inputs such as labor, mineral resources, or services. Foreign investors can withdraw their original capital during the life of the contract. The venture has no prescribed duration. In 2000 the Chinese government revised the Law of the People's Republic of China on Chinese-Foreign Contractual Joint Ventures. The revisions were done to be consistent with the general WTO framework. For instance, restrictions with respect to the balance of foreign exchange and expenditure and the requirement of local content were eliminated.

Wholly Foreign-Owned Enterprise. China allows total foreign ownership in industries in which foreign investment is considered beneficial to the country's economic development. Historically China has permitted, but not encouraged, this mode of FDI. To qualify as a WFO, the foreign investor must employ advanced technology and equipment, develop new products, use energy and raw materials economically, or upgrade products already existing in the country. Alternatively the value of the products exported each year must account for more than 50 percent of the total value of the products produced, and the foreign exchange account must show a balance or a surplus. As in the case of the Sino-foreign contractual joint ventures, in 2000 the Chinese government revised the Law of the People's Republic of China on Wholly Foreign-Owned Enterprises to be more consistent with the rules of the WTO.

To a foreign investor, the main advantage of a wholly foreign-owned enterprise is autonomy of operations, important if the investor wants to integrate its Chinese venture into its global operations. Such autonomy also facilitates some transactions that minimize tax liabilities, such as transfer-pricing, whereas a joint-venture partner with dissimilar financial interests complicates the same functions. For a foreign investor unfamiliar with local market conditions (including the Chinese output and input markets), the main disadvantage of a wholly foreign-owned enterprise is the lack of a Chinese partner that can provide the necessary local contacts and information.

Joint Development. A joint development venture is also referred to as a cooperative development venture. A JD is typically set up between a

Chinese corporation or a ministry under the Chinese central government and one or more foreign partners to explore and develop natural resources such as coal, oil, and natural gas. The arrangement creates no new legal entities. Typically the foreign partner must shoulder all risks and costs of exploration. The foreign partner receives compensation in the share form of output (for example, oil). The venture normally bears production costs, which are deducted from income before the foreign partner is compensated. The JD is generally not an important form of foreign direct investment in China—though fairly significant for recent U.S. direct investment. For example, cumulatively U.S. firms invested $2.059 billion in the mining and utilities industry by 2002, or 20 percent of total U.S. direct investment in China up to that year.

Foreign-Funded Joint-Stock Limited Company. Laws also provide for the establishment of foreign-funded joint-stock limited companies. Foreign companies, enterprises, or individuals (foreign shareholders) can set up such a company jointly with Chinese companies, enterprises, or individuals (Chinese shareholders). According to the Provisional Regulations on the Establishment of Foreign-Funded Joint-Stock Limited Companies (promulgated by the Ministry of Foreign Trade and Economic Cooperation, or MOFTEC, January 10, 1995), the capital stock of a typical limited company is made up of equal-value shares contributed by both Chinese and foreign shareholders. The foreign shareholders own at least 25 percent of the total value of the shares. The company is a legal entity and considered a foreign-invested enterprise (all laws relevant to foreign-invested enterprises apply). A limited company can be established by promotion or by public offering. It must set up a board of directors and a board of supervisors. Foreign-funded enterprises (Sino-foreign equity joint ventures, Sino-foreign contractual joint ventures, and wholly foreign-owned enterprises) can apply to transform themselves into limited companies. The companies can issue shares (such as B shares) in China as well as overseas—and can raise capital through the issuance of additional shares. The form of organization is closer in spirit to the modern public firm found in the United States or Western Europe. Shareholders' interests are supposed to play a dominant role (Hong Kong 1996b).

Special Economic Zones, Open Cities, and Open Coastal Areas

Guangdong and Fujian were the first provinces given permission to accept FDI. In 1979 and 1980, four special economic zones were set up. The original four SEZs were Shantou, Shenzhen, and Zhuhai in the Province of Guangdong, and Xiamen in the Province of Fujian. The SEZs adopted Hong Kong's traditional corporate income or profit tax rate of 15 percent, perhaps in part to attract investors from Hong Kong, the bulk of the initial foreign investors. Until 1984 the standard tax rate applied to foreign investors was 15 percent inside the SEZs but 30 percent outside the SEZs. In addition, until 1996, customs duties on equipment and raw materials used by foreign enterprises in the SEZs were also exempted. The exemption was eliminated in 1996, in part because of a desire to implement the international norm of national treatment—that is, treating both domestic and foreign firms the same way. In 1998, with a continued global financial crisis and weakened export markets and foreign direct investment inflows, the tax exemptions were reinstated with the same privileges extended to qualified domestic enterprises. As mentioned earlier, those tax privileges will be made consistent with the tax system facing domestic enterprises to meet the requirement of national treatment under the WTO.

In 1984 fourteen open coastal cities (OCCs) were set up: Tianjin, Qinhuangdao, Dalian, Shanghai, Nantong, Lianyungang, Ningbo, Wenzhou, Fuzhou, Qingdao, Yantai, Guangzhou, Zhanjiang, and Beihai (Fung 1997). In 1984 twelve economic and technology districts (ETDs) were set up, which also used a 15 percent profit-tax rate to lure industrial enterprises. Foreign-invested enterprises could receive the same treatment in those districts as in the SEZs. Then in 1985 open coastal economic areas (OCEAs) were set up in the Yangtze River Delta, Pearl River Delta, and Fujian River Delta. Two years later Liaodong Peninsula and Shandong Peninsula also became OCEAs. In the areas the tax rate on profits was typically 24 percent. The open coastal economic areas had more favorable tax rates than the inland areas but less favorable tax rates than the SEZs and the ETDs.

In 1988, Hainan Island became the fifth SEZ, and in 1990, the Shanghai area (Pudong New Zone) was designated to offer attractive terms to foreign investors. In 1992, in response to the high-profile visit of the late Deng Xiaoping to southern China and his encouragement of deeper economic reforms, six cities along the Yangtze River (called the open cities along the Yangtze) and eighteen capital cities of autonomous regions and provinces (called the open provincial and regional capital cities) were also given the freedom to offer more attractive terms to foreign investors (Cheng 1995). Sometimes the areas distinguished between *productive* and *nonproductive* direct investment, applying different profit tax rates to each. A productive investment project involves industrial manufacturing and excludes investment projects in agriculture or in service industries such as tourism (Zheng 1993). According to an empirical study by Fung, Iizaka, Lin, and Siu (2002), for the years 1990–99, U.S. direct investments did respond significantly to ETDs. However, there is no evidence that SEZs and OCCs significantly influence U.S. direct investment in China.

In theory SEZs are the most open areas, followed by the OCCS and then by the OCEAs. But in practice the preferential policies gradually spread to many other areas and situations. For example, the 15 percent tax rate on profits was used outside SEZs for enterprises that engaged in high technology, for ventures with an investment greater than $30 million, and for investments in energy, transportation, and port facilities (Sung 1991). Table 3-1 compares the tax treatments for foreign direct investment in the different areas of China. As indicated, some tax rules are being revised. For example, tariff exemptions for imports of machinery and equipment into China by foreign direct investors and joint ventures were eliminated in 1996. But in 1998 they were reinstated to stimulate more economic activities. With China in the WTO, reports indicate that by 2005, incentives applicable specifically to foreign firms will be extended to all firms, domestic and foreign, under the principle of national treatment.

The New FDI Guidelines and Industrial Policy

In 1995, the passage of a set of important laws concerning foreign direct investment seemed to indicate a substantial change in China's FDI policy. The laws were the Interim Provisions on Guidance for Foreign Investment and its companion, Guiding Catalogue of Industries for Foreign Investment

TABLE 3-1

TAX TREATMENT FOR FDI IN DIFFERENT AREAS OF CHINA

	Special Economic Zones and Pudong New Zone
Profit tax rate	15%
Profit tax exemption and reduction	For enterprises with a term of more than 10 years, no taxes paid for the first 2 profitable years; tax rate reduced to 7.5% for the subsequent 3 years
Scope of exemption and reduction of consolidated industry and commerce taxes (CT), value-added tax (VAT), and import duty	No CT on exports except crude oil, refined petroleum products, and other products specified by the government No import duties on machinery and equipment, raw materials and parts, etc., needed by the enterprises No CT on imported machinery and equipment, raw materials, parts, transport equipment, and all other inputs needed for production; CT on all other imports reduced by 50% CT replaced by VAT in 1994; for exports resulting from processing and assembly, VAT rebate of 17%, reduced to 9% in 1996, but increased to 17% in 1999 For joint ventures formed after April 1, 1996, imported machinery and equipment subjected to all taxes and tariffs[a]
Lane use fees	5 yuan per square meter No fee for rural counties if foreign investment for infrastructure and conversion of coastal beaches and swamps

SOURCE: Chung-Hua Institution for Economic Research 1994; Cheng 1995; Fung and Lau 1997; Silver 1997; Howell, Nuechterlein, and Hester 1995.

Open Coastal Cities and Economic and Technology Districts	Other Open Economic Cities and Areas
For productive and scientific-research related projects: 24% For nonproductive projects: 30%	Sino-foreign equity joint ventures: 30% Sino-foreign contractual joint ventures and wholly foreign-owned enterprises: 20–40% plus 10% local profit tax
Same rules as SEZs	No exemption
Same rules as SEZs	Same rules as SEZs
For export-oriented industries: no fee for 10 years, then 5 yuan per square meter For advanced technology enterprises: no fee for 5–10 years, then 5 yuan per square meter For other industrial enterprises, warehousing, and transportation enterprises: 10 yuan per square meter For commercial, residential, and office buildings: 12 yuan per square meter For investment in commerce, services, and tourism: 15 yuan per square meter	1–15 yuan per square meter Export-oriented and high-technology industries possibly exempted for 5 years High-technology development projects possibly exempted Investment in energy, port facilities, infrastructure, and conversion of beaches and swamps possibly exempted Investment in education, culture, science and technology, medical and health care, and other social welfare services possibly given special treatment

a. Projects signed October 1, 1995, through December 31, 1997, and valued less than US$30 million enjoyed a grace period. Imports of related capital equipment are still tax- and tariff-free.

(both promulgated jointly by the State Planning Commission, the State Economic and Trade Commission, and the Ministry of Foreign Trade and Economic Cooperation on June 20, 1995). China, like many developing countries earlier, wanted to attract high-technology FDI; the set of laws seemed to codify that vision. But some observers believe that the laws were disguised FDI-related industrial policy (Cheng 1995; Silver 1997). Other analysts believe that China, in an effort to join the World Trade Organization, was moving away from preferences given to FDI in some geographic areas. For example, the termination (since rescinded) of tax and import duty exemptions on the imports of capital equipment by foreign-invested firms in 1996 can be interpreted as a way of implementing the principle of national treatment under the WTO; that is, applying the same treatment to both domestic and foreign investors.

The most recent changes to the guidelines occurred in March 2002, when the State Development Planning Commission, the State Economic and Trade Commission, and the Ministry of Foreign Trade and Economic Cooperation promulgated the Catalogue for the Guidance of Foreign Investment Industries, which was approved by the State Council. The previous 1997 catalogue was abrogated at the same time. According to the new guidelines, for FDI purposes industries (and related economic activities) would continue to be classified into four categories: encouraged, permitted, restricted, and prohibited. Any industry or activity that was not encouraged, restricted, or prohibited would automatically fall in the permitted category. A permitted FDI project does not enjoy preferential administrative, legal, and tax treatments. The new catalog increased the number of projects in the encouraged category from 186 to 262. It also decreased those in the restricted category from 112 to 75. The catalogue contained provisions to encourage foreign investment in the western and interior regions. For example, the type and number of industries allowed in the interior regions will be more relaxed. Furthermore, certain service industries will be open to foreign investment, in accordance with the provisions of the WTO.

The government encourages projects with new agricultural technology; those developing energy, transportation, and key raw materials; projects with new and advanced technology; those meeting the demands of the international market; projects tapping human and natural resources in the central and western regions; and projects using recyclable resources and new technology in pollution control. The list of specified industries includes engineering plastics and plastic alloys, high-quality paper and cardboard, textile weaving and dyeing, large equipment for railway construction, construction and management of nuclear power stations, microelectronics technology, design of integrated circuits and large-scale production of integrated circuits, manufacture of recordable compact disks, manufacture of telecommunication system equipment, design and manufacture of civilian planes, and construction of nuclear-power plants.

Projects that are restricted include those that adopt out-of-date technologies and projects that are unfavorable to ecological environmental improvement. Explicitly restricted industries include production of cigarettes, production of Vitamin B1 and B2, satellite television receivers, distribution and sale of audiovisual products, foreign trade companies, and bank and finance companies.

Prohibited projects include enterprises that jeopardize state security, pollute, or involve products made with China's proprietary technical processes or technology. The prohibited industries include processing of green tea, postal services, construction of power network, and weapons manufacturing. However, as a result of China's accession to the WTO, many sectors, such as telecommunications, financial services, and distribution, will also gradually open. In the telecommunications industry, as of the end of 2003, China permits up to 50 percent foreign equity share for value-added services (such as Internet services) and paging services.

The Chinese government has issued occasional industry-specific directives that seem aimed at improving the competitiveness of domestic Chinese producers. National guidelines set up in 1997 restrict the extent of foreign market shares in the domestic beer and machinery industries. The Ministry of Machine Industry was reported to have an internal list of seventy-seven enterprises that are to remain wholly Chinese-owned. Unconfirmed reports in 1997 indicated that the ministry plans to place quotas and import licenses on certain machinery products (Silver 1997).

The State Council recently announced policies to shore up support for the domestic film company, China Lucky Film Corporation. The policies under consideration include reduced tariffs for imports of inputs and state loans. Starting July 1, 1997, new tariffs imposed on beer, photographic film, and videocassette recorders were reportedly intended to provide more protection for domestic firms (Silver 1997).

Although China seemed to be moving toward protecting its domestic enterprises, other measures aimed at liberalizing the market. On December 1, 1996, China made its currency convertible for the settlement of current accounts (Fung and Lau 1997). Foreign exchange may be freely bought and sold in the market to facilitate export and import of goods and services. The change eases transactions for many foreign direct investors. The yuan or renminbi does remain nonconvertible for settling capital accounts. And the East Asian currency crisis of 1997–98 demonstrated that keeping the yuan nonconvertible for capital accounts was a wise move on the part of the Chinese economic policymakers.

In early 1997 the Chinese government approved the first joint Sino-foreign insurance company, Zhong Hong Life, a joint venture between the Hong Kong subsidiary of Canada's Manulife Financial and China International Trust and Investment Corporation. Other foreign insurance companies also operate in China, including the American Insurance Group (AIG), Aetna, and Tokio Fire and Marine Insurance Company. In October 1996 joint venture trading companies were allowed to form in Shanghai and Shenzhen. This was a first step toward addressing the continuing complaints by foreign investors that foreign-invested firms have limited ability to engage in the trade and distribution of their products. In early 1999 two additional U.S. insurance companies, John Hancock and Chubb, received licenses to operate in China. As chapter 1 notes, distribution and financial services (including banking and insurance)—two areas where the United States would like to see greater market liberalization—will continue to be open for foreign direct investment. Under China's WTO accession agreement, there will be no restrictions on geography, quantity of sales, and forms of establishment for foreign retail sales by the end of 2004. In addition, foreign banks can conduct domestic currency business with local individuals by the year 2006.

Although with the new FDI guidelines and other internal directives, China may appear to be moving toward an industrial policy regime, other significant policy initiatives make the Chinese economy more market-friendly and ease investing in China by foreign firms. The dual aspects typify the evolution of Chinese reforms in general and reforms in the investment regime in particular. The policy zigzag also in part reflects the needs of China's different domestic constituencies. Looking at one or two changes in isolation may not give an accurate picture of the policy direction. Perhaps even more important, the restrictions in China's investment regime highlight the benefits and the importance of China's entry into the WTO (Fung and Lau 1997; Brecher and Gelb 1997). Chinese entry into the WTO will make many of the policies that target specific industries illegal; such policies will have to be phased out gradually. For example, before China's entry into the WTO, ownership and management in any form of telecommunication services were not allowed. But as mentioned, with Internet and paging services, ownership can currently rise up to 50 percent. The benefits of the phase-out of this and other restrictions will accrue to not only the Chinese economy but also the foreign direct investors.

Recent Initiatives on FDI

In terms of new initiatives, the most relevant ones are related to the WTO agreement and implementation. Most laws and measures have already been brought into conformity with the Agreement on Trade-Related Investment Measures (TRIMs). Investment restrictions such as trade and foreign exchange balancing requirements, local content requirements, and export performance requirements have been eliminated. As mentioned earlier, investment in wholesale trade and retail trade has been progressively relaxed. For example, in wholesale trade, majority ownership in joint ventures with no geographic or quantitative restrictions is now allowed. Similarly, majority ownership in joint ventures in retail services is now permitted in several Special Economic Zones and other cities. In telecommunication, foreigners can now own up to 50 percent of the joint ventures in value-added services and paging services. In banking, foreign banks can conduct yuan or renminbi business with local firms. By 2006, foreign banks can conduct yuan business with local individuals. In insurance, wholly owned subsidiaries of foreign non–life insurance companies are now permitted. Thus restrictions regarding foreign direct investment in industries and the service sectors in China are increasingly relaxed.

Legislation, Local Variations, and Enforcement of FDI Regulations

Laws relating to foreign investment are a subset of the so-called economic laws—laws adopted by the Chinese state to regulate the economy. Economic laws are in turn part of the administrative laws in China. Administrative laws, like other laws, must ultimately conform to the Constitution of the People's Republic of China. The major categories of administrative laws in China are the sectoral administrative laws, which regulate sectors of the economy, politics, and society. The regulations include customs, finance, prices, labor, education, and industry. Foreign investment laws cut across several of these aspects.

Two types of structures have the authority to enact laws. The first is related to state power: the National People's Congress (NPC), its standing committee, and the people's congresses of provinces, municipalities, and autonomous regions. The second structure is the administrative organ: the State Council, its commissions, and ministries; the governments of provinces, municipalities, and autonomous regions; and lower-level local governments. In general, laws issued by the state power organs take precedence over those made by administrative organs. Legislation from the administrative organs should complement those issued by the state power structures. The administrative organs are supposed to issue regulations to implement laws passed by the supreme lawmaking body, the NPC.

The constitution specifically grants the State Council, the highest administrative body, the power to issue administrative regulations so that laws can be implemented. Under article 89 of the constitution, the State Council adopts administrative measures, enacts administrative rules and regulations, and issues decisions and orders in accordance with the constitutions and statutes. The Chinese constitution empowers the State Council to enact any regulation necessary to implement laws, in part because typical Chinese laws enacted by the NPC are terse and require more detailed rules and regulations for implementation. Some legal scholars interpret the lawmaking function of the State Council as its inherent power, distinct from additional lawmaking power conferred by the National People's Congress (Corne 1997). The inherent power, though different from the legal tradition prevailing in the United States, is not unique to China. For example, under the French legal system, the executive branch has the power to make regulations, even though the legislature has not conferred such power.

Thus the State Council, although it represents the executive branch, also has legislative authority. The council has two distinct lawmaking powers: inherent power in the constitution and power delegated by the NPC. The executive branch has both legislative and executive power, but laws created by the administrative body supposedly cannot create new rights or obligations.

The NPC has approximately three thousand members. They are not elected directly but chosen by the provincial people's congresses. The standing committee of the NPC consists of a group of approximately 155 members and conducts NPC business when the NPC is not in session. Since drafts of laws are circulated for comments from central and local government commissions and ministries, a wide spectrum of the Communist Party elite have an opportunity to do so. Popular input is rare. Although the NPC is the supreme lawmaking body, traditionally it has not acted as a completely independent organ. The NPC is often viewed as rubber-stamping the rulings of the party leaders and the State Council. Recently, under a new leadership of the standing committee, the NPC has grown more independent and has even issued several criticisms of the government's administration of laws (for details, see, for example, Melloan 1997).

Legally the State Council lies in the next tier of lawmaking behind the NPC. Some regulations may require the State Council to seek the approval of the NPC if the regulations are sufficiently important. The 1986 Provisions of the State Council of the People's Republic of China for the Encouragement of Foreign Investment is such an example. Formally the NPC will review the regulations and issue its opinions.

Various commissions and ministries can also enact secondary legislation. And those entities issue more laws than other legislative or executive bodies. Many regulations and laws from the State Council and its commissions and ministries were never officially promulgated or published. They were meant to be seen by government officials only, even though they could affect nongovernmental parties. For example, documents such as Certain Provisions of the Ministry of Foreign Economic

FIGURE 3-1

HIERARCHY OF FORMAL AND INFORMAL FDI LEGISLATION

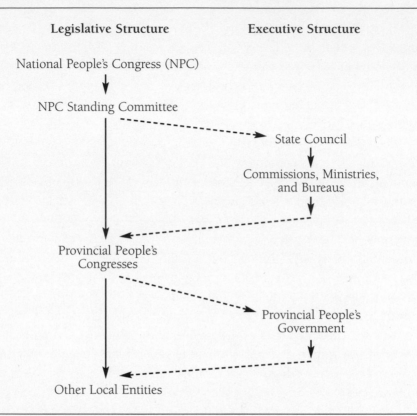

SOURCE: Adapted from Corne 1997.

Relations and Trade in Regard to Administration of the Adjustment of Import and Export Licenses, Administrative Measures of the PRC Customs in Regard to Bonded Areas and Storage of Goods, and Measures of the PRC Customs in Regard to the Administration of the Processing Trade of Bonded Factories were originally unpublished. Written copies of many laws, regulations, circulars, measures, and rules were difficult to obtain. Unless connected to the right governmental offices, a person would not know the contents of such regulations. Recently China has committed itself to publishing all such measures relevant to trade and foreign investment. Although problems continue, the system of legislation on foreign investment has significantly improved. Figure 3-1 presents the hierarchy of legislation on foreign direct investment.

Figure 3-1 shows that the highest legislative body is the National People's Congress. Next is the NPC's standing committee, followed by the highest executive structure, the State Council. The council is also empowered to issue laws and regulations. Next are the council's commissions, ministries, and bureaus. The provincial and local people's congresses and governments can also enact laws. Finally, other local entities such as county, township, and village governments can issue notices and resolutions narrow in scope but nonetheless with an impact on the implementation of FDI laws in various localities.

The approval process for applications for FDI involves different authorities. First, the Ministry of Foreign Trade and Economic Cooperation as well as relevant local governments screen an application. A feasibility study follows approval by MOFTEC and local governments. Both the central and the local governments must approve the study results. MOFTEC then leads an interagency meeting with various ministries to discuss the application. Any contract is based on both the proposal and the feasibility study (Howell, Nuechterlein, and Hester 1995; CIER 1996). In March 2003 Hu Jintao officially became the president of the People's Republic of China, having been elected the general secretary of the Chinese Communist Party in November 2002. It has been reported that there will be some streamlining of the State Council. The twenty-nine ministries of the State Council are expected to be slashed to twenty-one. Furthermore, the State Economic and Trade Commission, whose role is to manage sectors and enterprises still under the direct control of the state, is expected to be abolished.

While China's laws and regulations on FDI have become more transparent, they still are seen as vague, sometimes arbitrary, and not always internally consistent. Criticism also covers enforcement and the need to have good *guanxi,* or connections, in the government. Some complaints relate to the drafting and enactment of administrative laws, lack of input from industries (both domestic and foreign), the use of internal regulations, the vagueness of the laws, and inconsistencies between local and central laws.

A major problem in implementing FDI laws occurs because various government agencies may have a great deal of leeway in interpreting imprecise language. The Sino-Foreign Joint-Venture Law and other implementing regulations did not explicitly restrict how much technology transfer could count as contributions by the foreign partners toward the joint venture's registered capital. The Ministry of Foreign Economic Relations and Trade (MOFERT, currently named the Ministry of Foreign Trade and Economic Cooperation, MOFTEC) apparently chose to interpret the lack of clarity to mean that proprietary technology by the foreign partners cannot count for more than 20 percent of registered capital. The interpretation appeared in a MOFERT document in 1988 but was not issued to any interested parties. The example illustrates two problems with FDI laws. First, because the original laws were not absolutely clear, subsequent interpretations seemed arbitrary. Second, the interpretations were frequently not made public. Since then China has agreed to make its laws more transparent and publish all relevant documents (Corne 1997; Kuzmik 1992).

A related problem is that ministries and provincial and local governments can issue clarifications or specifications to conform the laws to local practice. Local specifications can be inconsistent with one another and even with the interpretations of the central government and the original laws. The State Council's Encouragement of Foreign Investment Provisions guarantees foreign investors management autonomy in recruiting local staff. To recruit and dismiss staff, foreign-invested firms need only report to a local labor bureau for filing. The Ministry of Labor interpreted the provisions to mean that recruitment should be carried out with the *assistance* of the local labor bureau. Conversely, the Shanghai Municipal People's Government interpreted autonomy to mean that recruitment should be implemented under the *guidance* of the local labor bureau. The frequency of conflicting interpretations has diminished, but they are still significant obstacles to foreign firms conducting business in China.

Finally, private investors often find a way to circumvent pitfalls in the practice of law in China. To avoid using the Chinese courts, more lawyers for foreign direct investors write dispute arbitration clauses into commercial contracts. A foreign company can stipulate that at least one foreign arbitrator sit on a three-member panel of the arbitration body. The arbitration rules follow the rules of the Chinese International Economic and

Trade Arbitration Commission in Beijing. The arbitration judges often use U.S. or European commercial codes. In essence international commercial laws can be imported into China through other channels. And since China has joined the WTO, its disputes on foreign direct investment with other countries are now settled by the dispute settlement panels of the WTO.

4

General Characteristics of FDI in China

This chapter provides general information about the nature and the trend of foreign direct investment in China as a background against which U.S. direct investment takes place. Table 4-1 and figure 4-1 present contracted and realized foreign direct investment flows in China. *Contracted investment* refers to the amount of investment committed in signed contracts. For various reasons those contracts may not all come to fruition (for example, the foreign party, the Chinese party, or both may not be able to raise the necessary capital). *Realized investment* refers to the total amount of foreign direct investment that actually materializes and arrives in China. Realized investment in principle cannot be larger than contracted investment on a cumulative basis. However, because of the time lag between commitment and actual arrival, the realized investment in a given year can exceed the contracted investment of the same year (for example, in a year with rapidly falling new commitments). In practice, realized investment has always been less than contracted investment of the same year.

In 2002, China was the largest recipient of FDI in the world. According to official Chinese sources, both contracted and realized foreign direct investment have been rising since economic reform began in 1979. The early years (1979–83) were a period of learning for the government, followed in 1984–85 by significant expansion in both contracted and realized FDI, sometimes at triple-digit rates. However, expansion did not last long as foreign investors quickly became unhappy with the difficulty of obtaining imported materials and machinery as well as their inability to sell to the domestic market. Contracted investment tumbled by 52 percent in 1986. Although realized investment continued to increase, it did so at a much slower rate. Foreign investors responded favorably to new laws to encourage foreign direct investment (the Provisions of the State Council on

42

TABLE 4-1
**CONTRACTED AND REALIZED FOREIGN DIRECT INVESTMENT
FLOWS TO CHINA, 1979–2003**

	Contracted FDI (US$ billion)	Realized FDI (US$ billion)	Number of Contracts
1979–82	6.01	1.17	922
1983	1.73	0.64	470
1984	2.65	1.26	1,856
1985	5.93	1.66	3,073
1986	2.83	1.87	1,498
1987	3.71	2.31	2,233
1988	5.30	3.19	5,945
1989	5.60	3.39	5,779
1990	6.60	3.49	7,273
1991	11.98	4.37	12,978
1992	58.12	11.01	48,764
1993	111.44	27.52	83,437
1994	82.68	33.77	47,549
1995	91.28	37.52	37,011
1996	73.28	41.73	24,556
1997	51.00	45.26	21,001
1998	52.10	45.46	19,799
1999	41.22	40.32	16,918
2000	62.38	40.72	22,347
2001	69.19	46.69	26,140
2002	82.77	52.74	34,171
2003	115.07	53.51	41,081
Total	840.87	499.60	464,801

SOURCE: PRC, National Bureau of Statistics 2001, 2002, 2003.

the Encouragement of Foreign Direct Investment); FDI resumed its increase in 1987.

The tragic events at Tiananmen Square in June 1989 interrupted FDI growth—but not for long. The absolute level of investment continued to increase. In the early 1990s foreign direct investment took off with huge increases in contracted FDI between 1991 and 1993 and in realized FDI a

FIGURE 4-1

CONTRACTED AND REALIZED FOREIGN DIRECT INVESTMENT INTO CHINA,
1983–2003

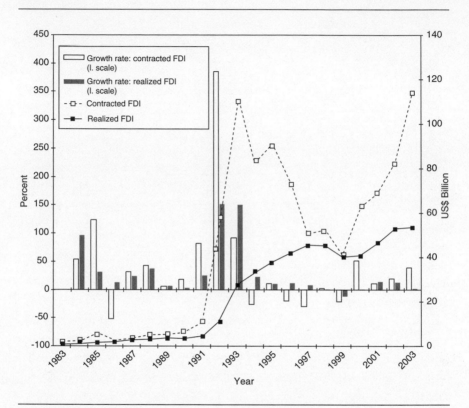

SOURCE: Table 4-1; PRC, National Bureau of Statistics 2001, 2002, 2003.

year later. In 1991 contracted investment increased 82 percent. In 1992 contracted investment increased almost fourfold while realized investment rose by more than 150 percent, with continued strong growth in 1993. The increases in 1992 and 1993 probably resulted from Deng Xiaoping's tour of southern China when he reaffirmed the open-door policy and encouraged faster economic growth and reform. The rates of growth could not be sustained; 1994 witnessed the beginning of a retrenchment in contracted FDI. In both 1996 and 1997, contracted investment dropped more than 20 percent. Realized FDI continued to increase in 1995 and 1996, but at a 10 percent rate of growth. By 1998 and 1999 both contracted and realized foreign direct investment became quite flat, partly because of the East Asian currency crisis. Despite the slowdown, contracted and realized direct investments in 2003 were approximately ten and twelve times the levels of 1991. With China's impending and then actual entry into the WTO, there has been a rush of foreign capital into the Chinese market. In 2003, realized foreign direct investment reached $53.51 billion.

Analysts have suggested several possible reasons for the slowdown in the rate of growth of foreign direct investment before China successfully negotiated to enter the WTO. Some reductions resulted from the elimination and reduction of the tax and import duty exemption and the reduction of privileges traditionally given to foreign direct investors. With China in the WTO, the same tax privileges have to be given to all firms. The Chinese government indicated in late 2002 that such equal treatment will be implemented very soon. A fundamental reason for the previous slowdown was the unsustainably high rates of growth of foreign direct investment in the early 1990s. The pace was so rapid that excess capacities might have built up in certain sectors, with a need for a correction, that is, a period of slower growth. Some investors complained about the continued difficulty of dealing with changing rules and regulations governing FDI. Still others criticized the level of corruption. But the negative factors had been part of the Chinese investment environment for a long time. Since 1992 discussions between the United States and China regarding market access and Chinese efforts to join the World Trade Organization have led to some relief in that area, diminishing over time. The East Asian currency crisis, which began in Thailand in mid-year 1997, severely affected direct investment inflows into China from the East Asian countries, including Hong Kong, which had been responsible for more than half of all FDI in China. However, with China in the World Trade Organization, the situation has changed dramatically. As mentioned earlier, realized foreign direct investment reached $53.51 billion in 2003.

Despite the previous "correction," China managed to accumulate a total stock of realized foreign direct investment worth more than $446.3 billion by the end of 2002. The cumulative number of contracts came to more than 423,720. FDI enterprises employed more than 18 million people.

In general the large proportion of disguised foreign direct investment or the so-called Chinese capital round-tripping has significantly distorted the FDI figures reported by the government. For various reasons, including the desire to take advantage of the favorable tax and tariff treatments given to foreign direct investors, some Chinese enterprises transferred funds, legally or illegally, out of China and then reinvested the funds in China as FDI. Such investment of Chinese origin is only camouflaged as foreign direct investment. One World Bank (1993) estimate indicates that 25 percent of the foreign direct investment might have originated from China. Others (Shih 1989; Hsueh and Woo 1991) estimate that approximately 40 percent of Hong Kong's direct investment in China actually came from the mainland. Between 1992 and 1995 the average share of realized FDI in China accounted for by Hong Kong was 58.16 percent. The 40 percent estimate means that approximately 23 percent of total FDI in China originated in China itself by round-tripping through Hong Kong, although Hong Kong is not the only possible source of round-tripped Chinese capital. Taking such capital round-tripping into account would reduce realized FDI flows into China in 1998 from $45.6 billion to $34.2 billion. But the proportion of round-tripped capital might have been much lower than 25 percent since 1998 because of the relatively poor economic performance of Chinese domestic enterprises in China and their affiliates in Hong Kong.

One obvious implication of the capital round-tripping is the exaggerated extent of China's foreign direct investment. Undoubtedly FDI is important to China's economic development, but China's dependence on foreign capital is actually less than assumed because a significant portion of foreign capital is actually of domestic origin. The round-tripping also implies that a significant part of the FDI inflow is actually not a real inflow in the Chinese balance of payments figures.

FDI Distribution by Location and Mode of Investment

Most FDI is located in the south and coastal areas despite efforts by the government to diversify the locations of foreign direct investment and lure FDI inland and toward the central and western regions. Table 4-2 shows the distribution of foreign direct investment by province, municipality, and autonomous region in 1999, 2000, 2001, and 2002. In 2002, Guangdong received the largest amount of realized foreign direct investment, more than 21 percent of the total foreign direct investment in China. The three

TABLE 4-2

REALIZED FOREIGN CAPITAL FLOWS BY PROVINCE, MUNICIPALITY, AND AUTONOMOUS REGION, 1999–2002

Location	1999 Realized FDI (US$ million)	1999 Rank by Value of Realized FDI	2000 Realized FDI (US$ million)	2000 Rank by Value of Realized FDI	2001 Realized FDI (US$ million)	2001 Rank by Value of Realized FDI	2002 Realized FDI (US$ million)	2002 Rank by Value of Realized FDI
Guangdong	11,658 (28.9%)	1	11,281 (27.7%)	1	11,932 (25.5%)	1	11,334 (21.5%)	1
Jiangsu	6,078 (15.1%)	2	6,426 (15.8%)	2	6,915 (14.8%)	2	10,190 (19.3%)	2
Shandong	2,259 (5.6%)	5	2,971 (7.3%)	5	3,521 (7.5%)	5	4,734 (9.0%)	3
Shanghai	2,837 (7.0%)	4	3,160 (7.8%)	4	4,292 (9.2%)	3	4,272 (8.1%)	4
Fujian	4,024 (10.0%)	3	3,432 (8.4%)	3	3,918 (8.4%)	4	3,838 (7.3%)	5
Liaoning	1,062 (2.6%)	9	2,044 (5.0%)	6	2,516 (5.4%)	6	3,412 (6.5%)	6
Zhejiang	1,233 (3.1%)	8	1,613 (4.0%)	8	2,212 (4.7%)	7	3,076 (5.8%)	7
Beijing	1,975 (4.9%)	6	1,684 (4.1%)	7	1,768 (3.8%)	9	1,725 (3.3%)	8
Tianjin	1,764 (4.4%)	7	1,166 (2.9%)	9	2,133 (4.5%)	8	1,582 (3.0%)	9
Hubei	915 (2.3%)	11	944 (2.3%)	10	1,189 (2.5%)	10	1,427 (2.7%)	10

SOURCE: PRC, Economic Information and Agency 2000b, 2001b; PRC, Asia Economic Information and Consultancy Ltd. 2002; PRC, National Bureau of Statistics 2001, 2002, 2003.

NOTE: Figures in parentheses below the foreign direct investment figures refer to the shares of the 1999, 2000, 2001, and 2002 total realized foreign direct investment.

regions with the most foreign direct investment (Guangdong, Jiangsu, and Shandong) accounted for almost half of total realized foreign direct investment in China that year. Moreover, the combined share of the top ten (of a possible thirty-one) recipients of foreign direct investment came to

TABLE 4-3

MODES OF FDI IN CHINA (CONTRACTED BASIS), 1986–2003 (US$ billion)

Year	EJV	CJV	WFO	JD
1986	1.38 (48.5)	1.36 (47.9)	0.02 (0.72)	0.08 (2.85)
1987	1.95 (52.6)	1.28 (34.6)	0.47 (12.70)	0.005 (0.13)
1988	3.13 (59.2)	1.62 (30.7)	0.48 (9.07)	0.05 (1.11)
1989	2.66 (47.5)	1.08 (19.3)	1.65 (29.5)	0.20 (3.64)
1990	2.70 (41.0)	1.25 (19.0)	2.44 (37.1)	0.19 (2.94)
1991	6.08 (50.8)	2.14 (17.9)	3.67 (30.6)	0.09 (0.77)
1992	29.1 (50.1)	13.3 (22.8)	15.7 (27.0)	0.04 (0.07)
1993	55.2 (49.6)	25.5 (22.6)	30.5 (27.5)	0.30 (0.28)
1994	40.2 (48.6)	20.3 (24.6)	21.9 (26.5)	0.24 (0.3)
1995	39.7 (43.5)	17.8 (19.5)	33.7 (36.8)	0.06 (0.07)
1996	31.9 (43.5)	14.3 (19.5)	26.8 (36.6)	0.29 (0.40)
1997	20.7 (40.6)	12.1 (23.6)	17.7 (34.6)	0.40 (0.79)
1998	17.3 (33.3)	11.6 (22.5)	21.7 (41.7)	0.08 (0.15)
1999	13.5 (32.8)	6.8 (16.5)	20.7 (50.2)	0.06 (0.1)
2000	19.6 (31.4)	8.1 (13.0)	34.3 (55.0)	0.1 (0.2)
2001	17.5 (25.34)	8.3 (12.00)	43.0 (62.14)	0.02 (0.03)
2002	18.5 (22.35)	6.2 (7.49)	57.3 (69.23)	0.06 (0.07)
2003	25.51 (22.18)	7.48 (6.50)	81.61 (70.97)	0.09 (0.07)

SOURCE: PRC, Asia Economic Information and Consultancy Ltd. 2003.

NOTE: Figures in parentheses are percentages of total contracted FDI. EJV refers to equity joint venture, CJV refers to contractual joint venture, WFO refers to wholly foreign-owned enterprise, and JD refers to joint development.

86.5 percent. In 2002, more than 87 percent of the total stock of realized FDI was concentrated in the eastern and southeastern part of China.

As described in chapter 3, foreign direct investment can occur in several forms: Sino-foreign equity joint venture (EJV), Sino-foreign contractual joint venture (CJV), wholly foreign-owned enterprise (WFO), joint development (JD), and foreign-funded joint-stock limited company. The foreign-funded joint-stock limited company is relatively new—the Ministry of Foreign Trade and Economic Cooperation authorized that form in 1995. Only scattered data are available on the magnitude of investment in the foreign-funded joint-stock limited company. Tables 4-3 and 4-4 present the FDI distributions by mode on a contracted and realized basis.

TABLE 4-4

MODES OF FDI IN CHINA (REALIZED BASIS), 1986–2003 (US$ billion)

Year	EJV	CJV	WFO	JD
1986	0.80 (42.9)	0.79 (42.3)	0.016 (0.87)	0.26 (13.89)
1987	1.49 (64.2)	0.62 (26.8)	0.025 (1.06)	0.18 (7.92)
1988	1.98 (61.9)	0.78 (24.4)	0.23 (7.08)	0.21 (6.64)
1989	2.04 (60.1)	0.75 (22.2)	0.37 (11.0)	0.23 (6.84)
1990	1.89 (54.1)	0.67 (19.3)	0.68 (19.6)	0.24 (7.01)
1991	2.30 (52.7)	0.76 (17.5)	1.14 (26.0)	0.17 (3.87)
1992	6.11 (55.6)	2.12 (19.3)	2.52 (22.9)	0.25 (2.27)
1993	15.35 (55.8)	5.24 (19.0)	6.51 (23.7)	0.42 (1.50)
1994	17.93 (53.1)	7.12 (21.1)	8.04 (23.8)	0.68 (2.0)
1995	19.08 (50.8)	7.54 (20.1)	10.32 (27.5)	0.59 (1.57)
1996	20.75 (49.7)	8.11 (19.4)	12.61 (30.2)	0.26 (0.61)
1997	19.5 (43.1)	8.93 (19.7)	16.2 (35.8)	0.34 (0.75)
1998	18.3 (40.4)	9.72 (21.5)	16.5 (36.6)	0.18 (0.39)
1999	15.8 (39.3)	8.23 (20.4)	15.5 (38.6)	0.38 (0.01)
2000	14.3 (35.1)	6.60 (16.2)	19.3 (47.4)	0.38 (0.9)
2001	15.74 (33.57)	6.21 (13.25)	23.9 (50.93)	0.51 (1.09)
2002	14.99 (28.42)	5.06 (9.59)	31.7 (60.11)	0.27 (0.52)
2003	15.39 (29.07)	3.84 (7.25)	33.38 (63.05)	0.03 (0.06)

SOURCE: PRC, Asia Economic Information and Consultancy Ltd. 2003.

NOTE: Figures in parentheses are percentages of the total realized FDI. EJV refers to equity joint venture, CJV refers to contractual joint venture, WFO refers to wholly foreign-owned enterprise, and JD refers to joint development.

Tables 4-3 and 4-4 show that in 2003, on a realized basis, wholly foreign-owned enterprise was the dominant mode of investment in China, accounting for more than 63 percent of the realized foreign direct investment; on a contracted basis, the wholly foreign-owned enterprise also took the lead in 2003. Both the equity joint venture and the contractual joint venture were equally important in the mid-1980s. But their shares have declined. On a contracted basis, equity joint ventures accounted for 22.2 percent in 2003, while on a realized basis, its share was 29.1 percent in the same year. The contractual joint venture mode has declined even more. On a realized basis it accounted for only 7.3 percent of the total FDI in 2003, down from

TABLE 4-5

REALIZED FDI FLOWS BY REGION AND MODE, 2002 (US$ million)

Location[a]	Equity Joint Venture	Contractual Joint Venture	Wholly Foreign-Owned Enterprise	Joint-Stock Limited Company	Total by Regional Data[b]	Total by National Data
Beijing	552.42	298.88	941.27	NA	1,792.57	1,724.64
Tianjin	NA	NA	NA	NA	1,003	1,581.95
Hebei	520.13	90.93	213.39	NA	824.45	782.71
Shanxi	58.89	91.13	99.14	NA	249.16	211.64
Inner Mongolia	54.95	24.83	53.35	10.15	143.28	177.01
Liaoning	1,793	271	1788	33	3,916	3,411.68
Jilin	157.12	41.48	10.67	7.76	317.03	244.68
Heilongjiang	216.46	43.24	132.36	NA	945.56	355.11
Shanghai	1,190	510	3,065	264	5,029	4,272.29
Jiangsu	2,609.69	292.41	7,406.98	57.07	10,366.15	10,189.60
Zhejiang	1,231.06	105.15	1,823.81	NA	3,160.02	3,076.10
Anhui	157.37	15.93	200.01	NA	375.23	383.75
Fujian	846.69	115.87	3,162.40	124.99	4,249.95	3,838.37
Jiangxi	367.98	37.65	681.62	NA	160.00	1,081.97
Shandong	1,420	390	37.2	60	5,590	4,734.04
Henan	274.21	83.26	146.68	NA	504.15	404.63
Hubei	536.28	277.31	580.68	7.24	1,401.51	1,426.65
Hunan	419.53	140.02	471.34	NA	1,030.89	900.22
Guangdong	2,891.91	2,374.78	7,314.52	89.50	13,110.71	11,334.00

continued on next page

42 percent in 1986. The wholly foreign-owned enterprise increased from a negligible amount in 1986 to more than 63 percent in 2003. On a realized basis it accounted for almost 63.05 percent of the total foreign direct investment in 2003, significantly larger than the 29.07 percent of the equity joint venture. Its share of total foreign direct investment, on both a contracted and realized basis, is expected to increase further. Joint development has become less and less important, with less than 0.1 percent of FDI in 2003. On a cumulative basis, up to the year 2003, 41.2 percent of realized

TABLE 4-5 (*continued*)
REALIZED FDI FLOWS BY REGION AND MODE, 2002 (US$ million)

Location[a]	Equity Joint Venture	Contractual Joint Venture	Wholly Foreign-Owned Enterprise	Joint-Stock Limited Company	Total by Regional Data[b]	Total by National Data
Guangxi	149.74	82.92	194.94	57.12	484.72	417.26
Hainan*	40.64	38.81	151.28	NA	231	511.96
Chongqing	161.49	56.48	61.48	1.44	282.17	195.76
Sichuan	373.29	88.76	181.60	15.60	659.25	555.83
Guizhou	21.25	0.75	15.00	NA	27.00	38.21
Yunnan	54.71	11.93	45.02	NA	111.66	111.69
Tibet	NA	NA	NA	NA	2.93	NA
Shaanxi	175.91	124.47	110.26	NA	410.64	360.05
Gansu	35.38	0.05	16.85	NA	52.28	61.21
Qinghai	31.43	40.04	76.20	NA	147.67	47.26
Ningxia	15.74	3.11	3.15	NA	22.00	22.00
Xinjiang	8.17	0.44	12.03	NA	20.64	18.99
All Regions	16,385.44	5,651.63	28,996.23	727.87	56,620.62	52,471.26
National total[c]	14,992.00	5,058.00	31,725.00	697.00	52,472.00	52,742.86

SOURCE: PRC, Asia Economic Information and Consultancy Ltd. 2003.

* Data for Hainan is based on contractual value, as the realized value is not available.

a. The ordering of the regions in this table is done according to Chinese practice, which approximately corresponds to going first from north to south and then from east to west.

b. The row total (equity joint venture, contractual joint venture, wholly foreign-owned enterprise, and joint-stock limited company) does not necessarily equal the total by regional data because of the omission of the categories of joint development and others.

c. The national total row does not add to the national total because of the omission of joint exploration (US$271 million).

FDI was in equity joint ventures, 16.8 percent in contractual joint ventures, 40.2 percent in wholly foreign-owned enterprises, and 1.4 percent in joint development.

Data on realized FDI in the forms of equity joint ventures, contractual joint ventures, and wholly foreign-owned enterprises can be obtained for most regions. Some data on direct investment in the form of joint-stock limited companies have been gathered for a few select regions. Table 4-5 presents those data. The table was compiled from reports of the departments of foreign trade and economic cooperation of the various provinces, municipalities, and autonomous regions (except for the total by national data and national total). Occasional unexplained discrepancies occur between the foreign direct investment data obtained from regional sources and from national sources (for example, compare columns 6 and 7). Fortunately the discrepancies are relatively small. In 2002 the sum total FDI reported by the individual regions comes to $52.471 billion, whereas the figure reported by the national authorities is $52.743 billion. The difference is negligible. Despite some possible inconsistencies, the data may still be useful for our comparative purposes.

Table 4-6 uses the data in table 4-5 to derive the percentage distribution of the modes of FDI of each region. Overall in 2002, the wholly foreign-owned enterprise became the predominant mode of foreign direct investment in China. On a disaggregated basis the WFO was the dominant mode in sixteen regions, whereas the EJV was a close second, being most popular in fourteen regions. The WFO enterprise has become more important than the CJV in twenty-six of the thirty-one regions, including eight of the ten most popular destinations (Jiangsu, Guangdong, Shanghai, Shandong, Zhejiang, Hebei, Liaoning, and Fujian). The contractual joint venture has remained more popular than the wholly foreign-owned enterprise in three regions: Jilin, Shandong, and Shaanxi.

Table 4-6 also shows that in 2002, Inner Mongolia, Liaoning, Jilin, Jiangsu, Shanghai, Fujian, Hubei, Shandong, Hubei, Guangdong, Guangxi, Chongqing, and Sichuan had small amounts of FDI in the mode of joint-stock limited company. As discussed in chapter 3, the foreign-funded joint-stock limited company is a relatively new mode of foreign direct investment in China but is expected to become more prevalent gradually.

FDI Distribution by Sector

Table 4-7 examines the distribution of contracted foreign direct investment by sector from 1997 through 2002, and shows that more than 60 percent was concentrated primarily in the manufacturing sector. The next highest share, approximately 8–10 percent, was in real estate. Beyond those two

TABLE 4-6

DISTRIBUTION OF REALIZED FDI FLOWS BY REGION AND MODE, 2002
(percent)

Location	Equity Joint Venture	Contractual Joint Venture	Wholly Foreign-Owned Enterprise	Joint-Stock Limited Company
Beijing	30.82	16.67	52.51	NA
Tianjin	NA	NA	NA	NA
Hebei	63.09	11.03	25.88	NA
Shanxi	23.64	36.57	39.79	NA
Inner Mongolia	38.35	17.33	37.23	7.08
Liaoning	45.79	6.92	45.66	0.84
Jilin	49.56	13.08	3.37	2.45
Heilongjiang	22.89	4.57	14.00	NA
Shanghai	23.66	10.14	60.95	5.25
Jiangsu	25.18	2.82	71.45	0.55
Zhejiang	38.96	3.33	57.72	NA
Anhui	41.94	4.25	53.30	NA
Fujian	19.92	2.73	74.41	2.94
Jiangxi	229.99	23.53	426.01	NA
Shandong	25.40	6.98	0.67	1.07
Henan	54.39	16.51	29.09	NA
Hubei	38.26	19.79	41.43	0.52
Hunan	40.70	13.58	45.72	NA
Guangdong	22.06	18.11	55.79	0.68
Guangxi	30.89	17.11	40.22	11.78
Hainan	17.59	16.80	65.49	NA
Chongqing	57.23	20.02	21.79	0.51
Sichuan	56.62	13.46	27.55	2.37
Guizhou	78.70	2.78	55.56	NA
Yunnan	49.00	10.68	40.32	NA
Tibet	NA	NA	NA	NA
Shaanxi	42.84	30.31	26.85	NA
Gansu	67.67	0.10	32.23	NA
Qinghai	21.28	27.11	51.60	NA
Ningxia	71.55	14.14	14.32	NA
Xinjiang	39.58	2.13	58.28	NA
National total	28.42	9.59	60.15	1.32

SOURCE: Authors' calculations using table 4-5.

TABLE 4-7

CONTRACTED FDI BY SECTOR, 1997–2002 (US$ million)

	1997	1998	1999	2000	2001	2002
National total	51,004	52,102	41,223	62,380	69,195	82,768
Farming, forestry, animal husbandry, and fishing	1,065 (2.09%)	1,204 (2.31%)	1,472 (3.57%)	1,483 (2.38%)	1,762 (2.55%)	1,688 (2.04%)
Mining and quarrying	717 (1.41%)	852 (1.64%)	322 (0.78%)	506 (0.81%)	644 (0.93%)	381 (0.46%)
Manufacturing	27,065 (53.1%)	30,827 (59.2%)	25,332 (61.5%)	44,254 (70.9%)	48,847 (70.59%)	59,270 (71.61%)
Electric power, gas, and water production and supply	3,656 (7.17%)	1,968 (3.78%)	1,635 (3.97%)	1,227 (1.97%)	2,134 (3.08%)	1,475 (1.78%)
Construction	3,120 (6.12%)	1,750 (3.36%)	1,096 (2.66%)	831 (1.33%)	1,823 (2.63%)	1,058 (1.28%)
Geological prospecting and water conservancy management	21.8 (0.04%)	23.5 (0.05%)	54 (0.13%)	15 (0.02%)	13 (0.02%)	31 (0.04%)
Transportation, storage, postal, and telecommunications services	2,622 (5.14%)	2,301 (4.42%)	1,114 (2.70%)	1,417 (2.27%)	884 (1.28%)	1,529 (1.85%)
Wholesale and retail trade and catering services	1,839 (3.61%)	1,314 (2.52%)	1,204 (2.92%)	1,435 (2.30%)	1,398 (2.02%)	1,663 (2.01%)
Banking and insurance			37 (0.09%)	79 (0.13%)	86 (0.12%)	460 (0.56%)
Real estate	6,222 (12.2%)	6,648 (12.76%)	4,178 (10.1%)	5,232 (8.39%)	5,031 (7.27%)	7,217 (8.72%)
Social services	2,669 (5.23%)	3,012 (5.78%)	3,017 (7.32%)	4,255 (6.82%)	4,289 (6.20%)	4,988 (6.03%)
Health care, sports, and social welfare	143 (0.28%)	141 (0.27%)	67 (0.16%)	154 (0.25%)	133 (0.19%)	258 (0.31%)
Education, culture and arts, radio, film, and TV	69.7 (0.14%)	22.1 (0.04%)	72.6 (0.18%)	83.3 (0.13%)	72 (0.10%)	109 (0.13%)
Scientific research and technical services	138 (0.27%)	851 (1.6%)	134 (0.33%)	250 (0.40%)	654 (0.95%)	534 (0.65%)
Other sectors	1,656 (3.25%)	1,211 (2.36%)	1,713 (4.2%)	1,502 (2.41%)	1,425 (2.06%)	2,108 (2.55%)

SOURCE: PRC, Economic Information and Agency 2002b; PRC, National Bureau of Statistics 1999, 2001, 2002, 2003.

NOTE: Figures in parentheses are the shares of the total flows of foreign direct investment in 1997, 1998, 1999, 2000, 2001, and 2002. Figures and percentages may not add to totals because of rounding.

TABLE 4-8

FOREIGN CAPITAL IN CHINA (CONTRACTED BASIS), 1979–2002

(US$ billion)

	FDI	External Loans	Other Foreign Investments
1979–83	7.7	15.1	1.2
1984	2.7	1.9	0.2
1985	5.9	3.5	0.4
1986	2.8	8.4	0.5
1987	3.7	7.8	0.6
1988	5.3	9.8	0.9
1989	5.6	5.2	0.7
1990	6.6	5.1	0.4
1991	12.0	7.2	0.5
1992	58.1	10.7	0.6
1993	111.4	11.3	0.5
1994	82.7	10.7	0.4
1995	91.3	11.3	0.6
1996	73.3	8.0	0.4
1997	51.0	5.9	4.2
1998	52.1	8.4	2.7
1999	41.2	8.4	2.4
2000	62.4	NA	8.8
2001	69.2	NA	2.8
2002	87.8	NA	2.0

SOURCE: PRC, National Bureau of Statistics 2001, 2002, 2003.

sectors, FDI was scattered across various sectors with single-digit or even lower percentage shares. No obvious systematic pattern appears.

Distribution of Foreign Capital by Type

Consider the importance of foreign direct investment relative to other forms of foreign capital in China. Tables 4-8 and 4-9 depict the extent of external loans and other foreign investments compared with FDI. *Other foreign investments* in Chinese statistics refers to equity shares issued

TABLE 4-9

FOREIGN CAPITAL IN CHINA (REALIZED BASIS), 1979–2002 (US$ billion)

	FDI	External Loans	Other Foreign Investments
1979–83	1.8	11.8	0.9
1984	1.3	1.3	0.2
1985	1.7	2.7	0.3
1986	1.9	5.0	0.4
1987	2.3	5.8	0.3
1988	3.2	6.5	0.5
1989	3.4	6.3	0.4
1990	3.5	6.5	0.3
1991	4.4	6.9	0.3
1992	11.0	7.9	0.3
1993	27.5	11.2	0.3
1994	33.8	9.3	0.2
1995	37.5	10.3	0.3
1996	41.7	12.7	0.4
1997	45.3	12.0	7.1
1998	45.5	11.0	2.1
1999	40.3	10.2	2.1
2000	40.7	10.0	8.6
2001	46.9	NA	2.8
2002	52.7	NA	2.3
1979–02	446.2	147.3	30.0

SOURCE: PRC, National Bureau of Statistics 2001, 2002, 2003.

abroad, international leasing, compensation (barter) trade, and processing and assembly. *External loans* include loans from foreign governments,
loans from international organizations, export credits, commercial loans
from foreign banks, and the value of bonds and other debt instruments
issued to investors in foreign countries.

Tables 4-8 and 4-9, as well as figure 4-2, show that before the 1990s,
foreign capital flows into China primarily took the form of external
loans, most long-term. (The external loans during the period were primarily in the form of official development assistance, ODA.) Between
1979 and 1991, external loans accounted for 66 percent of total foreign

FIGURE 4-2

FORMS OF FOREIGN CAPITAL IN CHINA

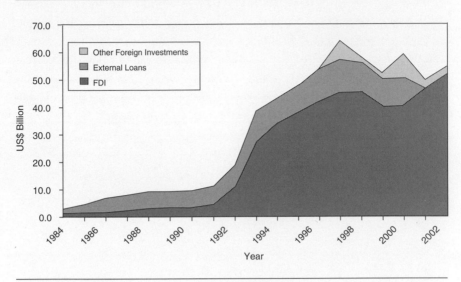

SOURCE: Table 4-9; PRC, National Bureau of Statistics 2001, 2002, 2003.

capital used by China, with FDI comprising only 29 percent. However, in 1992 the value of realized FDI flow began to exceed the value of realized external loans. Since then, realized FDI has grown at a much faster rate than realized external loans. By 2000 the value of realized FDI flow was more than four times that of external loans. During the period 1992–2002, FDI accounted for 79 percent of foreign capital, compared with 17 percent for external loans—a complete reversal of the situation in the earlier period. Other foreign investments were a rather insignificant proportion of the total foreign capital inflow. However, in 1997 other foreign investments abruptly increased by almost seventeenfold. The increase may have been due to increased issuance of equity shares overseas. In 1998 and 1999 the importance of other foreign investments came down considerably. Nonetheless, the amount was still much higher than the historical norm. Possibly 1997 represented an abnormal startup year. Undoubtedly the practice of Chinese enterprises' issuing equity shares overseas is expected to continue. But in 2000 that form of investment shot up again, even though by 2002, the amount came down to $2.3 billion.

There is little doubt that the practice of Chinese enterprises' issuing equity shares overseas is expected to continue in the foreseeable future.

Cumulatively the stock of realized FDI is more than twice the stock of realized external loans. The large proportion of FDI in the Chinese use of foreign capital, coupled with the relatively long maturity of its external loans, explains in part why China was relatively insulated from the East Asian currency crisis of 1997–98. Since the bulk of the foreign capital in China takes the form of direct investment in plants, equipment, and structures, foreign investment in China is oriented toward the long term and cannot be easily withdrawn, unlike external loans—especially short-term ones.

5

General Characteristics of
U.S. Direct Investment

Chapter 4 highlighted the general trend and characteristics of *foreign* direct investment in China. This chapter focuses on aspects and characteristics of *U.S.* direct investment in China. To obtain a comprehensive as well as a comparative view of U.S. direct investment, including the magnitude and characteristics of such investments, we rely on various data sources: the U.S. Department of Commerce annual and benchmark surveys on U.S. direct investment abroad; three surveys of comparative foreign direct investments in China conducted by the Chung-Hua Institution for Economic Research, Taipei; and FDI data contained in the *Almanac of China's Foreign Economic Relations and Trade*, published by the government of the People's Republic of China.

We discuss here the U.S. annual and benchmark surveys conducted by the Bureau of Economic Analysis of the U.S. Department of Commerce (chapter 6 details three CIER surveys). The benchmark survey of U.S. direct investment abroad is conducted once every five years (the most recent published benchmark survey occurred in 1994). It covers virtually the entire population of U.S. direct investment abroad in terms of its dollar value. The survey covers all U.S. parent companies and all foreign affiliates with assets, sales, or net income of $3 million or more. Survey results include reported or estimated data for 2,658 nonbank U.S. parent companies and for 21,300 nonbank foreign affiliates. The U.S. parent companies are fully consolidated business enterprises. (For more discussion of the survey, see U.S. Department of Commerce 1997a.) The Department of Commerce also conducts annual surveys of U.S. direct investment abroad, but the surveys contain less detailed information.

TABLE 5-1

STATUS OF U.S. DIRECT INVESTMENT IN CHINA,
BASED ON HISTORICAL COST, 1989–2002

	Direct Investment Outflow to China (U.S. data) (US$ million)	Direct Investment Position in China (U.S. data) (US$ million)	Total Realized FDI to China (Chinese data) (US$ million)	Share of Total FDI Inflow to China (percent)
1989	100	436	3,392	2.95
1990	30	354	3,487	0.86
1991	40	426	4,366	0.92
1992	74	563	11,007	0.67
1993	556	916	27,520	2.02
1994	1,232	2,557	33,770	3.65
1995	261	2,765	37,520	0.70
1996	933	3,848	41,730	2.24
1997	1,250	5,150	45,260	2.76
1998	1,497	6,350	45,460	3.29
1999	1,947	9,401	40,320	2.35
2000	1,817	11,140	40,720	4.46
2001	1,225	11,387	46,880	2.61
2002	914	10,294	52,743	1.73

SOURCE: Bargas 2000; U.S. Department of Commerce 1994b, 1996d, 1998d, 1999c, 2000c, 2001a, and 2003b; authors' calculations, using data from table 4-1.

NOTE: Wherever available, the latest revised figures are used.

Table 5-1 shows the extent of such investments over time, based on official U.S. government survey data.

In column 2, table 5-1 first presents the direct investment outflow from the United States to China for various years, based on official U.S. data. The statistics include outflows of equity capital, reinvested earnings, and outflow of intercompany debt. *Equity capital outflows* are net increases in U.S. parent companies' equity in their affiliates in China. *Reinvested earnings* of affiliates in China are the differences between their earnings and their distributed earnings. Reinvested earnings reflect an increase of investment by the U.S. parent companies in their affiliates in China. *Intercompany debt outflows* refer to the difference between increases in U.S. parent companies' receivables from their affiliates in China and increases in U.S. parent companies' payables to their affiliates in China. Intercompany debt outflows thus reflect the net contribution in the form of loans by the U.S. parent companies to their affiliates in China.

Table 5-1 shows that U.S. direct investment outflow to China suffered a decline of 70 percent in 1990 as a result of the Tiananmen incident in June 1989. (The decline may also be attributed in part to the tension between China and the United States because of the U.S. visit of Teng-Hui Lee of Taiwan and China's subsequent test-firing of missiles across the Taiwan Straits.) The outflow in 1992 remained smaller than in 1989. However, a major upsurge in U.S. direct investment outflow to China occurred in 1993 as well as in 1994. The increase was due at least in part to the southern tour by the late Chinese leader Deng Xiaoping, who signaled to everyone (including foreign investors) that economic reforms in China not only would continue but also would accelerate (Lau 1997). By 2002 U.S. direct investment outflow to China was more than nine times that of 1989. But the U.S. direct investment flow to China plunged almost 80 percent in 1995; that drop was partially reversed in 1996. Since then, U.S. direct investment flow to China has continued to grow. By 2002 it amounted to $0.9 billion, with a share of almost 2 percent in the total FDI inflow to China.[1]

Table 5-1 also shows that U.S. direct investment outflow to China was a slight proportion of total foreign direct investment inflows into China—less than 5 percent in the highest year, 2000 (see column 5). Column 3 presents the aggregate U.S. direct investment position in China, based on official U.S. data. Basically the U.S. direct investment position in China is defined as U.S. parent companies' equity in and net outstanding loans to their affiliates in China. It is a measure of the total stock of financing provided by the U.S. parent companies through either equity or debt. The estimates are based on historical or book values, rather than current market values. (Detailed estimates of U.S. direct investment in China are given only on the basis of historical costs in the various surveys by the U.S. government.) Equity owned by the U.S. parent companies includes capital stock, additional paid-in capital, retained earnings, and cumulative translation adjustments. Translation adjustments represent gains and losses due to changes in the U.S. dollar–renminbi exchange rates, which are applied in assessing assets and liabilities when converting renminbi, the Chinese currency, into U.S. dollars.

What is the relationship between U.S. direct investment outflow and the U.S. direct investment position? Basically the change in the U.S. direct investment position (that is, the stock of U.S. direct investment in China) from one year to the next reflects the capital outflow from the United States to China for that year plus adjustments resulting from capital gains and losses.[2] Based on official U.S. estimates presented in table 5-1, the U.S. direct investment position in China significantly declined in 1990 because of the tragic Tiananmen incident, as confidence about China's direction plummeted.[3] Despite the setback, the stock of U.S. direct investment in China has been rising rapidly since 1992. By 2002 the stock of U.S. direct investment in China amounted to $10.3 billion, almost twenty-four times the 1989 figure. To put those figures in perspective, the total U.S. direct investment position abroad, at historical cost, was $1.52 trillion at the end of 2002; the U.S. direct investment position in China of $10.3 billion in 2002 was less than 0.7 percent of the U.S. total.

Table 5-2 presents official Chinese data on direct investment inflow from the United States, on both contracted and realized bases. U.S. government estimates of the extent of U.S. direct investment in China (column 4) are significantly lower than the official estimates of the Chinese government. Even the trends in the figures appear different. The official Chinese data series are also smoother than the official U.S. data series. What makes the two data series so different?

As discussed in chapter 4, China's official FDI figures are contaminated by Chinese capital that leaves China and returns "camouflaged" as "foreign" direct investment. The problem of capital round-tripping affects the magnitude of Hong Kong direct investment in China (since much of Chinese capital first goes to Hong Kong) and the magnitude of total foreign direct investment. It can also affect to some extent U.S. direct investment as reported in official Chinese statistics. The so-called U.S. partner of a Sino-U.S. joint venture actually is the (formal or informal) foreign affiliate of a Chinese entity (U.S.-China Business Council 1990). In more and more cases the "foreign" partners of joint ventures are of Chinese origin. In

TABLE 5-2
CONTRACTED AND REALIZED U.S. DIRECT INVESTMENT IN CHINA,
1989–2002 (US$ million)

	Contracted U.S Direct Investment (Chinese data)	Realized U.S. Direct Investment (Chinese data)	Realized U.S. Direct Investment (U.S. data)
1989	641	284	100
1990	358	456	30
1991	548	323	40
1992	3,121	511	74
1993	6,813	2,063	556
1994	6,010	2,491	1,232
1995	7,471	3,083	261
1996	6,916	3,443	933
1997	4,937	3,239	1,250
1998	6,484	3,898	1,497
1999	6,116	4,387	1,947
2000	8,001	4,384	1,817
2001	7,515	4,433	1,225
2002	8,156	5,424	914

SOURCE: PRC, Economic Information and Agency 1999b, 2000b, 2001b; PRC, Asia Economic Information and Consultancy Ltd. 2002, 2003; Lardy 1994; table 5-1.

general, Chinese multinational corporations have become more important. According to one estimate, Chinese enterprises now have more than 5,500 foreign affiliates; together they hold more than $200 billion of foreign assets. As an example, the Fujian Corporation is reported to have set up affiliates in Australia, Canada, Japan, and Thailand (Wilson 1996). Chapter 8 discusses Chinese investments in the United States.

What are other plausible sources of discrepancies between the official U.S. and Chinese direct investment data series? First, some Chinese officials reportedly exaggerate the value of some FDI because an ability to attract more foreign funds could enhance their careers. Second, evaluating a foreign firm's contribution in the form of intangible assets such as technology transfer is often difficult. The Chinese figures may reflect a different valuation than those of the United States. (See chapter 3 for a

FIGURE 5-1

CONTRACTED AND REALIZED U.S. DIRECT INVESTMENT IN CHINA

(US$ million)

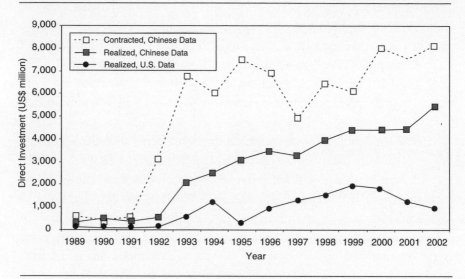

SOURCE: PRC, Economic Information and Agency 1999b, 2000b, 2001b; PRC, Asia Economic Information and Consultancy Ltd. 2002, 2003; Lardy 1994; tables 5-1 and 5-2.

discussion of some legal issues involved in FDI in the form of technology transfer.) Third, the official U.S. figures do not necessarily include debts incurred directly by affiliates of U.S. firms in the process of making their direct investments. A Hong Kong subsidiary of a U.S. firm may receive a contribution of capital of $15 million from its parent but may borrow in Hong Kong another $15 million to make a direct investment of $30 million. If the U.S. parent guarantees a loan, official U.S. statistics may include it. U.S. statistics will show a direct investment outflow of $15 million, whereas the Chinese statistics will show a realized U.S. direct investment of $30 million.

Figure 5-1 plots both contracted and realized U.S. direct investment flows against time. The figure shows, as expected, that realized direct investment lags behind contracted direct investment by at least one year. In 1990, 1994, 1996, 1999, and again in 2001, contracted investment declined, but realized investment continued to rise. In 1991 contracted investment rose, but realized investment declined, similarly for 2000.

Moreover, cumulatively less than half of the contracted direct investment is eventually realized. Figure 5-1 also shows the large discrepancy between the official U.S. and Chinese data on U.S. direct investment outflows to China.

Geographical Distribution of U.S. Direct Investment

Where is U.S. direct investment in China located? Table 5-3 highlights the locations. The top ten regions by value in 2002 were (in descending order): Jiangsu (17.63 percent), Shandong (15.77 percent), Liaoning (13.46 percent), Guangdong (11.82 percent), Shanghai (9.60 percent), Zhejiang (7.93 percent), Tianjin (4.20 percent), Fujian (3.08 percent), Beijing (2.35 percent), and Sichuan (1.56 percent). For 1998 the corresponding ranking was Shanghai (27 percent), Liaoning (12 percent), Jiangsu (9.6 percent), Beijing (7 percent), Zhejiang (6.9 percent), Tianjin (5.8 percent), Fujian (5.3 percent), Sichuan (4.8 percent), Shandong (4.7 percent), and Guangdong (3.5 percent). All the top ten regions for U.S. direct investment in 1998 and 2002 overlapped. Nine of the top ten regions were coastal municipalities and provinces. The top three regions in 2002 (Jiangsu, Shandong, and Liaoning) accounted for $4.07 billion, or 46.86 percent of total U.S. contracted direct investment in China that year. Despite Chinese government efforts to lure foreign investment to the inland provinces and regions, U.S. direct investment (measured by contracted value) still concentrated along coastal regions of China.

The geographical distribution of U.S. direct investment in China may be compared with the geographical distribution of all foreign direct investment. For the 2002 U.S. top ten regions, table 5-4 lists the rankings for U.S. direct investment in 1995, 1996, 1998, and 2001, together with their ranks as locations for all foreign direct investment.[4] Similarly, for the 2002 top ten regions which received the most FDI, table 5-5 lists the rankings in 1995, 1996, 1998, and 2001, together with their ranks as locations for U.S. direct investment. Table 5-4 shows an overlap of seven of the top ten regions for the United States for all five years. Table 5-5 shows a similar overlap for nine of the top ten regions for all foreign direct investment. The tables illustrate the persistence of locational preferences.

TABLE 5-3

LOCATION OF U.S. DIRECT INVESTMENT IN CHINA, 1998, 2001, AND 2002

	Number of U.S. Contracts			Region's Share of Total U.S. Contracts (%)			Region's Share of All Contracts (%)			Total Value of U.S. Contracts (US$ million)		
	1998	2001	2002	1998	2001	2002	1998	2001	2002	1998	2001	2002
Beijing	120	159	218	7.0	6.4	6.8	3.3	4.4	4.0	413	369	204
Tianjin	216	110	113	12.7	4.4	3.6	4.3	2.4	2.5	346	863	365
Hebei	NA	76	65	NA	3.1	2.0	3.5	1.9	1.4	152	57	100
Shanxi	16	10	10	0.9	0.4	0.3	0.5	0.3	0.2	11	28	25
Inner Mongolia	NA	13	12	NA	0.5	0.4	0.5	0.3	0.3	NA	111	16
Liaoning	236	235	295	13.9	9.5	9.3	8.6	6.4	6.3	710	1,242	1,170
Jilin	43	19	28	2.5	0.8	0.9	1.9	1.3	1.0	NA	76	54
Heilongjiang	40	36	32	2.3	1.5	1.0	1.3	0.9	0.6	30	81	113
Shanghai	221	263	332	13.0	10.6	10.4	7.5	9.4	8.8	1,596	598	834
Jiangsu	NA	391	642	NA	15.8	20.1	9.2	13.7	17.0	568	1,604	1,532
Zhejiang	146	318	415	8.6	12.9	13.0	4.9	8.8	9.9	409	492	689
Anhui	NA	30	48	NA	1.2	1.5	1.0	1.0	1.0	NA	60	76
Fujian	73	88	97	4.3	3.6	3.0	10.1	6.4	5.3	316	221	268
Jiangxi	NA		NA	NA		0.0	1.7	1.2	1.7	53	25	65
Shandong	188	311	394	11.0	12.6	12.4	6.9	11.7	11.9	280	700	1,370
Henan	48	28	33	2.8	1.1	1.0	1.7	0.9	0.8	91		52
Hubei	51	39	NA	3.0	1.6	0.0	1.7	1.3	1.4	94	124	92
Hunan	28	41	NA	1.6	1.7	0.0	2.1	1.3	1.2	61	127	64
Guangdong	169	211	276	9.9	8.5	8.7	22.0	20.3	19.9	209	602	1,027
Guangxi	16	23	33	0.9	0.9	1.0	1.3	1.1	0.8	47	37	84
Hainan	8		NA	0.5		0.0	0.9	0.7	0.7	126		NA
Chongqing			16			0.5			0.4			23
Sichuan	31		62	1.8		2.0	1.2	1.4	1.0	285		136
Guizhou	NA		NA	NA		0.0	0.4	0.2	0.2	13	28	2
Yunnan	13	16	9	0.8	0.6	0.3	0.6	0.5	0.4	55	69	56
Tibet	1		1	0.1		0.0	0.0	NA	0.0	0		0
Shaanxi	29	34	32	1.7	1.4	1.0	·1.0	0.9	0.6	NA	125	105
Gansu	NA	7	11	NA	0.3	0.4	0.3	0.3	0.2	NA	4	44
Qinghai	3	8	4	0.2	0.3	0.1	0.1	0.2	0.1	26	15	75
Ningxia	1		2	0.1		0.1	0.2	0.1	0.1	6		7
Xinjiang	6	7	7	0.4	0.3	0.2	0.2	0.2	0.2	17	13	43
All regions	1,703	2,473	3,187	100.0	100.0	100.0	98.8	100.0	100.0	5,916	7,668	8,689

SOURCE: PRC, Economic Information and Agency 1999b; PRC, Asia Economic Information and Consultancy Ltd. 2002, 2003.

Region's Share of Total Value of U.S. Contracts (%)			Region's Share of Total Value of All Contracts (%)			Average Size of U.S. Contracts (US$ million)			Average Size of All Contracts (US$ million)		
1998	2001	2002	1998	2001	2002	1998	2001	2002	1998	2001	2002
7.0	4.8	2.4	7.9	3.9	3.3	3.4	2.3	0.9	6.3	2.4	2.0
5.8	11.3	4.2	5.9	3.0	2.5	1.6	7.8	3.2	3.6	3.4	2.5
2.6	0.7	1.2	2.4	1.2	1.4	NA	0.8	1.5	1.8	1.6	2.4
0.2	0.4	0.3	0.8	0.4	0.3	0.7	2.8	2.5	4.1	4.0	3.5
NA	1.4	0.2	0.3	0.4	0.2	NA	8.5	1.4	1.4	3.5	2.3
12.0	16.2	13.5	8.4	6.0	6.3	3.0	5.3	4.0	2.6	2.5	2.4
NA	1.0	0.6	1.0	0.8	0.6	NA	4.0	1.9	1.3	1.7	1.4
0.5	1.1	1.3	1.1	0.6	0.4	0.8	2.2	3.5	2.2	1.6	1.7
27.0	7.8	9.6	11.2	10.7	10.8	7.2	2.3	2.5	3.9	3.0	3.0
9.6	20.9	17.6	14.5	21.8	23.7	NA	4.1	2.4	4.2	4.2	3.4
6.9	6.4	7.9	3.5	7.3	8.1	2.8	1.5	1.7	1.9	2.2	2.0
NA	0.8	0.9	0.5	0.9	1.0	NA	2.0	1.6	1.2	2.5	2.4
5.3	2.9	3.1	9.6	7.2	4.7	4.3	2.5	2.8	2.5	3.0	2.1
0.9	0.3	0.7	0.8	0.8	1.8	NA		NA	1.3	1.7	2.5
4.7	9.1	15.8	4.2	9.7	8.7	1.5	2.3	3.5	1.6	2.2	1.8
1.5		0.6	1.0	0.9	0.9	1.9		1.6	1.6	2.8	2.6
1.6	1.6	1.1	1.0	1.3	1.2	1.8	3.2	NA	1.6	2.5	2.0
1.0	1.7	0.7	2.1	1.4	1.1	2.2	3.1	NA	2.6	2.8	2.1
3.5	7.8	11.8	17.6	16.2	18.4	1.2	2.9	3.7	2.1	2.1	2.2
0.8	0.5	1.0	1.2	0.9	0.6	3.0	1.6	2.6	2.4	2.1	1.8
2.1		NA	0.3	0.2	0.3	15.8		NA	0.8	0.8	1.0
		0.3			0.6			1.5			3.2
4.8		1.6	1.4	1.4	1.0	9.2		2.2	3.1	2.8	2.5
0.2	0.4	0.0	0.3	0.1	0.2	NA		NA	2.1	1.5	2.4
0.9	0.9	0.6	0.6	0.4	0.3	4.2	4.3	6.2	2.8	2.1	1.7
0.0		0.0	NA	NA	0.0	0.0		0.0	NA	NA	0.4
NA	1.6	1.2	0.7	1.1	0.9	NA	3.7	3.3	2.0	3.3	3.6
NA	0.1	0.5	0.2	0.2	0.1	NA	0.6	4.0	1.2	2.2	2.2
0.4	0.2	0.9	0.2	0.3	0.1	8.8	1.9	0.1	3.3	4.2	3.5
0.1		0.1	0.1	0.1	0.1	6.0		3.4	1.4	2.4	3.1
0.3	0.2	0.5	0.3	0.2	0.2	2.8	1.8	6.1	3.0	2.4	2.3
100.0	100.0	100.0	99.0	100.0	100.0	3.5	3.1	3.3	2.6	2.6	2.4

NOTE: The number and value of U.S. contracts by region are taken from regional sources. They do not add to the national totals. The national total number and value of U.S. contracts for 1998, 2001, and 2002 are, respectively, 2,238 and US$6.483 billion, 2,606 and US$7.515 billion, and 3,363 and US$8.156 billion.

TABLE 5-4

TOP-RANKED REGIONS FOR U.S. DIRECT INVESTMENT IN CHINA,
1995, 1996, 1998, 2001, AND 2002

	Rank by Contracted Amount of FDI									
	1995		1996		1998		2001		2002	
Region	U.S.	All	U.S.	All	U.S.	All	U.S.	All	U.S.	All
Jiangsu	1	2	1	2	3	2	1	1	1	1
Shandong	4	5	7	5	9	8	4	4	2	4
Liaoning	7	6	3	6	2	5	2	7	3	6
Guangdong	2	1	4	1	10	1	5	2	4	2
Shanghai	3	3	2	3	1	3	6	3	5	3
Zhejiang	6	8	6	8	5	9	7	5	6	5
Tianjin	8	7	5	7	6	7	3	9	7	9
Fujian	9	4	12	4	7	4	9	6	8	7
Beijing	5	9	11	10	4	6	8	8	9	8
Sichuan	12	12	14	15	8	13	–	10	10	14

SOURCE: PRC, Economic Information and Agency 1997b, 1998b, 2000b; PRC, Asia Economic
Information and Consultancy Ltd. 2002, 2003.
NOTE: Data for U.S. direct investment in Liaoning in 1998 include only those of Dalian and Shenyang.

TABLE 5-5

TOP-RANKED REGIONS FOR FDI IN CHINA,
1995, 1996, 1998, 2001, AND 2002

	Rank by Contracted Amount of FDI									
	1995		1996		1998		2001		2002	
Region	All	U.S.	All	U.S.	All	U.S	All	U.S.	All	U.S.
Jiangsu	2	1	2	1	2	3	1	1	1	1
Guangdong	1	2	1	4	1	10	2	5	2	4
Shanghai	3	3	3	2	3	1	3	6	3	5
Shandong	5	4	5	7	8	9	4	4	4	2
Zhejiang	8	6	8	6	9	5	5	7	5	6
Liaoning	6	7	6	3	5	2	7	2	6	3
Fujian	4	9	4	12	4	7	6	9	7	8
Beijing	9	5	10	11	6	4	8	8	8	9
Tianjin	7	8	7	5	7	6	9	3	9	7
Jiangxi	–	–	21	20	19	17	19	22	10	18

SOURCE: PRC, Economic Information and Agency 1997b, 1998b, 2000b; PRC, Asia Economic
Information and Consultancy Ltd. 2002, 2003.
NOTE: Data for U.S. direct investment in Liaoning in 1998 include only those of Dalian and Shenyang.

In 1998 nine of the top ten destinations for U.S. direct investment and for all FDI overlapped each other.

Locational preferences of U.S. and all foreign direct investors have two notable differences, and they have to do with the roles played by Guangdong and Fujian. While Guangdong has until recently been the most popular destination of all foreign direct investment (see table 5-5), it has never been the most popular destination for U.S. direct investment. Instead, Jiangsu and Liaoning have been the most popular destinations for U.S. direct investment in terms of the total value of contracts (see table 5-4). And although Fujian has consistently been among the top seven most popular destinations of all foreign direct investment, it has never been a particularly important destination for U.S. direct investment—it ranked eighth in 2002, seventh in 1998, twelfth in 1996, and ninth in 1995.

Table 5-3 also provides data on the average size of contracted direct investment. The average size of U.S. contracted direct investment was $3.9 million in 1998, $3.1 million in 2001, and $3.3 million in 2002. But in 1995, the average size of the U.S. contract was $1.9 million. The average size for all FDI was $2.6 million, $2.6 million, and $2.42 million, respectively, for 1998, 2001, and 2002. The figures indicate that over time the size of a typical U.S. direct investment in China has grown much more significantly than that of direct investment from other countries: by the end of the 1990s, a typical U.S. direct investment would be larger than a typical direct investment from other countries and regions. But between 1998 and 2001, the average size of the U.S. contracted direct investment actually declined. In table 5-11, we present similar information as contained in table 5-3 for the years 1996 and 1997.

Factors in Locational Choice

A survey conducted by the National Bureau of Statistics of the People's Republic of China for CIER in 1993 asked foreign-invested firms to identify the principal factors influencing their location decision in China. Table 5-6 summarizes the results, which indicate that the most important factor influencing the location decision for U.S.-invested firms as well as foreign-invested firms was a "better tax break." The factor was the most often cited for all major countries and regions of origin of FDI in China.

TABLE 5-6

IMPORTANCE OF FACTORS IN SELECTION OF LOCATION OF DIRECT INVESTMENT, 1992 (percent of firms citing the specific factor)

Factors	United States	Hong Kong	Japan	Singapore	Taiwan	Others	All
Better tax break	50.8	53.4	54.5	66.7	47.7	54.5	52.4
Better infra-structure	50.8	41.5	30.9	33.3	37.7	48.5	40.9
Lower trans-portation cost	32.8	36.7	36.7	47.6	31.6	31.8	35.1
Lower land price or rent	27.8	34	41.8	28.6	35.8	36.1	34.2
Similarity in language/dialect	13.1	33.5	14.5	33.3	41.3	19.7	32.1
Higher quality of labor	39.3	28.4	38.2	28.6	25.1	28.8	28.9
Local availability of resources	24.6	18.2	21.8	19.1	19.1	22.7	19.2
Efficiency of the local government	16.4	20.2	20	0	20.1	10.6	18.9
Cluster of investors from the same country	11.5	16.7	10.9	0	18.1	15.2	16.3
Others	16.4	7.9	16.3	4.8	13.2	16.6	9.6
Number of cases	61	648	55	21	215	66	1,066

SOURCE: CIER 1993.

The second most frequently cited factor for all foreign-invested firms was "better infrastructure," followed by "lower transportation cost," "lower land price or rent," and "similarity in language/dialect," in that order. U.S.-invested firms, however, considered "better infrastructure" as important as "better tax break"; "similarity in language/dialect" was, as expected, relatively unimportant. Moreover, "higher quality of labor" ranked ahead of "lower transportation cost" and "lower land price or rent." "Local availability of resources" was also a factor cited more often by U.S.-invested firms than the other foreign-invested firms.

The CIER survey questions on locational choice did not explicitly consider "low wage rate." Does U.S. direct investment go to China to take advantage of low wages? Or do the U.S. direct investors go to China to sell in China's domestic market? We can shed some light on the questions by examining China's top ten regions of U.S. direct investment and their local per-capita income as well as the local cost of labor (table 5-7). Not too surprisingly, a high per-capita gross domestic product positively correlates with a high wage rate. U.S. direct investment seems to be locating primarily where local income per capita and wage rates are both high. In 1998, except for Sichuan, the top ten regions with the highest amounts of contracted U.S. direct investment were also among the top ten regions with the highest per-capita incomes; seven of the top ten regions for U.S. direct investment were among the ten regions with the highest wage rates. The facts contradict the hypothesis that U.S. direct investment is primarily motivated by low wage rates but agree with the hypothesis that firms want an entry into the domestic Chinese market. According to CIER (1996), in 1995 U.S. firms in China sold 84.5 percent of the value of their output in the *domestic* Chinese market and only 8.4 percent to the home market (see the discussion in chapter 6).

Other factors may affect the choice of location for U.S. direct investment in China. The factors include the availability of infrastructure, including transportation, telecommunications, and power, and the quality of human capital. Generally speaking, the east and southeast coastal regions of China, the favorite locations of U.S. (and other foreign) direct investors, also rank high in the other dimensions.

Types of Investment

In what modes has U.S. direct investment taken place? Direct investment can take the form of one of five modes: equity joint venture, contractual joint venture, wholly foreign-owned enterprise, joint development, and the more recently introduced foreign-funded joint-stock limited companies. Table 5-8 presents the available data from two sources: the U.S.-China Business Council, for the years 1979–89; and the Chung-Hua Institution for Economic Research (CIER), for the years 1992, 1993, and 1995. The

TABLE 5-7

TOP TEN REGIONS FOR U.S. DIRECT INVESTMENT IN CHINA,
1998, 2001, AND 2002

Region	Per-Capita GDP (US$)	Average Monthly Wage Rate (US$)
1998		
Shanghai (24.62%)	3,412 (1)	137 (1)
Liaoning (10.96%)	1,127 (8)	72 (11)
Jiangsu (8.76%)	1,210 (7)	83 (8)
Beijing (6.37%)	2,232 (2)	125 (2)
Zhejiang (6.31%)	1,358 (4)	98 (6)
Tianjin (5.34%)	1,788 (3)	100 (5)
Fujian (4.87%)	1,252 (6)	86 (7)
Sichuan (4.39%)	524 (24)	66 (16)
Shandong (4.32%)	981 (9)	69 (13)
Guangdong (3.22%)	1,346 (5)	111 (3)
2001		
Jiangsu (21.35%)	1,556 (6)	119 (9)
Liaoning (16.53%)	1,450 (8)	102 (13)
Tianjin (11.48%)	2,428 (3)	144 (6)
Shandong (9.31%)	1,261 (9)	100 (14)
Guangdong (8.00%)	1,654 (5)	157 (5)
Shanghai (7.96%)	4,504 (1)	219 (1)
Zhejiang (6.55%)	1,766 (4)	119 (4)
Beijing (4.91%)	3,075 (2)	192 (2)
Fujian (2.94%)	1,490 (7)	121 (8)
Hunan (1.69%)	729 (17)	97 (17)
2002		
Jiangsu (18.78%)	1,738 (6)	136 (8)
Shandong (16.80%)	1,406 (9)	114 (14)
Liaoning (14.34%)	1,568 (8)	117 (11)
Guangdong (12.60%)	1,815 (5)	179 (5)
Shanghai (10.23%)	4,909 (1)	241 (2)
Zhejiang (8.44%)	2,034 (4)	189 (4)
Tianjin (4.47%)	2,703 (3)	164 (6)
Fujian (3.29%)	1,630 (7)	134 (9)
Beijing (2.51%)	3,436 (2)	220 (3)
Sichuan (1.66%)	696 (26)	113 (15)

SOURCE: PRC, Economic Information and Agency 1999b, 2002b, 2003; PRC, National Bureau of Statistics 1999, 2002, 2003; Asian Development Bank 1997; table 5-3.

NOTE: In column 1, figures in parentheses are the percentage shares of total U.S. contracted foreign direct investment in China in 1998, 2001, and 2002, respectively; in column 2, figures in parentheses are the rankings of regional per-capita income in China in 1998, 2001, and 2002; in column 3, figures in parentheses are rankings of regional wage rates in China in 1998, 2001, and 2002.

TABLE 5-8

DISTRIBUTION OF U.S. DIRECT INVESTMENT IN CHINA BY MODES OF INVESTMENT, SELECTED YEARS (percent)

	Equity Joint Venture	Contractual Joint Venture	Wholly Foreign-Owned	Joint Development
		By Value		
(Contracted)				
1979–89	30.5	31.9	8.6	29.1
(Contracted) 1992	NA	NA	NA	NA
(Contracted) 1993	NA	NA	NA	NA
(Realized) 1995	72.6	25.1	2.3	NA
		By Number of Contracts or Firms		
(Contracted)				
1979–89	76.1	13.1	6.9	3.9
(Realized) 1992	85.3	3.3	11.5	NA
(Realized) 1993	84.2	4.9	11.0	NA
(Realized) 1995	83.3	5.6	11.1	NA

SOURCE: 1979–89 data from the U.S.-China Business Council 1990; 1992, 1993, and 1995 data from CIER 1993, 1994, 1996.

NOTE: The 1979–89 data refer to contracted as opposed to realized direct investment. The CIER surveys did not include JDs. Percentages may not add to 100 due to rounding.

information contained in both sets of data reflects the distribution by mode of the cumulative stock of U.S. direct investment rather than its annual flow and is not directly comparable to the information in tables 4-3 and 4-4 for all FDI in China.

In terms of contracted value, from 1979 to 1989, U.S. direct investment was almost evenly divided among equity joint ventures, contractual joint ventures, and joint development. Wholly U.S.-owned enterprises were only about 8.6 percent of the total.[5] Comparable stock figures are not available for all foreign direct investment. But cumulating the contracted investments in table 4-3 from 1986 through 1989 would give a breakdown of EJVs, 52.4 percent; CJVs, 30.7 percent; WFOs, 15 percent; and JDs, 1.9 percent (data from earlier years unavailable). In terms of the number of ventures, the predominant mode of U.S. direct investment was equity joint venture, at 76.1 percent, followed by contractual joint venture and then wholly owned enterprise. On average, equity joint ventures tend to be smaller investments in terms of value, and wholly owned enterprises and joint development tend to be larger.

In the 1990s, according to the CIER surveys, in terms of the stock of realized value the equity joint venture has remained the dominant mode of U.S. direct investment; its share was approximately three-quarters, followed by CJVs at 25 percent, and WFOs at 2.3 percent (excluding joint development). Comparable stock figures are not available for all FDI. But cumulating the realized investments in table 4-4 from 1986 through 1995 gives the breakdown of EJVs, 53.7 percent; CJVs, 20.5 percent; WFOs, 23.2 percent; and JDs, 2.5 percent. The proportion of the stock of U.S. direct investment accounted for by WFO in the CIER survey is low and may have been the result of low response rates by WFOs compared with other modes of direct investment. In terms of the number of ventures, however, the wholly owned enterprise has overtaken the contractual joint venture to become the second most popular mode of U.S. direct investment, at approximately 11 percent. That shift is consistent with the general trend in China of the rising of the wholly foreign-owned enterprise in importance over time for all foreign direct investment (see chapter 4).

Table 5-9 examines the distribution of U.S. direct investment in China by sectors. Based on U.S. government estimates, the bulk of U.S. direct investment in China is in the *manufacturing* industries. In 2001 and 2002, 67.6 percent and 59.9 percent, respectively, of the total U.S. direct investment position (the cumulative stock of U.S. direct investment), valued at historical cost, were in manufacturing; and 15.58 percent and 20 percent, respectively, were in mining and utilities. The investment in mining and utilities reflects one motive of U.S. multinationals in China—to extract relatively untapped natural resources and other raw materials—in this case, oil. Within the direct investment in manufacturing, 40.74 percent and 24.79 percent were in electronics and other electrical equipment in 2001 and 2002, respectively. Electronic and other electrical equipment has become the sector with the most U.S. direct investment since 1995.

Comparable data on direct investment position by sector are not available for all FDI. Table 4-7 indicated that in 2002, FDI as a whole was concentrated in the manufacturing sector, with a share of 71.61 percent.

TABLE 5-9

U.S. DIRECT INVESTMENT POSITION IN CHINA BY SECTORS, BASED ON HISTORICAL COSTS (US$ million)

	1999	2000	2001	2002
All industries	9,401	11,140	11,387	10,294
Mining	773	1,404	1,287	1,514
Utilities	589	583	487	545
Total manufacturing	5,787	7,076	7,698	6,161
Food	280	286	330	392
Chemicals	995	1,122	1,045	1,196
Primary and fabricated metals	223	157	140	121
Machinery	212	218	201	212
Computer and electronic products	2,402	3,500	3,999	1,942
Electrical equipment, appliances, and components	396	458	640	610
Transportation equipment	627	652	615	746
Wholesale trade	386	378	410	536
Information	46	79	105	99
Depository institutions	62	64	161	329
Finance (except deposit institutions and insurance)	11	43	D	29
Professional, scientific, and technical services	306	245	120	65
Other industries	1,440	1,267	D	1,016

SOURCE: Bargas 2000; U.S. Department of Commerce 2003c.

NOTE: D indicates that the data in the cell have been suppressed to avoid the disclosure of data of individual companies.

The closest comparisons for U.S. direct investment are 59.9 percent in manufacturing in 2002 (on a stock basis). The broad sectoral distribution of U.S. direct investment in China does not appear to differ significantly from that of all FDI in China.

U.S. firms in China reportedly signed 3,474 direct investment contracts in 1995, 2,517 in 1996, 2,188 in 1997, 2,238 in 1998, 2,606 in 2001, and 3,363 in 2002. Table 5-10 highlights Fortune 500 U.S. companies that made direct investments in China in 1995, 1996, 1998, 1999, 2000, and 2001, including Ford Motors, General Electric, IBM, Mobil, DuPont, Hewlett-Packard, Procter & Gamble, Bell Atlantic, Lucent Technologies, and Motorola.

Smaller U.S. firms have also begun to invest in China. Those include the Aluminum Company of America, Sida Corporation, and Armstrong World Industries Delaware, Inc. Clearly the largest U.S. corporations have been leaders in investing in China. For example, Motorola (China) Tianjin Co. Ltd. is the largest foreign-invested electronics firm in China, with sales revenue of 16.3 billion yuan (almost $2 billion) in 1997. Other large U.S. corporations such as the AIG Group, Chrysler, General Motors, Intel, and Microsoft have been prominent U.S. direct investors.[6]

Table 5-10

U.S. Fortune 500 Direct Investment in China, 1995, 1996, 1998, 1999, 2000, 2001

Rank within U.S. Fortune 500	U.S. Corporation	Value of Investment/Revenue (US$ million)	Venture
		1995	
7	General Electric	8.16	GE Shanghai Drive Systems Co. Ltd.
		2.4	Chengdu GE Medical Systems (Xinan) Co. Ltd.
8	Mobil	29.8	Mobil (Taicang) Petrochemical Terminalling Co. Ltd.
64	RJR Nabisco Holdings	21.13	Beijing Nabisco Food Co., Ltd.
128	Emerson Electric	4.83	Hangzhou Wanshili Knitting
159	Whirlpool	16.23	Whirlpool Narcissus
219	Microsoft	2.6	Microsoft (China) Co., Ltd.
230	Ingersoll-Rand	23.56	Torrington Wuxi Bearings Co., Ltd.
287	Seagate Technology	30	Seagate Technology Co., Ltd.
473	Stanley Works	11.2	Beijing Jinzhou Engineering Machinery Equipment Co.
		1996	
2	Ford Motors	11.34	Jiangxi Fuchang Air Condition Systems Co., Ltd.
14	DuPont	14.85	DuPont (Qingdao) Nylon Co., Ltd.
79	Rockwell	7.2	Shanghai Rockwell Collins Navigation & Communication Co., Ltd.
223	Nike	20	Nike Sports and Fitness (Suzhou) Co., Ltd.
497	Pacific Enterprise	30	Fujian Dongshan Pacific Jinluan Gulf Hotel Co., Ltd.
		1998	
5	General Electric	77.49	General Electric Appliance Plastic (China) Co., Ltd.
6	IBM	184.58	IBM (China) Co., Ltd.
14	Hewlett-Packard	219.29	China Hewlett-Packard Co., Ltd
		83.59	Packard Electric Shanghai Co., Ltd.

continued on next page

TABLE 5-10 *(continued)*
U.S. FORTUNE 500 DIRECT INVESTMENT IN CHINA, 1995, 1996, 1998, 1999, 2000, 2001

Rank within U.S. Fortune 500	U.S. Corporation	Value of Investment/Revenue (US$ million)	Venture
		1998 *(continued)*	
		118.08	Hewlett-Packard Computer Products (Shanghai) Co., Ltd.
17	Procter & Gamble (P&G)	583.81 90.93 74.98	P&G (G.Z.) Co., Ltd. P&G Paper (G.Z.) Co., Ltd. Procter & Gamble Personal Cleansing (Tianjin), Ltd.
25	Bell Atlantic	601.65	Shanghai Bell Telephone Equipment MFG. Co., Ltd.
33	Lucent Technologies	131.63 117.13	Lucent Technologies of Shanghai, Ltd. Lucent Technologies Qingdao Tele-communications System Co., Ltd.
34	Motorola	2,366.40	Motorola (China) Electronics, Ltd.
51	Johnson & Johnson	80.42	Shanghai Johnson, Ltd.
54	Pepsico	108.74	Shanghai Pepsi-Cola Beverage Co., Ltd.
63	Xerox	59.00	Xerox of Shanghai Limited
73	Coca-Cola	68.05 68.30 58.12	Tianjin Coca-Cola Bottling Co., Ltd. Beijing Coca-Cola Beverage Co., Ltd. Wuhan Coca-Cola Beverage Co., Ltd.
87	Ameritech	73.12	Amertek Computers (S.Z.) Co., Ltd.
106	Pfizer	55.77	Pfizer Pharmaceuticals Co., Ltd.
134	McDonald's	57.68	Beijing McDonald's Corporation
155	Whirlpool	104.75	Shunde Whirlpool SMC Microwave Products Co., Ltd.
244	Seagate Technology	1,009.06 566.85	Seagate Technology (Shenzhen) Co., Ltd. Seagate Technology International Wuxi Co., Ltd.
308	Avon Products	77.12	Avon Products (G.Z.) Co., Ltd.
		1999	
6	IBM	203.35 210.83	IBM (China) Co., Ltd. Shenzhen IBM Technology Products Co., Ltd.

continued on next page

TABLE 5-10 *(continued)*
U.S. FORTUNE 500 DIRECT INVESTMENT IN CHINA, 1995, 1996, 1998, 1999, 2000, 2001

Rank within U.S. Fortune 500	U.S. Corporation	Value of Investment/Revenue (US$ million)	Venture
		1999 *(continued)*	
13	Hewlett-Packard	226.62	China Hewlett-Packard Co., Ltd.
		94.48	Packard Electric Shanghai Co., Ltd.
		187.28	Hewlett-Packard Computer Products (Shanghai) Co., Ltd.
		67.63	Shanghai Hewlett Packard, Ltd.
22	Lucent Technologies	181.97	Lucent Technologies of Shanghai, Ltd.
		163.63	Lucent Technologies Qingdao Tele-communications System Co., Ltd.
		59.05	Lucent Technology (China) Co., Ltd.
23	Procter & Gamble (P&G)	218.36	P&G China, Ltd.
		85.91	P&G Paper (G.Z.) Co., Ltd.
		68.57	Tianjin P&G Co., Ltd.
33	Bell Atlantic	729.99	Shanghai Bell Telephone Equipment MFG. Co., Ltd.
		372.19	Shanghai Bell Alcart Mobile Communication System, Ltd.
37	Motorola	2,174.20	Motorola (Tianjin) Electronics, Ltd.
43	Johnson & Johnson	70.73	Shanghai Johnson, Ltd.
		79.08	Johnson (China) Co., Ltd.
76	Pepsico	104.20	Shanghai Pepsi-Cola Beverage Co., Ltd.
83	Coca-Cola	69.87	Tianjin Coca-Cola Bottling Co., Ltd.
		68.61	Beijing Coca-Cola Bottling Co., Ltd.
		68.00	Wuhan Coca-Cola Bottling Co., Ltd.
87	Xerox	78.91	Xerox of Shanghai Limited
		90.88	Shenzhen Xerox High-Tech Co., Ltd.
124	Eastman Kodak	69.96	Kodak Electronics (Shanghai) Co., Ltd.
151	Anheuser-Busch	98.60	Budweiser (Wuhan) International Beer Co., Ltd.
164	Whirlpool	127.56	Shunde Whirlpool SMC Microwave Products Co., Ltd.
256	Seagate Technology	796.93	Seagate Technology (Shenzhen) Co., Ltd.
		918.47	Seagate Technology International Wuxi Co., Ltd.

continued on next page

TABLE 5-10 *(continued)*
U.S. FORTUNE 500 DIRECT INVESTMENT IN CHINA, 1995, 1996, 1998, 1999, 2000, 2001

Rank within U.S. Fortune 500	U.S. Corporation	Value of Investment/Revenue (US$ million)	Venture
		1999 *(continued)*	
261	SCI Systems	104.63	SCITECH Group Company Limited
418	Copper Industries	292.51	Jiangxi Copper Co., Ltd.
		181.45	Jinlong Copper Co., Ltd.
479	Phoenix Home Life Mutual INS.	127.95	Phoenix Co., Ltd.
		2000	
8	IBM	72.63	IBM (China) Co., Ltd.
		279.24	Shenzhen IBM Technology Products Co., Ltd.
10	Verizon Communications	756.87	Shanghai Bell Telephone Equipment MFG. Co., Ltd.
19	Hewlett-Packard	181.86	Hewlett-Packard Computer Products (Shanghai) Co., Ltd.
		401.06	Shanghai Hewlett Packard, Ltd.
		236.40	China Hewlett-Packard Co., Ltd.
28	Lucent Technologies	113.58	Lucent Technologies of Shanghai, Ltd.
		100.56	Lucent Technology (China) Co., Ltd.
31	Procter & Gamble (P&G)	472.03	P&G (G.Z.) Co., Ltd.
		90.16	P&G Paper (G.Z.) Co., Ltd.
		169.90	P&G (China), Ltd.
		85.43	Guangzhou P&G Oral Healthcare Products Co., Ltd.
34	Motorola	2,855.34	Motorola (Tianjin) Electronics, Ltd.
48	Dell Computer	235.30	Dell Computer (China) Co., Ltd.
56	E.I. Du Pont De Nemours	88.93	Suzhou Du Pont Polyester Co., Ltd.
57	Johnson & Johnson	92.18	Johnson & Johnson (China) Co., Ltd.
57	Delphi Automotive	73.37	Shanghai Delphi Auto Air-Conditioning Systems Co., Ltd.
93	Coca-Cola	75.17	Tianjin Coca-Cola Bottling Co., Ltd.
		73.11	Beijing Coca-Cola Bottling Co., Ltd.

continued on next page

TABLE 5-10 *(continued)*
U.S. FORTUNE 500 DIRECT INVESTMENT IN CHINA, 1995, 1996, 1998, 1999, 2000, 2001

Rank within U.S. Fortune 500	U.S. Corporation	Value of Investment/Revenue (US$ million)	Venture
		2000 *(continued)*	
		173.00	Coca-Cola (China) Beverage Co., Ltd.
94	Pepsico	103.15	Shanghai Pepsi-Cola Beverage Co., Ltd.
109	Xerox	76.16	Xerox of Shanghai Limited
		78.00	Shenzhen Xerox High-Tech Co., Ltd.
139	Solectron	76.75	Solectron (Suzhou) Technology Co., Ltd.
141	Eastman Kodak	217.84	Kodak (China) Shareholding Co., Ltd.
159	Anheuser-Busch	105.25	Budweiser (Wuhan) International Beer Co., Ltd
181	Whirlpool	134.30	Shunde Whirlpool SMC Microwave Products Co., Ltd.
201	Colgate-Palmolive	128.84	Guangzhou Colgate Palm & Olive Co., Ltd.
212	Nike	81.20	Nike (Suzhou) Sports Products Co., Ltd.
230	SCI Systems	76.08	SCI Electronic (Kunshan) Co., Ltd.
285	Seagate Technology	606.19	Seagate Technology (Shenzhen) Co., Ltd.
		663.10	Seagate Technology International Wuxi Co., Ltd.
383	Copper Industries	326.77	Jiangxi Copper Co., Ltd.
		197.53	Jinlong Copper Co., Ltd.
		2001	
1	Wal-Mart Stores	118.34	Shenzhen Wal-Mart Pearl River Store Co., Ltd.
9	IBM	102.48	IBM (China) Co., Ltd.
		241.57	Shenzhen IBM Technology Products Co., Ltd.
11	Verizon Communications	782.73	Shanghai Bell Telephone Equipment MFG. Co., Ltd.
		206.37	Shanghai Bell Alcart Mobile Communication
28	Hewlett-Packard	178.40	China Hewlett-Packard Co., Ltd.
		96.89	Packard Electric Shanghai Co., Ltd.

continued on next page

TABLE 5-10 (*continued*)
U.S. FORTUNE 500 DIRECT INVESTMENT IN CHINA, 1995, 1996, 1998, 1999, 2000, 2001

Rank within U.S. Fortune 500	U.S. Corporation	Value of Investment/Revenue (US$ million)	Venture
		2001 (*continued*)	
		360.70	Hewlett-Packard Computer Products (Shanghai) Co., Ltd.
		507.09	Shanghai Hewlett Packard Ltd.
35	Procter & Gamble (P&G)	454.05	P&G (G.Z.) Co., Ltd.
		104.20	P&G Paper (G.Z.) Co., Ltd.
		143.23	P&G (China), Ltd.
46	Compaq Computer	143.76	Compaq (Shanghai), Ltd.
47	Johnson & Johnson	120.54	Johnson (China) Co., Ltd.
56	Motorola	3,769.74	Motorola (Tianjin) Electronics Limited
		347.56	Hangzhou Motorola Mobile Telecom. Equipment Co., Ltd.
63	Pepsico	95.57	Shanghai Pepsi-Cola Beverage Co., Ltd.
70	E.I. Du Pont De Nemours	116.56	Suzhou Du Pont Polyester Co., Ltd.
		97.73	Dupont China Group Co., Ltd.
76	Lucent Technologies	292.43	Lucent Technologies of Shanghai, Ltd.
		351.62	Qingdao Lucent Technology & Communications Equipment Inc.
		129.42	Shanghai Lucent Technology International Trade Co., Ltd.
		93.98	Shanghai Lucent Technological Optical Fiber Co., Ltd.
99	Coca-Cola	155.36	Coca-Cola (China) Beverage Co., Ltd.
110	Solectron	607.20	Solectron (Suzhou) Technology Co., Ltd.
120	Xerox	100.15	Xerox of Shanghai Limited
		118.88	Shanzhen Xerox High-Tech Co., Ltd.
155	Eastman Kodak	402.34	Kodak (China) Shareholding Co., Ltd.
159	Anheuser-Busch	142.15	Budweiser (Wuhan) International Beer Co., Ltd
186	Whirlpool	136.24	Shunde Whirlpool SMC Microwave Products Co., Ltd.

continued on next page

TABLE 5-10 (continued)

U.S. FORTUNE 500 DIRECT INVESTMENT IN CHINA, 1995, 1996, 1998, 1999, 2000, 2001

Rank within U.S. Fortune 500	U.S. Corporation	Value of Investment/Revenue (US$ million)	Venture
		2001 (continued)	
204	Nike	99.80	Nike (Suzhou) Sports Products Co., Ltd.
207	Colgate-Palmolive	207.65	Guangzhou Colgate Palm & Olive Co., Ltd.
222	SCI Systems	112.44	SCITECH Group Company Limited
292	United Auto Group	131.81	United Auto Electronic Ltd.
		117.69	Xiamen King Long United Automobile Industry Co., Ltd.
377	Black & Decker	112.66	Black and Decker (Suzhou) Tools, Ltd.
386	Copper Industries	246.11	Jinlong Copper Co., Ltd.
		106.66	Huludao East Copper Co., Ltd.
		196.59	Changzhou Kinyuan Copper Co., Ltd.
		94.80	Zhangjiagang United Copper Co., Ltd.

SOURCE: *Fortune* 1996, 1997, 1999, 2000, 2001, 2002. PRC, Economic Information and Agency 1999a, 2000a, 2001a; PRC, Asia Economic Information and Consultancy Ltd. 2002.

NOTE: The values of investment are stated for 1995 and 1996. The revenues for the joint ventures are stated for the years 1998, 1999, 2000, and 2001.

TABLE 5-11

LOCATION OF U.S. DIRECT INVESTMENT IN CHINA, 1996 AND 1997

	Number of Contracts		Region's Share of Total U.S. Contracts (%)		Region's Share of All Contracts (%)		Value of Contracts (US$ million)	
	1996	1997	1996	1997	1996	1997	1996	1997
Beijing	144	124	5.80	7.05	3.50	3.80	161.4	129.8
Tianjin	197	208	8.00	11.82	4.50	5.00	492	300
Hebei	110	NA	4.40	NA	3.40	3.00	325.1	180.1
Shanxi	23	25	0.90	1.42	0.50	0.70	53.2	21.4
Inner Mongolia	21	19	0.80	1.08	0.50	0.50	24.6	7.4
Liaoning	267	NA	10.80	NA	7.20	8.10	720	NA
Jilin	37	NA	1.50	NA	1.70	1.90	106.5	NA
Heilongjiang	NA	56	NA	3.18	2.20	1.80	NA	91.4
Shanghai	313	250	12.60	14.21	8.50	8.60	939.3	939.5
Jiangsu	354	275	14.30	15.63	11.00	9.90	1,460	804.3
Zhejiang	178	125	7.20	7.11	4.90	4.10	488.3	103.9
Anhui	53	46	2.10	2.62	1.40	1.30	42.9	32.6
Fujian	50	67	2.00	3.81	8.10	10.90	136	601
Jiangxi	15	30	0.60	1.71	1.50	1.90	32.1	56.1
Shandong	255	179	10.30	10.18	8.90	7.60	433	200
Henan	59	71	2.40	4.04	1.90	1.90	230.7	116.9
Hubei	42	NA	1.70	NA	2.20	1.90	55.9	NA
Hunan	28	30	1.10	1.71	1.80	1.90	20.6	51
Guangdong	130	125	5.30	7.11	18.80	17.80	554.4	199.3
Guangxi	22	21	0.90	1.19	1.30	1.40	37.5	95.4
Hainan	22	14	0.90	0.80	1.00	1.00	25.1	16
Sichuan	78	39	3.20	2.22	1.90	1.20	98.3	46
Guizhou	11	6	0.40	0.34	0.40	0.40	16.2	3.4
Yunnan	19	13	0.80	0.74	0.60	0.60	53.6	28.1
Tibet	NA	NA	NA	NA	0.10	NA	NA	NA
Shaanxi	46	27	1.90	1.53	1.10	0.90	191.1	52.1
Gansu	NA	NA	NA	NA	0.50	0.30	NA	NA
Qinghai	2	2	0.10	0.11	0.10	0.10	0.9	6.3
Ningxia	NA	NA	NA	NA	0.10	0.10	NA	NA
Xinjiang	NA	7	NA	0.40	0.30	0.20	NA	3.5
All regions	2,476	1,759	100	100	100	98.80	6,699	4,085.5

SOURCE: PRC, Economic Information and Agency 1998b, 1999b.

NOTE: The number and value of U.S. contracts by region are taken from regional sources.
They do not add to the national totals. The national total number of U.S. contracts for 1997 and

Region's Share of Total Value of U.S. Contracts (%)		Region's Share of Total Value of All Contracts (%)		Average Size of U.S. Contracts (US$ million)		Average Size of All Contracts (US$ million)	
1996	1997	1996	1997	1996	1997	1996	1997
2.40	3.18	2.40	3.30	1.1	1	2.1	2.1
7.30	7.34	5.30	7.50	2.5	1.4	3.6	3.6
4.90	4.41	2.80	2.20	3	NA	2.5	1.8
0.80	0.52	1.70	0.60	2.3	0.9	10.5	2
0.40	0.18	0.30	0.30	1.2	0.4	1.5	1.3
10.70	NA	5.80	8.60	2.7	NA	2.4	2.6
1.60	NA	0.90	1.00	2.9	NA	1.6	1.2
NA	2.24	1.00	1.20	NA	1.6	1.3	1.5
14.00	23.00	13.70	10.40	3	3.8	4.8	3
21.80	19.69	14.60	18.00	4.1	2.9	4	4.4
7.30	2.54	4.30	2.40	2.7	0.8	2.6	1.4
0.60	0.80	0.70	0.80	0.8	0.7	1.5	1.4
2.00	14.71	8.90	8.90	2.7	9	3.3	2
0.50	1.37	0.50	1.30	2.1	1.9	1.1	1.6
6.50	4.90	7.40	6.40	1.7	1.1	2.5	2
3.40	2.86	1.70	1.20	3.9	1.6	2.5	1.5
0.80	NA	1.30	1.30	1.3	NA	1.8	1.6
0.30	1.25	0.60	1.70	0.7	1.7	1.1	2.1
8.30	4.88	21.30	15.10	4.3	1.6	3.4	2.1
0.60	2.34	1.00	2.90	1.7	4.5	2.3	5.1
0.40	0.39	0.40	0.60	1.1	1.1	1.1	1.3
1.50	1.13	0.90	0.50	1.3	1.2	1.5	1.1
0.20	0.08	0.20	0.20	1.5	0.6	1.3	1.3
0.80	0.69	0.30	0.50	2.8	2.2	1.3	2.1
NA	NA	0.00	NA	NA	NA	0.6	NA
2.90	1.28	0.80	1.30	4.2	1.9	2	3.6
NA	NA	0.10	0.20	NA	NA	0.7	1.7
0.00	0.15	0.00	0.10	0.4	3.1	0.9	2.4
NA	NA	0.10	0.00	NA	NA	1.5	0.4
NA	0.09	0.10	0.10	NA	0.5	1.6	0.8
100	100	99	98.60	2.7	2.3	3	2.4

1996 is, respectively, 2,188 and 2,517, and the total value of U.S. contracts is US$4.937 and 6.916 billion.

6

Comparison of
Foreign Direct Investment

Chapters 4 and 5 examine the trends and the characteristics of U.S. and aggregate foreign direct investment in China. This chapter focuses precisely on comparisons of U.S. direct investment with other countries, comparing the features of U.S. direct investment with those of direct investment from Hong Kong, Japan, Singapore, and Taiwan—economies that are significant sources of direct investment inflows into China.

How important is U.S. direct investment in China? How large is U.S. direct investment compared with that of other countries? Table 6-1 compares the direct investment of the most important direct investor countries and regions in China on the basis of official Chinese data. Hong Kong has consistently been the largest and most important single source of FDI with an average of more than half the aggregate FDI flow into China over the 1993–2002 period. However, a significant proportion of the Hong Kong direct investment, an estimated 40 percent (see Shih 1989; Hsueh and Woo 1991), originates in Mainland China. But even discounting Hong Kong direct investment by 40 percent, it remains by far the largest "foreign" direct investor in China. In 2002 Hong Kong nominally accounted for 34 percent of aggregate FDI; if the reported Hong Kong direct investment of $17.86 billion is reduced by 40 percent to $10.7 billion, Hong Kong still accounts for almost 21 percent of the adjusted aggregate foreign direct investment in that year (taking into account the effect of the reduction of Hong Kong direct investment on aggregate FDI). Even with the adjustment, Hong Kong is more than twice as important as the United States, the second largest source of direct investment in 2002, with $5.4 billion, about 10.3 percent of the adjusted aggregate FDI.

However, the relative importance of the foreign countries and regions investing in Mainland China has gradually but clearly shifted. Hong Kong and Taiwan, the traditional sources of direct investment, have seen their combined share decline from almost three-quarters in 1993 to less than half in 2002. The U.S. share remained fairly constant at approximately 8 percent through the mid-1990s but rose above 10 percent in 2002. The combined share of the other industrialized countries—the European Union and Japan—has increased dramatically from approximately 7 percent in 1993 to more than 14 percent in 2002. The share of the Association of Southeast Asian Nations (ASEAN) countries has doubled from approximately 3.5 percent to more than 6 percent in 2002. Those shifts relate to the gradual evolution of the objectives of the foreign direct investors. The early foreign direct investors, primarily from Hong Kong and Taiwan, were generally interested in Mainland China as a manufacturing base for exports that had become too expensive to produce at their respective homes—for example, electrical appliances, garments, shoes, and toys. However, the later foreign direct investors include many from the advanced industrialized countries that bring with them advanced technology and know-how and aim to sell in the large domestic Chinese market.

The direct investment figures in table 6-1 are taken from official Chinese government sources. (Chapter 4 has discussed some potential problems.) Table 6-1 has the merit of consistency and allows a comparative impression of the relative importance of the various countries and regions as sources of FDI as well as its evolution. Information from the official sources does not allow a detailed comparison of various characteristics of the direct investments from different countries and regions. To do so, we turn to the surveys conducted by the Chung-Hua Institution for Economic Research in 1993, 1994, and 1996 (for the years 1992, 1993, and 1995, respectively).

The rest of this chapter uses comparative data primarily derived from surveys conducted by the National Bureau of Statistics of the People's Republic of China for CIER in 1993, 1994, and 1996. The surveys provide significantly more detailed and comprehensive information than that in official Chinese sources. The central Chinese government does not handle all FDI projects. Provincial and local governments handle some smaller projects; the details are not forwarded to the central government itself. Because the CIER surveys, unlike central government data, include

TABLE 6-1

REALIZED FOREIGN DIRECT INVESTMENT FLOWS, 1993–2002 (US$ billion)

	1993	1994	1995	1996
Hong Kong	17.27	19.67	20.06	20.68
	(62.77%)	(58.25%)	(53.46%)	(49.56%)
Japan	1.32	2.08	3.11	3.68
	(4.80%)	(6.16%)	(8.29%)	(8.82%)
Taiwan	3.14	3.39	3.16	3.47
	(11.41%)	(10.04%)	(8.42%)	(8.32%)
United States	2.06	2.49	3.08	3.44
	(7.49%)	(7.37%)	(8.21%)	(8.24%)
ASEAN	1.00	1.87	2.62	3.18
	(3.63%)	(5.54%)	(6.98%)	(7.62%)
European Union	0.67	1.54	2.14	2.74
	(2.44%)	(4.56%)	(5.70%)	(6.57%)
Total	27.515	33.767	37.521	41.725

SOURCE: PRC, Economic Information and Agency 1993, 1994, 1995, 1996, 1997a, 1998a, 1999a, 2000a, 2001a, 2002b, 2003.

NOTE: As of 2002, the European Union consists of Austria, Belgium, Denmark, Finland, France, Germany, Greece, Ireland, Italy, Luxembourg, Netherlands, Portugal, Spain, Sweden, and the United Kingdom. ASEAN consists of Brunei, Indonesia, Malaysia, Philippines,

smaller FDI projects systematically excluded from central government data, they can be used to correct for the effects of such omissions.

To implement the surveys, CIER contracted with the PRC National Bureau of Statistics (NBS) to conduct a five-year longitudinal study of all foreign investor firms in the manufacturing sector. In the initial survey conducted in 1993, NBS compiled a list of 30,000 FDI cases from all major cities; 22,740—all in manufacturing—had accurate addresses. With the criteria of size, origin of foreign investors, and industrial classification, the CIER team selected a stratified sample of 1,200 cases. NBS recruited 1,500 interviewers to gather the needed information from the firms; 1,066 usable questionnaires were collected. The original survey doubled the number of Taiwanese firms, so firms from Taiwan were overrepresented in the sample. Whenever appropriate, weights were attached to data on the Taiwanese firms to reflect their overrepresentation.

In the second survey, NBS updated its original list of firms and found 70,000 FDI cases in all major cities. The bureau conducted a follow-up

1997	1998	1999	2000	2001	2002
20.63	18.51	16.36	15.50	16.72	17.86
(45.58%)	(40.71%)	(40.58%)	(38.07%)	(35.67%)	(33.86%)
4.33	3.4	2.97	2.92	4.35	4.19
(9.57%)	(7.48%)	(7.37%)	(7.17%)	(9.28%)	(7.94%)
3.29	2.92	2.60	2.30	2.98	3.97
(7.27%)	(6.42%)	(6.44%)	(5.65%)	(6.36%)	(7.5%)
3.24	4.17	4.22	4.38	4.43	5.42
(7.16%)	(9.17%)	(10.46%)	(10.76%)	(9.45%)	(10.28%)
3.42	4.21	3.29	2.84	2.97	3.22
(7.56%)	(9.26%)	(8.15%)	(6.98%)	(6.34%)	(6.11%)
4.17	3.98	4.48	4.48	4.18	3.71
(9.21%)	(8.75%)	(11.00%)	(11.00%)	(8.92%)	(7.03%)
45.257	45.463	40.319	40.71	46.88	52.74

Singapore, Thailand, and Vietnam. Laos and Myanmar joined ASEAN in 1997, and
Cambodia joined in 1999. For consistency purposes, Cambodia, Laos, and Myanmar
have been excluded from the ASEAN data in this table. The realized FDI figure for the EU
in 1998 excludes direct investment from Ireland. Figures in parentheses refer to the share in
total FDI.

study of the original 1,066 cases and drew a sample of 500 new cases
from the second list; only 943 usable questionnaires were collected
from the original 1,066 cases, and 484 from the 500 newly added cases.
Some original firms declined to be interviewed again, while others had
relocated without a forwarding address. Some original firms had withdrawn from China entirely for financial or other reasons. Thus, the
second survey in 1994 makes available 1,427 usable questionnaires.
In 1996 a follow-up survey of the 1,427 firms produced 1,166 usable
questionnaires.[1]

In the CIER surveys only three types of direct investment were studied:
equity joint venture, contractual joint venture, and wholly foreign-owned
enterprise. The surveys did not include joint development because of the
small number of such cases and also because almost all JD ventures were
in the mining sector and the CIER surveys focused on foreign-invested
firms in the manufacturing sector.[2] Most information (though not all)
comparing U.S. direct investment with direct investment from the other

TABLE 6-2
MODES OF FDI BY PLACE OF ORIGIN, 1992, 1993, AND 1995
(percent of firms)

Modes	United States			Hong Kong			Japan		
	1992	1993	1995	1992	1993	1995	1992	1993	1995
EJV	85.2	84.2	83.3	79.5	78.4	80.3	85.5	84.9	85.0
CJV	3.3	4.9	5.6	12.2	12.1	11.7	5.5	6.1	5.0
WFO	11.5	11.0	11.1	8.3	9.5	7.9	9.1	9.1	10.0
Number of cases	61	82	72	648	771	605	55	66	60

SOURCE: CIER 1993, 1994, 1996.

countries and regions in the CIER surveys is given, not in value, but in the number of firms. Comparing the number of firms across various dimensions (by type of investment, industry, etc.) also shows similarities and differences among countries.

Comparison by Type, Industrial Distribution, and Size

Table 6-2 presents the distribution of the type of FDI by origin for 1992, 1993, and 1995. The distribution across the three years does not appear to differ appreciably. In 1995, 83.3 percent of U.S. firms were engaged in EJVs, 11.1 percent in WFOs, and 5.6 percent in CJVs.[3] In terms of the number of firms, the EJV was clearly the most popular form of U.S. direct investment and the most common mode of direct investment for all foreign direct investors (including Hong Kong and Taiwan). The second most popular mode of direct investment for U.S. firms and for all foreign firms combined was the WFO. However, U.S. companies had a relatively higher concentration of investment in the EJV and a relatively lower concentration in the WFO. Among all foreign investors surveyed, Japan had the highest percentage of firms in the EJV (85 percent), with the United States a close second (83.3 percent). For the WFO, Singaporean firms came in first (36.4 percent), followed by firms from Taiwan (21.4 percent). U.S. firms came in a distant third, with 11.1 percent. U.S. firms are

Singapore			Taiwan			Others			All		
1992	1993	1995	1992	1993	1995	1992	1993	1995	1992	1993	1995
66.7	48.0	54.6	69.3	69.3	75.0	80.3	80.2	72.8	77.8	76.7	78.6
4.7	8.0	9.1	5.1	6.0	3.5	9.1	8.9	17.3	9.6	9.7	9.0
28.6	44.0	36.4	25.6	24.7	21.4	10.6	10.9	9.9	12.6	13.7	12.5
21	25	22	215	300	228	66	101	81	1,066	1,345	1,068

NOTE: EJV: equity joint venture; CJV: contractual joint venture; WFO: wholly foreign-owned enterprises; totals may not add to 100% due to rounding.

more likely to participate in equity joint ventures partially because compared with other foreign firms, they tend to sell their products in the domestic Chinese market rather than export them. Selling in China requires good information about the Chinese consumers, including other Chinese enterprises. A domestic Chinese partner may prove more useful to U.S. firms.

Table 6-3 details the type of joint-venture partners by the country or region of origin of the foreign investors. Chinese state-owned enterprises (SOEs) are uniformly the first choice as joint-venture partners for all major foreign direct investors, including the United States, Hong Kong, Japan (tied for first place for collective enterprises in 1992), Singapore, and Taiwan in 1992, 1993, and 1995. Singapore had the greatest preference for SOEs—almost 80 percent of the firms had state-owned enterprises as partners in 1995. Singapore also had the highest degree of aversion to collective enterprises (CEs) as partners—none of the Singapore firms had one as a joint venture partner in 1995. The pattern of U.S. preference for joint-venture partners does not differ from the average pattern for all foreign direct investors. In 1995, 41 percent of the partners of U.S. firms were SOEs; 33 percent, CEs; and 22 percent, township and village enterprises (TVEs). For all foreign direct investors, 42 percent of the partners were SOEs; 31 percent, CEs; and 23 percent, TVEs, in a pattern virtually identical to that of the United States. The pattern for Hong Kong was similar. In 1993 and 1995, Japan-invested firms had somewhat higher proportions of

TABLE 6-3

TYPES OF JOINT-VENTURE PARTNER BY ORIGIN OF DIRECT INVESTMENT,
1992, 1993, AND 1995 (percent of firms)

Partner	United States			Hong Kong			Japan		
	1992	1993	1995	1992	1993	1995	1992	1993	1995
SOE	48.2	42.3	41.3	45.7	44.1	43.1	32.7	51.7	46.3
CE	25.9	26.8	33.3	27.1	29.6	30.1	32.7	27.6	35.2
TVE	16.7	19.7	22.2	20.8	22.0	23.7	12.2	19.0	14.8
PE	7.4	0.0	0.0	3.3	1.5	1.3	14.3	1.7	1.9
Others	1.8	11.3	3.2	3.1	2.8	1.8	8.1	0.0	1.9
All	100	100	100	100	100	100	100	100	100
Number of cases	54	71	63	582	673	552	49	58	54

SOURCE: CIER 1993, 1994, 1996.

joint ventures with SOEs and CEs and somewhat lower proportion of joint ventures with TVEs than the average. Taiwan in contrast had the lowest proportion of joint ventures with SOEs (35 percent on average) but the highest proportion of joint ventures with both CEs (34 percent on average) and TVEs (24 percent on average). Taiwanese firms are more likely to invest in the far-flung regions in China because they are more willing and able to work with the provincial or local governments due to their cultural, ethnic, and language affinity.

U.S. firms concentrate on Shanghai, Jiangsu, and Shandong[4] but do invest in other parts of China. Direct investors from other countries and regions are concentrated even more heavily in the coastal areas. Firms from different countries and regions may have different locational preferences because of different marketing strategies. Hong Kong and Taiwanese firms traditionally export most of their output and therefore prefer to invest in coastal areas with convenient export facilities. Japanese and U.S. firms tend to set their eyes on the domestic Chinese market and have a relatively larger presence in other parts of China to be closer to potential customers.

Table 6-4 breaks down the distribution of invested industries by country or region of origin. For FDI as a whole, the two industries with the most foreign direct investment are electrical and electronic products and

Singapore			Taiwan			Others			All		
1992	1993	1995	1992	1993	1995	1992	1993	1995	1992	1993	1995
66.6	64.3	78.6	34.8	35.4	35.8	51.8	50.6	44.6	44.0	43.5	42.4
20.0	7.1	0.0	32.9	33.7	34.1	17.2	20.5	24.6	27.6	29.1	30.5
6.7	21.4	21.4	21.3	24.2	25.0	13.8	25.3	21.5	19.5	22.3	23.2
0.0	0.0	0.0	9.7	1.4	2.3	8.6	1.2	4.6	5.5	1.4	1.6
6.7	7.1	0.0	1.3	5.2	2.8	8.6	2.4	4.6	3.4	3.7	2.3
100	100	100	100	100	100	100	100	100	100	100	100
15	14	14	155	211	176	58	83	65	913	1,110	924

NOTE: SOE: state-owned enterprises; CE: collective enterprises; TVE: township and village enterprises; PE: private enterprises.

the apparel industry, followed by textiles, food, and plastics. The distribution appears quite stable, without major changes across 1992, 1993, and 1995. In 1992, U.S. direct investment projects were most found in electrical and electronic products (13.1 percent), followed by food and textiles (both at 9.8 percent). In 1993 the apparel industry (11.7 percent) and machinery (11.7 percent) became the most important sectors, followed by electrical and electronic products (10.4 percent) and food (9.1 percent).[5] In 1995 U.S. direct investment was more evenly distributed among electrical and electronic products (9.7 percent), apparel (9.7 percent), food (9.7 percent), and machinery (9.7 percent).[6] Due to its advantage in technology, the United States had a larger share of its direct investment in machinery than any other country or region.

The industrial distribution of Japanese direct investors had a similar pattern. In 1995 Japan had higher concentrations of investment in electrical and electronic products (16.7 percent), apparel (11.7 percent), textiles (8.3 percent), precision instruments (8.3 percent), industrial chemicals (6.7 percent), chemical products (6.7 percent), and food (6.7 percent), with lower concentrations in machinery (1.7 percent). Unlike the United States and Japan, Singapore's direct investment focused on a few industries: non-metallic mineral products, electrical and electronic products, and food and kindred products. As expected, both Hong Kong and Taiwanese firms were

TABLE 6-4

SELECTION OF INDUSTRIES BY PLACE OF ORIGIN OF DIRECT INVESTMENT,
1992, 1993, AND 1995 (percent of firms)

Industry	United States			Hong Kong			Japan		
	1992	1993	1995	1992	1993	1995	1992	1993	1995
Food and food products	9.8	9.1	9.7	5.7	5.7	5.8	7.3	6.5	6.7
Beverage and tobacco	6.6	5.2	5.6	0.3	1.2	0.7	1.8	3.2	3.3
Textiles	9.8	3.9	5.6	13.9	13.7	14.1	7.3	6.5	8.3
Apparel	6.6	11.7	9.7	16.0	15.9	15.5	10.9	11.3	11.7
Leathers, fur, and related products	1.6	1.3	1.4	6.3	3.3	5.0	0.0	0.0	0.0
Wood, bamboo, and nonmetallic furniture	3.3	3.9	4.2	2.5	2.2	2.6	7.3	1.6	6.7
Paper products, printing	3.3	3.9	4.2	3.7	5.8	4.1	1.8	3.2	1.7
Industrial chemicals	0.0	3.9	1.4	2.0	5.8	3.0	1.8	8.1	6.7
Chemical products	6.6	1.3	2.8	4.9	1.6	4.3	7.3	4.8	6.7
Petroleum and coal products	1.6	1.3	1.4	0.5	0.7	0.7	0.0	0.0	0.0
Rubber products	1.6	0.0	1.4	1.7	1.3	1.3	1.8	0.0	1.7
Plastic products	6.6	3.9	5.6	7.4	6.8	6.9	0.0	1.6	1.7
Nonmetallic mineral products	6.6	6.5	5.6	2.8	3.0	3.3	5.5	6.5	5.0
Primary metals	1.6	2.6	2.8	0.8	0.4	1.0	3.6	3.2	1.7
Fabricated metal products	6.6	5.2	5.6	4.0	3.5	4.3	3.6	3.2	3.3
Machinery	3.3	11.7	9.7	4.5	6.9	4.6	1.8	8.1	1.7
Electrical and electronic products	13.1	10.4	9.7	16.4	12.1	14.9	20.0	19.4	16.7
Transport equipment	6.6	3.9	4.2	1.0	1.7	1.5	7.3	1.6	6.7
Precision instruments	1.6	2.6	1.4	3.0	2.6	2.6	9.1	6.5	8.3
Other	3.2	7.8	8.3	2.6	5.8	3.8	1.8	4.8	1.7
Total	100	100	100	100	100	100	100	100	100
Number of cases	61	77	72	648	692	605	55	62	60

SOURCE: CIER 1993, 1994, 1996.

	Singapore			Taiwan			Others			All		
	1992	1993	1995	1992	1993	1995	1992	1993	1995	1992	1993	1995
	23.8	22.7	18.2	7.9	9.9	9.2	10.6	5.6	6.9	7.0	7.1	7.2
	0.0	0.0	0.0	0.5	0.8	0.0	0.0	1.1	0.0	0.8	1.4	0.9
	0.0	0.0	0.0	9.8	8.3	7.4	13.6	15.6	13.9	12.2	11.5	11.4
	0.0	4.6	0.0	11.6	15.0	12.7	10.6	10.0	11.1	13.7	14.6	13.7
	9.4	4.6	9.1	8.4	5.1	7.0	3.0	4.4	2.8	6.0	3.5	4.8
	4.8	4.6	0.0	4.7	4.4	5.7	1.5	2.2	2.8	3.2	2.8	3.6
	0.0	13.6	9.1	3.3	5.5	3.9	1.5	6.7	5.6	3.3	5.7	4.2
	0.0	0.0	0.0	1.4	5.1	3.1	3.0	7.8	4.2	1.8	5.7	3.1
	4.8	0.0	4.6	5.6	1.6	3.9	4.6	2.2	2.8	5.3	1.8	4.2
	0.0	0.0	0.0	0.0	0.0	0.0	0.0	0.0	0.0	0.4	0.5	0.5
	4.8	0.0	4.6	0.0	1.2	0.4	3.0	2.2	2.8	1.5	1.2	1.3
	0.0	4.6	0.0	6.5	7.1	9.6	7.6	4.4	8.3	6.7	6.2	7.1
	19.0	9.1	22.7	3.7	2.4	3.9	3.0	4.4	1.4	3.7	3.5	4.0
	0.0	0.0	0.0	1.4	0.0	1.3	0.0	1.1	1.4	1.0	0.7	1.2
	4.8	4.6	4.6	4.2	5.9	6.1	6.1	4.4	5.6	4.3	4.2	4.8
	4.8	0.0	4.6	3.3	5.5	2.6	1.5	1.1	1.4	3.8	6.4	4.2
	23.8	22.7	18.2	16.7	11.1	12.2	10.6	8.9	8.3	16.2	12.1	13.7
	0.0	0.0	0.0	3.6	2.8	4.4	3.0	2.2	2.8	2.3	2.1	2.6
	0.0	4.6	4.6	3.3	1.6	3.1	9.1	2.2	5.6	3.7	2.6	3.2
	0.0	4.6	0.0	4.1	6.7	3.5	7.6	13.3	12.5	3.1	6.6	4.4
	100	100	100	100	100	100	100	100	100	100	100	100
	21	22	22	215	253	229	66	100	72	1,066	1,196	1,060

TABLE 6-5

INDUSTRIES RANKED BY COUNTRY OR REGION OF ORIGIN OF DIRECT
INVESTMENT, 1995

	United States	Hong Kong	Japan	Singapore	Taiwan	Others
1	Electrical[a]	Apparel	Electrical	Nonmetallic	Apparel	Textiles
2	Apparel[a]	Electrical	Apparel	Electrical[b]	Electrical	Other
3	Food[a]	Textiles	Textiles[c]	Food[b]	Plastic	Apparel
4	Machinery[a]	Plastic	Precision[c]	Leather[d]	Food	Electrical[d]
5	Other	Food	Food[e]	Paper[d]	Textiles	Plastic[d]

SOURCE: CIER 1996.
a. Tied for first place.
b. Tied for second place
c. Tied for third place.
d. Tied for fourth place.
e. Tied for fifth place. Other industries tied for fifth include wood, industrial chemicals, chemical products, and transportation equipment.

more heavily concentrated in apparel and textiles than U.S.-invested firms, but they also had a higher concentration in electrical and electronic products and plastic products.

Table 6-5 specifically identifies the five industries with the highest shares of direct investment from specific countries and regions of origin in 1995. Electrical and electronic products and food and kindred products were among the top five for all countries and regions and for foreign direct investors as a whole. Apparel was among the top five for all countries and regions except Singapore. Textiles were among the top five for all except Singapore and the United States. Plastic products were found in the top five for every place of origin except Japan, Singapore, and the United States. The selections of industries for investment were remarkably similar; technological advantages might explain some exceptions. For example, the United States has a technological advantage in machinery; Japan, in precision instruments.

Table 6-6 concerns the size of FDI projects and the origin of the direct investment. Although the average size is small, the project tends to increase. In 1995, 46 percent of FDI projects had an initial investment value less than $500,000, down from 53 percent in 1992. At the upper end of the distribution, 3.3 percent had an initial investment value greater than $10 million, up from 0.4 percent in 1992. The common assumption that investment projects of U.S. firms are probably larger than those of other foreign investors is not exactly the case. According to CIER data, although in 1995 the United States had the most investment projects greater than $10 million (5.6 percent), it also had the most projects less than $500,000 (57 percent). More than half the U.S investors invested less than $500,000. Thus U.S. direct investors are overrepresented at both the lowest and the highest ends. In contrast Singapore had a much lower share of its direct investments in the lowest-size category, whereas Taiwan had a much lower share of its direct investments in the highest-size category. The size distributions of both Hong Kong and Japan did not significantly differ from the size distribution of all FDI in China.

Sources of Capital, Technology, and Intermediate Inputs

Do U.S. and other foreign investors import their machinery and equipment from the parent companies, or do they purchase them locally? If U.S. firms import most of their capital goods from home, they will increase demand for U.S.-made machinery and equipment. Other things being equal, the U.S. economy would more likely benefit from U.S. direct investment in China (chapter 8 discusses related issues such as U.S. transfer of technology).

Table 6-7 presents data on the sources of the principal machinery and equipment used by foreign firms for 1992, 1993, and 1995. The firms were questioned about the sources of principal machinery and equipment and asked to provide the percentage distribution by value of five possible sources: (1) parent company; (2) other firms at home; (3) other foreign firms in China; (4) domestic Chinese firms; and (5) others. Table 6-7 shows that U.S.-invested firms in China on average imported more than one-third of their equipment by value from home (22 percent from parent companies and 14 percent from other companies) in 1995. The share appeared quite stable over time. U.S. direct investment in China did increase the export demand for U.S. capital goods. However, U.S firms had

TABLE 6-6

DISTRIBUTION BY SIZE OF INITIAL INVESTMENTS OF FDI FIRMS BY ORIGIN, 1992, 1993, AND 1995 (percent of firms)

	Less than US$0.5 million			US$0.51–1.0 million			US$1.01–2.0 million		
	1992	1993	1995	1992	1993	1995	1992	1993	1995
United States	49.2	54.6	56.9	14.8	16.7	15.3	8.2	10.6	6.9
Hong Kong	53.5	46.6	46.0	20.9	23.5	24.1	12.6	15.5	13.7
Japan	49.1	45.6	43.3	14.6	17.5	21.7	14.6	14.0	13.3
Singapore	33.3	33.3	36.4	38.1	28.6	27.3	4.8	4.8	0.0
Taiwan	54.2	43.5	42.4	20.0	27.2	28.0	13.1	17.6	15.7
Others	46.9	51.9	50.6	15.6	15.2	9.9	16.5	6.3	12.4
All	52.7	46.5	45.9	19.7	23.1	23.2	12.8	14.7	13.3
Number of cases	562	515	491	210	256	248	137	163	142

SOURCE: CIER 1993, 1994, 1996.

TABLE 6-7

SOURCE OF PRINCIPAL EQUIPMENT, 1992, 1993, AND 1995 (percent, weighted by the total value of investment at time of the survey)

Source	United States			Hong Kong			Japan		
	1992	1993	1995	1992	1993	1995	1992	1993	1995
Imported from parent company	25.2	23.1	22.4	56.4	24.8	36.8	69.9	50.7	38.8
Imported from other firms at home	9.2	13.7	13.8	16.2	12.7	8.1	15.3	12.7	17.5
Other foreign firms in China	8.2	2.2	5.4	4.4	5.9	6.7	2.3	0.4	7.5
Domestic companies	24.7	54.4	43.6	11.4	42.8	37.0	10.8	20.7	29.5
Others	32.8	6.6	14.8	11.6	13.8	11.6	1.7	15.6	6.7

SOURCE: CIER 1993, 1994, 1996.

the smallest share of their principal machinery and equipment supplied from the home country. For all foreign firms the share was 48 percent in 1995. All other foreign firms on average imported a greater proportion of principal machinery and equipment from home. Taiwanese firms in 1995 imported 62 percent of their equipment from home (47 percent from parent

US$2.01–5.0 million			US$5.01–10.0 million			More than US$ 10.0 million		
1992	1993	1995	1992	1993	1995	1992	1993	1995
26.2	10.6	13.9	1.6	3.0	1.4	0.0	4.6	5.6
8.4	8.1	9.3	4.2	2.6	3.6	0.5	3.7	3.3
9.0	15.8	13.3	10.9	1.8	3.3	1.8	5.3	5.0
19.0	28.6	22.7	4.8	4.8	9.1	0.0	0.0	4.6
8.6	8.4	9.6	3.6	2.9	2.6	0.5	0.4	1.8
9.0	12.7	14.8	12.1	10.1	8.6	0.0	3.8	3.7
9.9	9.4	10.6	4.5	3.3	3.7	0.4	3.1	3.3
105	104	113	48	36	40	4	34	35

Singapore			Taiwan			Others			All		
1992	1993	1995	1992	1993	1995	1992	1993	1995	1992	1993	1995
57.1	53.0	51.3	20.6	54.8	46.7	59.3	46.7	35.3	38.3	36.5	37.3
0.0	3.5	5.0	16.2	14.6	14.7	2.2	8.7	6.1	14.3	11.7	10.3
0.0	0.0	1.1	10.8	1.6	4.0	1.3	3.0	7.4	7.2	4.3	6.1
14.7	13.4	13.0	19.7	14.6	26.7	11.0	25.0	41.7	16.4	32.8	35.6
28.2	30.1	30.0	32.7	14.4	7.8	26.2	16.6	9.5	23.8	14.6	10.6

companies and 15 percent from other firms), while Japanese and Singaporean firms imported 56 percent.

While foreign-invested firms in China did import a significant part of their capital goods from home, the trend is to purchase an increasing share of machinery and equipment locally. As the Chinese economy becomes more developed, high-quality machinery and equipment are increasingly available. Foreign-invested firms in 1995 purchased 35.6 percent of machinery and equipment from local suppliers, up from 32.8 percent in 1993 (37.1 percent including foreign suppliers located in China) and 16.4 percent (23.6 percent including foreign suppliers located in China) in 1992. Conversely, foreign-invested firms in China brought 47.6 percent of their principal machinery and equipment from their home countries in 1995, down from 48.2 percent in 1993 and 52.6 percent in 1992.

Chinese government officials often complain that foreign-invested firms import too much second-hand machinery and not enough new machinery from their home countries: they want the transfer of more advanced technology from the industrialized countries. The CIER survey for 1992 asked foreign-invested firms about the age of equipment when they established their firms. Table 6-8 shows that approximately three-quarters of the firms installed new machinery and equipment. The age distribution of the machinery and equipment does not differ significantly across places of origin.

CIER surveys for 1993 and 1995 asked: "Was there any additional equipment installed at your plant last year [meaning 1993 or 1995]? If so, how old was it? Brand-new, less than 1 year old, between 1 to 3 years, between 3 to 5 years, and 5 years and above?" Table 6-9 summarizes the responses, which again show that the majority of foreign-invested firms installed new machinery and equipment. In 1995 (surveyed in 1996) almost 70 percent installed new equipment; the percentage is even higher for U.S firms, with a figure of 75 percent, itself an increase from 68 percent in 1993 (surveyed in 1994). Among all foreign-invested firms, those from Singapore consistently had the highest proportion of new machinery and equipment (100 percent in 1993 and 77 percent in 1995). The proportions of other firms are similar, with the possible exception of Hong Kong.

Where do U.S. and other foreign firms obtain their production technology? If U.S. firms bring technology to China from home, U.S. FDI becomes a vehicle for transferring more advanced technology into China. U.S. firms also benefit from sales of U.S. machinery and equipment as well as from license fees, royalty payments, and consultancy,

TABLE 6-8

AGE OF PRINCIPAL MACHINERY AND

EQUIPMENT INSTALLED AT ESTABLISHMENT OF FIRMS, 1992

(percent, weighted by total value of investment at time of survey)

	United States	Hong Kong	Japan	Singapore	Taiwan	Others	All
New	76.7	74.5	73.6	76.2	80.7	78.2	76.1
1 year old or less	8.3	7.4	11.3	9.5	5.8	1.6	7.0
1–3 years old	5.0	8.5	5.7	4.8	6.8	6.2	7.6
3–5 years old	5.0	4.1	1.8	0.0	5.3	7.8	4.4
5 years and older	5.0	5.5	7.6	9.5	1.4	6.2	4.9
Number of cases	60	636	53	21	207	64	1,041

SOURCE: CIER 1993.

NOTE: Surveys for 1993 and 1995 did not ask the same question.

maintenance, and service contracts. However, if those firms use local technology, the purpose of technology transfer is not served. The CIER surveys for 1992, 1993, and 1995 posed a question to foreign-invested firms: "What is the source of the principal technology used by your firm?"

Table 6-10 reveals that on average 36 percent of U.S.-invested firms used technology from their parent companies; 5 percent, technology from other U.S. firms; and the rest, primarily local technology—44 percent used technology provided by their Chinese joint-venture partners, and slightly less than 10 percent, by other domestic firms in China. A somewhat higher percentage of other foreign-invested firms, except those from Hong Kong, imported technology from parent companies. Hong Kong likely has less indigenous production technology that can be transferred; it has the highest degree of reliance on domestic Chinese firms for technology (60 percent in 1995). In contrast Japan, Singapore, Taiwan, and other countries relied much less on domestic Chinese firms.

The relatively advanced level of U.S. technology can explain the relatively lower percentage of U.S. firms using technology from the parent company. Technology imported from the United States might be inappropriate under China's prevailing economic conditions. The technology used

TABLE 6-9
AGE OF PRINCIPAL MACHINERY AND EQUIPMENT, 1993 AND 1995
(percent, weighted by total value of investment at time of survey)

	United States		Hong Kong		Japan	
	1993	1995	1993	1995	1993	1995
New	67.8	75.0	79.0	65.6	82.9	73.1
1 year old or less	8.5	5.6	6.3	6.1	2.4	7.7
1–3 years old	11.9	5.6	5.4	12.1	4.9	11.5
3–5 years old	6.8	5.6	5.6	9.9	4.9	0.0
5 years and older	5.1	8.3	3.7	6.4	4.9	7.7
Number of cases	59	36	461	314	41	26

SOURCE: CIER 1994, 1996.

by firms in East Asian countries may be more appropriate for China, given the stage of development of its economy.

While the degree of reliance on parent companies and other domestic firms has held steady at slightly above 40 percent for U.S. firms, foreign-invested firms as a whole showed a noticeable declining trend, from 47.7 percent in 1992 to 38.1 percent in 1995. The reliance on Chinese firms has been rising for both U.S. firms (from 49.1 percent in 1992 to 53.6 percent in 1995) and all foreign firms (from 46.1 percent in 1992 to 53.5 percent in 1995).

An important question related to the source of machinery and equipment and technology is the source of industrial supplies. The CIER surveys asked FDI firms for the percentage distributions of current sources of their principal industrial raw materials and semifinished goods by value. Table 6-11 shows that U.S. firms on average purchased less than 10 percent of principal industrial raw materials and semifinished goods from home in all three years of the survey (1992, 1993, and 1995). Instead they procured a large and rising share of such inputs from local suppliers, 76.1 percent in 1995. In contrast, in the same year Taiwanese, Japanese, and Hong Kong firms purchased 21.6, 20.8, and 19.1 percent of their principal supplies, respectively, from home. U.S. reliance on local supplies is much higher than that of other major direct investor countries and much higher than the

Singapore		Taiwan		Others		All	
1993	1995	1993	1995	1993	1995	1993	1995
100	76.9	79.2	73.5	79.2	70.7	78.8	69.1
0.0	0.0	5.7	9.8	5.6	5.2	5.9	6.7
0.0	0.0	9.0	10.6	4.2	8.6	6.5	10.7
0.0	0.0	1.4	3.8	5.6	12.1	4.5	7.7
0.0	23.1	4.7	2.3	5.6	3.4	4.2	5.7
15	13	211	132	72	58	859	579

NOTE: The survey for 1992 did not ask the same question.

norm of 67.8 percent in 1995. Correspondingly, its reliance on home supplies is the lowest among the major foreign direct investor countries. The reluctance of U.S. firms to purchase industrial raw materials and intermediate goods from home results in part from the great distance between China and the United States, producing higher transport costs and longer transport time when compared with local and other nearby sources of supply, and in part because many U.S. firms are in China precisely to exploit local natural resources. (U.S. firms cited local availability of resources much more often than other foreign firms as an important factor influencing their location decisions; see table 5-6.) U.S. firms may have purchased their principal industrial raw materials and semifinished goods not directly from the United States but indirectly through the affiliates of their U.S. parents in other countries and regions.

The same considerations of cost and time apply to other foreign investors, though perhaps to a lesser extent for neighboring countries and regions. Unsurprisingly in 1995, foreign-invested firms in China as a whole purchased more than 90 percent of needed industrial raw materials and semifinished goods from either local Chinese suppliers or from neighboring Asian countries and regions, including Hong Kong (12.4 percent), Taiwan (6.5 percent), and Japan (4.9 percent). As the Chinese economy becomes more developed, more industrial raw materials and

TABLE 6-10
SOURCE OF PRINCIPAL TECHNOLOGY USED BY FDI FIRMS,
1992, 1993, AND 1995 (percent of firms)

Source of Technology	United States 1992	1993	1995	Hong Kong 1992	1993	1995	Japan 1992	1993	1995
Parent company	32.2	37.3	38.0	33.8	29.5	25.9	45.3	54.8	44.8
Other companies at home	11.9	1.3	4.2	6.2	3.0	3.0	11.3	0.0	5.2
Third parties	0.0	0.0	1.4	4.5	3.1	2.7	1.9	3.2	1.7
Chinese partner of JV	44.0	45.3	43.7	44.0	43.9	46.0	35.8	19.4	32.8
Other FDI firms	0.0	0.0	0.0	1.9	2.0	2.0	1.9	1.6	0.0
Other domestic firms	5.1	10.7	9.9	5.9	12.3	13.0	3.8	8.1	12.1
Others	6.8	5.3	2.8	3.7	6.1	7.4	0.0	12.9	3.5
Number of cases	59	75	71	628	701	594	53	67	58

SOURCE: CIER 1993, 1994, 1996.

intermediate inputs will become available locally. The long-term outlook is for foreign-invested firms to purchase an increasingly greater share of necessary industrial supplies locally (the local supplier may be another foreign-invested firm). CIER data show that the proportion of industrial supplies of the foreign-invested firms purchased locally increased from 52.9 percent in 1992 to 62.6 percent in 1993 and 67.8 percent in 1995. The reliance on local supplies has been rising for the United States as well as every other major direct investor country or region.

Japan has declined significantly as a source of industrial supplies—from more than 20 percent in 1992 to less than 5 percent in 1995—primarily because Japanese investors substituted local for home supplies. Appreciation of the yen, which peaked at eighty yen to the U.S. dollar in 1995, might have caused the substitution. Firms imported 100 percent of industrial raw material and intermediate inputs for material processing and assembly, especially in the early days of FDI in China. But recently even such activities frequently use domestic raw material and intermediate inputs.

Singapore			Taiwan			Others			All		
1992	1993	1995	1992	1993	1995	1992	1993	1995	1992	1993	1995
57.1	39.1	42.9	53.6	55.2	46.8	56.3	44.2	47.4	40.1	38.1	34.1
4.8	0.0	4.8	11.6	4.6	7.3	1.5	1.2	1.3	7.6	2.9	4.0
4.8	0.0	0.0	0.5	1.2	1.4	3.1	1.2	4.0	3.2	2.3	2.3
28.5	34.8	33.3	24.2	26.8	32.3	30.0	34.9	30.3	38.5	38.3	40.8
0.0	0.0	0.0	1.0	1.5	0.0	1.5	1.2	0.0	1.6	1.7	1.2
0.0	13.0	9.5	7.7	7.3	9.0	6.1	12.8	6.6	6.0	10.9	11.5
4.8	13.0	9.5	1.4	3.5	2.3	1.5	4.7	10.5	3.1	5.9	6.1
21	27	21	207	261	220	64	108	76	1,032	1,427	1,040

Where do foreign-invested firms obtain their working capital? Table 6-12 presents responses from foreign-invested firms on the percentage distributions of their working capital by source, aggregated with the value of total investment at the time of the survey as weight. Somewhat surprisingly the CIER surveys show that U.S. and all foreign-invested firms relied on Chinese banks as the principal source. U.S.-invested firms in 1995 on average used Chinese banks for 45 percent of their working capital needs; all foreign-invested firms, 35.6 percent. Parent companies provided 20.7 percent of the working capital of U.S.-invested firms; 17.2 percent of all foreign-invested firms relied on parent companies. Other sources provided 20.1 percent and 22.8 percent of the working capital of U.S.- and all foreign-invested firms, respectively. U.S.-invested firms are quite similar to all foreign-invested firms in this respect.

In contrast, Japan-invested firms did not rely on domestic Chinese banks as their principal source of working capital. Instead in 1995 they relied heavily on Japanese banks in Japan as their principal source.

TABLE 6-11
SOURCES OF PRINCIPAL INDUSTRIAL RAW MATERIALS AND
SEMIFINISHED GOODS OF FDI FIRMS, 1992, 1993, AND 1995
(percent, weighted by total value of investment at survey)

Source	United States 1992	1993	1995	Hong Kong 1992	1993	1995	Japan 1992	1993	1995
Mainland China	64.1	66.2	76.1	51.3	68.4	67.0	29.7	54.9	68.3
United States	9.4	7.1	9.7	1.9	1.8	1.7	0.4	0.3	0.7
Hong Kong	6.4	6.2	3.9	28.7	17.0	19.1	0.4	1.4	0.3
Japan	10.8	13.1	3.7	4.2	2.6	4.2	67.2	41.3	20.8
Taiwan	2.1	1.2	2.2	10.0	2.2	2.8	1.9	0.0	1.0
Europe	1.0	2.5	0.8	0.5	2.4	1.0	0.0	0.2	2.1
Southeast Asia	0.1	0.2	0.6	0.6	1.0	0.6	0.1	0.6	0.3
Others	6.1	3.5	2.9	2.8	4.6	3.5	0.3	1.3	6.5

SOURCE: CIER 1993, 1994, 1996.

TABLE 6-12
SOURCES OF WORKING CAPITAL, 1992, 1993, AND 1995
(percent, weighted by total value of investment at survey)

Source	United States 1992	1993	1995	Hong Kong 1992	1993	1995	Japan 1992	1993	1995
Parent company	17.0	8.3	20.7	14.9	16.3	14.7	45.5	4.8	10.2
Banks at home	0.0	0.4	0.2	1.5	1.2	0.6	2.5	0.3	41.5
Chinese partner	16.2	8.8	13.7	16.5	21.8	19.0	2.0	2.8	10.9
Chinese banks	65.0	45.4	45.2	61.5	45.4	36.8	18.0	13.3	9.2
Foreign banks in China	0.0	0.0	0.2	0.6	2.1	5.0	27.9	1.6	0.9
Third parties	0.0	0.0	0.0	0.0	0.2	0.1	0.0	0.0	0.0
Others		1.8	37.2	20.1	5.0	13.1	23.8	4.1	77.2	27.3

SOURCE: CIER 1993, 1994, 1996.

Overall the reliance on banks, both domestic Chinese and foreign,
seemed to be declining. Singaporean and Taiwanese firms relied much
more heavily than other foreign firms on their parent companies as
sources of working capital. The Chinese joint-venture partners of the

Singapore			Taiwan			Others			All		
1992	1993	1995	1992	1993	1995	1992	1993	1995	1992	1993	1995
70.4	49.0	72.6	52.8	53.6	64.4	43.3	49.2	73.8	52.9	62.6	67.8
6.4	5.0	2.8	1.3	1.6	1.7	4.6	2.1	0.8	3.1	2.1	2.1
3.5	6.4	4.0	5.7	4.9	4.5	8.7	7.4	3.6	10.9	11.8	12.4
14.3	9.3	6.0	2.6	2.6	3.5	1.0	17.7	2.6	20.7	9.7	4.9
0.0	0.3	0.0	31.8	33.1	21.6	1.6	0.7	0.6	5.0	5.6	6.5
1.2	7.9	0.6	1.6	0.2	1.2	33.1	10.0	3.6	3.6	2.6	1.3
2.1	1.8	1.6	0.6	0.3	0.7	0.3	0.6	2.2	0.4	0.8	0.8
2.1	20.3	12.5	3.4	3.7	2.4	7.4	12.4	12.9	3.5	5.0	4.3

Singapore			Taiwan			Others			All		
1992	1993	1995	1992	1993	1995	1992	1993	1995	1992	1993	1995
35.4	43.9	27.1	40.9	30.9	29.5	15.1	16.2	12.4	24.0	16.8	17.2
0.0	0.0	5.5	0.8	2.8	0.9	1.1	6.2	0.1	1.5	1.7	4.4
4.0	7.3	5.0	9.0	10.0	13.5	2.8	6.1	5.2	11.7	15.3	15.5
48.6	35.8	50.7	45.7	38.5	35.9	46.3	55.9	40.7	50.3	41.2	35.6
0.0	3.8	0.0	0.1	2.3	2.9	28.3	2.3	7.7	8.0	2.0	4.0
0.0	0.0	0.0	0.0	1.0	3.5	0.0	2.0	0.0	0.0	0.4	0.6
12.0	9.3	11.8	3.5	14.5	13.9	6.5	11.3	34.0	4.6	22.8	22.8

foreign-invested firms were also significant sources of working capital in accounting for some 15 percent of the working capital of all foreign-invested firms. Taking together Chinese partners and Chinese banks, more than half of the working capital of U.S.- and foreign-invested firms

TABLE 6-13
DID PARENT COMPANY CLOSE DOMESTIC PLANTS, 1993 AND 1995?
(percent of firms)

Response	United States		Hong Kong		Japan	
	1993	1995	1993	1995	1993	1995
Yes	13.0	17.1	7.7	11.0	8.8	13.3
No	87.0	82.9	92.3	89.0	91.2	86.7
Number of cases	69	70	640	592	57	60

SOURCE: CIER 1994, 1996.

TABLE 6-14
DID PARENT COMPANY INCREASE INVESTMENT AT HOME, 1993 AND 1995?
(percent of firms)

Response	United States		Hong Kong		Japan	
	1993	1995	1993	1995	1993	1995
Yes	39.0	35.0	37.3	36.8	50.0	36.5
No	32.2	30.0	32.3	31.2	21.2	30.3
Don't know	28.8	35.0	30.3	32.1	28.9	32.7
Number of cases	59	60	600	536	52	52

SOURCE: CIER 1994, 1996.

came from domestic Chinese sources. Less than a quarter of their working capital came from home sources (parent companies and banks at home).

Does U.S. Direct Investment in China Affect Domestic Investment in the United States?

An important consideration of the impact of U.S. direct investment in China is whether such an investment leads to plant closings and hence reduces jobs in the United States. Table 6-13 reports data on plant closings at home by FDI firms in China. On the whole, U.S. companies that set up subsidiaries in China did not close down production lines at home and thus

Singapore		Taiwan		Others		All	
1993	1995	1993	1995	1993	1995	1993	1995
9.5	22.7	11.5	19.5	6.3	16.5	8.8	14.0
90.5	77.3	88.5	80.5	93.7	83.5	91.2	86.0
21	22	234	221	79	79	1,100	1,044

NOTE: The survey for 1992 did not ask the same question.

Singapore		Taiwan		Others		All	
1993	1995	1993	1995	1993	1995	1993	1995
42.2	41.2	41.5	41.1	40.3	62.9	39.3	37.6
36.8	17.7	27.4	27.2	36.1	18.4	31.1	30.0
21.1	41.2	31.1	31.7	23.6	19.3	29.7	32.4
19	17	212	180	72	62	1,014	907

NOTE: The survey for 1992 did not ask the same question.

did not displace jobs. Obviously there are some isolated counterexamples. For example, Black and Decker announced plant closings and specifically tied its moves to Asia and China to low wages. But CIER data reveal that 82.9 percent of the plants of U.S. firms remained in operation in 1995, while 17.1 percent of them closed production facilities at home. On average, 86 percent of direct investors in China from all countries continued their production at home in 1995. U.S. firms had only the third highest incidence of plant closings, after Singapore (22.7 percent) and Taiwan (19.5 percent). Direct investment in China did not necessarily lead to plant closings at home.

For particular industries and industry sectors, the impact can still be significant. All shoe factories in Taiwan, once the largest shoe exporter in the world, moved to China within a five-year period in the late 1980s and

TABLE 6-15

RELATIONSHIP BETWEEN THE PRINCIPAL PRODUCTS OF FDI FIRM AND PARENT COMPANY, 1993 AND 1995 (percent of firms)

Response	United States		Hong Kong		Japan	
	1993	1995	1993	1995	1993	1995
Same but downstream from parent company	8.6	10.7	6.4	5.7	0.0	3.8
Same but upstream from parent company	6.9	16.1	4.8	5.9	6.0	1.9
Identical but lower grade than parent company's	12.1	10.7	13.7	11.4	26.0	23.1
Identical but higher grade than parent company's	0.0	0.0	1.2	1.4	0.0	0.0
Identical and same grade as parent company's	10.3	7.1	14.4	19.4	28.0	32.7
Totally different types of products	62.1	55.4	59.5	56.3	40.0	38.5
Number of cases	58	56	563	510	50	52

SOURCE: CIER 1994, 1996.

early 1990s. The incidence of plant closings was higher in 1995 than in 1993. Since the 1993 and 1995 samples of foreign-invested firms were essentially the same, over time the likelihood of plant closings at home would probably rise. But the overall probability of plant closings must still be regarded as relatively low—less than 20 percent.

Does direct investment in China reduce a firm's investment at home? If U.S. direct investment leads to a reduction of domestic investment, it may cause a reduction in job creation in the longer run and may impede the technological upgrading of the domestic operations of those firms. CIER survey data show that in both 1993 and 1995 more U.S.-invested firms in China reported that their parent companies continued to expand investment at home than not. The U.S. figures are comparable to the overall average for all foreign-invested firms but lower than those of the Japanese, Singaporean, and Taiwanese firms (table 6-14).

Further, do Chinese subsidiaries of U.S. firms produce the same products as their parents? Table 6-15 shows that more than half the U.S. firms in China

Singapore		Taiwan		Others		All	
1993	1995	1993	1995	1993	1995	1993	1995
5.6	5.9	7.5	7.0	7.1	3.1	6.5	6.0
11.1	0.0	8.0	8.2	4.3	10.8	5.7	7.0
11.1	17.6	15.5	11.1	15.7	13.8	14.7	12.3
0.0	5.9	0.5	2.3	1.4	1.5	0.9	1.5
22.2	23.5	23.5	27.5	22.9	23.1	17.5	21.4
50.0	47.1	45.0	43.9	48.6	47.7	54.6	51.9
18	17	200	171	70	65	959	871

NOTE: The survey for 1992 did not ask the same question.

produced totally different products from those of the parent companies. In 1995, 55 percent of U.S. subsidiaries in China produced totally different types of products. Another 11 percent of the U.S. firms produced products of lower quality than those produced at home; 11 percent produced products downstream from their parent companies and used semifinished goods from their parent companies as inputs. Another 16 percent produced semifinished products used by their parent companies as intermediate inputs. Altogether, more than 90 percent of U.S.-invested firms did not directly compete with their parent companies. Most U.S. direct investment in China does not substitute for U.S. production at home. U.S. jobs have not been "exported" to China as a result of U.S. direct investment in China.

Although the percentages of all foreign-invested firms producing either totally different types of products or identical but lower-grade products (respectively, 52 percent and 12 percent in 1995) are comparable to those for the United States, a much larger percentage of all other foreign-invested firms produced products identical and of equal or higher grade than those

TABLE 6-16
**PRINCIPAL MARKET DESTINATIONS OF GOODS PRODUCED
BY FDI FIRMS IN CHINA, 1992, 1993, AND 1995**
(percent, weighted by total value of investment at time of survey)

	Year	Foreign Firms in China	Other Firms in China	United States
United States	1992	4.8	64.7	15.6
	1993	5.7	76.8	9.6
	1995	2.5	82.0	8.4
Hong Kong	1992	13.5	21.9	14.1
	1993	9.6	49.4	3.5
	1995	6.1	47.5	7.9
Japan	1992	10.6	19.2	18.6
	1993	22.6	30.8	1.2
	1995	34.9	30.7	0.3
Singapore	1992	2.2	53.1	8.0
	1993	5.5	59.7	2.6
	1995	5.1	53.6	2.1
Taiwan	1992	10.2	49.4	4.8
	1993	12.5	27.9	10.2
	1995	9.0	22.2	13.6
Others	1992	2.5	74.3	3.5
	1993	6.4	51.9	5.4
	1995	8.7	50.0	6.2
All	1992	9.6	42.9	9.1
	1993	11.0	46.5	4.7
	1995	10.4	44.6	7.4

SOURCE: CIER 1993, 1994, 1996.

of the parent companies. In contrast to the United States, only 38 percent of Japanese firms produced products totally different from their parent companies; moreover, 23 percent of the Japanese firms produced products of lower quality than the outputs of their parent companies. Even for Japanese firms, however, a majority produced products in China not competitive with and hence substitutable for the production of their parent companies at home. Taiwanese firms were likeliest to compete with or replace the production of parents at home—the combined percentage of firms producing totally different types of products or lower-grade products was 55 percent in 1995, the lowest of all major direct investor countries or

Hong Kong	Japan	Taiwan	European Union	Southeast Asia	Others
2.8	1.9	0.0	3.6	2.8	3.8
2.5	0.6	0.0	0.4	0.8	3.6
1.6	0.5	0.3	0.2	2.5	1.9
13.2	7.5	12.1	7.1	3.5	7.1
19.5	3.0	1.3	2.5	1.9	9.4
12.8	3.2	1.8	1.6	6.0	13.0
7.4	19.3	0.0	22.0	2.4	0.5
6.9	25.6	0.1	0.3	0.2	12.4
10.5	14.8	0.2	0.1	8.1	0.3
9.7	4.2	1.0	9.0	7.8	5.0
7.1	7.1	0.0	9.0	4.6	4.4
7.6	7.4	0.0	3.2	4.6	16.4
22.3	2.2	0.9	4.1	1.8	4.3
19.7	11.4	7.6	2.6	2.0	6.2
23.9	8.2	6.3	9.8	1.7	5.4
4.4	0.9	1.3	6.1	3.6	3.4
6.2	1.7	0.9	13.4	2.4	11.6
4.2	1.9	0.9	18.0	3.2	7.0
16.0	6.0	1.8	8.2	2.4	4.0
15.4	6.7	1.8	3.2	1.7	9.0
13.5	5.2	2.0	8.3	5.2	3.4

regions in China. Not unexpectedly, only 1.5 percent of foreign-invested firms (and 0 percent of U.S.-invested firms) produced products of higher grade than their parent companies, perhaps in part because of the demand conditions in the Chinese market and concerns about the quality of available inputs, including the labor force, as well as the adequacy of protection of intellectual property rights.

According to available data, most U.S. companies do not export their products to the United States for sale. The CIER surveys asked foreign-invested firms about sales of their goods by major market destinations. Table 6-16 tallies the aggregated responses with the value of total investment at the time of the surveys as weights.[7] In 1995, 85 percent of sales of U.S.-invested firms in China was to the domestic Chinese market (82 percent to domestic Chinese firms and 2.5 percent to foreign firms in China), up from 69.5 percent in 1992, and only 8.4 percent returned to the United States, down from an already low 15.6 percent in 1992. Moreover, the share of Chinese domestic sales has been rising, and the share of U.S. home market sales has been falling steadily for U.S.-invested firms. The trend is consistent with earlier empirical observation that U.S. direct investment in China does not compete with or substitute for domestic U.S. production and hence does not cause significant job losses at home.

In contrast, for all foreign-, including U.S.-, invested firms, only 55 percent of the sales involved the domestic Chinese market in 1995. The marketing behavior of U.S.-invested firms diverges from that of other foreign-invested firms. Despite the difference, the Chinese domestic market was still the largest market for Hong Kong (53.6 percent), Japanese (65.6 percent), Singaporean (58.7 percent), Taiwanese (31.2 percent), and all other foreign-invested firms (58.7 percent) in 1995. Moreover, the share of Chinese domestic sales has risen dramatically for Japanese firms. Part of the rise in Japanese and U.S. shares may be attributed to the fact that the export requirements on foreign-invested firms, commonly imposed as conditions for the approval of direct investment projects in China in the early days, substantially relaxed in the 1990s. Foreign-invested firms have been increasingly free to focus on the Chinese market.

The home market was the second most-important market for U.S.-invested firms (but only less than 10 percent) and for Hong Kong and Japanese firms. The latter had the highest share of sales back to home market of any foreign direct investor country or region, an average of 20 percent. However, the proportions of the exported goods from Hong Kong firms intended for the domestic Hong Kong market and for reexporting elsewhere were unknown. For all foreign-invested firms as a whole, Hong Kong was the second most important market, after the domestic Chinese market, with an average share of approximately 15 percent. For Japanese, Singaporean, Taiwanese, and other foreign firms, Hong Kong was either the second most important market (for firms from Singapore, Taiwan, and others) or the third (for firms from Japan). A significant proportion of those exports to Hong Kong was subsequently reexported elsewhere. Hong Kong, however, was not an important market for U.S.-invested firms. The European Union and the United States were the third and fourth most important markets for all foreign-invested firms as a whole but not important for Japanese firms. The European Union was also not an important market for U.S.-invested firms. For Hong Kong and Taiwanese firms, both the United States and the European Union were significant direct export markets.

Finally, the share of domestic sales of Taiwanese firms declined continuously from almost 60 percent in 1992 to just above 30 percent in 1995, then the lowest among all foreign-invested firms. Taiwan also had the lowest share of home market sales (6.3 percent in 1995), significantly below those of Japan (14.8 percent), Hong Kong (12.8 percent), and the United States (8.4 percent). Taiwanese firms apparently focused more on Mainland China as a manufacturing base for exports than on either the domestic Chinese market or China as a source of supply for the home market. Because of this, and because of Taiwan's legal barriers against imports from Mainland China, many parents of Taiwanese firms were export oriented compared to other direct investor countries and regions. In any case, Taiwan itself is not a large market for the light industrial manufactured goods, the bulk of Chinese exports.

Are U.S.-Invested Firms Profitable?

Do foreign-, and in particular U.S.-, invested firms make profits? Or are recent reports about the poor profitability of multinational corporations operating in China true?[8]

In general the analysis of profits of multinational corporations can be problematic because reported profits often reflect not only the underlying cost and market conditions but also practices such as transfer pricing. A parent company may deliberately underinvoice its exports to its affiliate abroad if such goods are faced with high tariffs in the host country. Its affiliate abroad may in turn underinvoice its exports to the parent or other affiliates in third countries to minimize profit and hence host-country tax liabilities, as well as to circumvent host-country capital controls. The study of the profitability of foreign-invested firms is further complicated by the fact that China is a transition economy where the rule of law is not fully established. As chapter 3 discusses, the enforcement of laws in China can be arbitrary. Firms may not wish to declare their profits truthfully for several reasons. First, underreporting of profits can lead to lower taxes. In addition to official taxes, foreign firms are often asked to make contributions to local communities. Local authorities may ask for help in building schools and hospitals, improving roads, and assisting in community services.

Some multinational corporations are primarily interested in the huge domestic market in China and may be willing to forgo profit in the short run to secure a significant market share in the long run. The strategy often combines aggressive pricing and massive advertising and promotion in the domestic Chinese market, which results in lower revenues, higher costs, and lower profits in the early years of the direct investment. Finally, multinational corporations sometimes use posting losses as a tactic to acquire greater control over joint ventures with Chinese enterprises. Sustained losses eventually require recapitalization; to the extent the Chinese joint-venture partner cannot meet the capital call, it will see its share of the equity and hence its control diluted in favor of the foreign partner, which often has deeper pockets.

For the CIER data used in this study, overall profitability may have been overstated because foreign-invested firms that closed due to their losses would no longer be represented in the survey sample. Hence, the proportion of loss-making enterprises is bound to be underestimated. A systematic tendency for an upward bias in the degree of profitability likely exists because of sample selection (only the survivors are included). Unfortunately, no hard data exist to help determine more definitively the direction of the *net* bias. On balance, based on anecdotal evidence (for example, continual capacity expansion by foreign-invested firms despite a history of losses), the reported profitability more likely understates the true and potential profitability than overstates it.[9]

Table 6-17 presents CIER data on the distribution of self-reported profitability of foreign-invested firms in China (by the number of firms). In 1995 more than half the foreign-invested firms made some profits; another 5 percent or so broke even; and the remaining 42 percent posted losses—with 29 percent incurring slight losses, and 13 percent, heavy

TABLE 6-17

PROFITABILITY OF FDI BY ORIGIN, 1995 (percent)

	Heavy Losses	Slight Losses	Break-even	Rate of Return on Capital			
				0–3%	3%–8%	8%–15%	>15%
United States	13.9	29.2	1.4	11.1	16.7	15.3	12.5
Hong Kong	13.7	30.0	6.2	17.5	16.8	9.3	6.5
Japan	12.1	15.5	3.5	13.8	17.2	12.1	25.9
Singapore	9.1	9.1	0.0	22.7	22.7	18.2	18.2
Taiwan	13.3	31.4	6.2	16.4	13.7	12.0	7.1
Others	12.5	27.5	3.8	18.8	13.8	15.0	8.8
All	13.3	28.8	5.4	16.8	16.1	11.1	8.5

SOURCE: CIER 1996.

losses.[10] The loss-making record of U.S.-invested firms was quite similar to that of all foreign-invested firms, at 43.1 percent.[11] But because the National Bureau of Statistics conducted the surveys, respondents might have understated the degree of profitability to decrease taxes and to avoid contributions.

Among the foreign firms making a profit, the distribution is further broken down by the rate of return on capital (measured in terms of the value of the original investment). U.S. firms performed somewhat better than the average foreign firm. According to table 6-17, 44.5 percent of U.S.-invested firms achieved a rate of return on capital exceeding 3 percent, as opposed to only 35.7 percent of all foreign-invested firms. Firms from Singapore and Japan had the best record in terms of making profit and avoiding loss. In 1995, 81.8 percent of Singaporean and 69 percent of Japanese firms made a profit. Taiwanese firms had the poorest performance, with a below-average proportion of firms making a profit (49.1 percent) and an above-average proportion making a loss (44.7 percent). Hong Kong firms had the second poorest performance but were not appreciably different from Taiwan-invested firms. (The accuracy of the responses of Hong Kong and Taiwanese firms is probably more suspect, because those firms have greater incentives to understate profits to avoid taxation as well as demands for contributions by local governments and distribution by Chinese joint-venture partners.) Japan had the largest percentage of its firms earning a profit rate of more than 15 percent in 1995, followed by Singapore. The United States came in third, with 12.5 percent of its firms earning a rate of return of more than 15 percent, followed by Taiwan and then Hong Kong.

Because the exact rates of return are not available (the surveyed firms were only asked to report their rates of return within specified ranges), calculating the mean rate of return for each investor country or region is impossible. The median rate of return for all investor countries and regions does lie between 0 and 3 percent. Japanese and Singaporean firms had median rates of return in the 3–8 percent range. Taiwanese firms had a median rate of return in the breakeven range. All other foreign firms, including U.S. firms, had a median rate of return in the 0–3 percent range. For U.S. direct investors abroad, that range of rate of return appears relatively low.[12]

Although Hong Kong and Taiwan share a similar culture and language with the workers and government officials in Mainland China, they still had lower reported average rates of profit than those of Japan and U.S.-invested firms. Firms from Hong Kong and Taiwan do tend to be small and lack multinational experience. In contrast, Japanese and U.S.-invested firms are usually larger and technologically more advanced. They are often subsidiaries of successful companies in their home countries. Some have considerable foreign experience and generally may be better managed and able to adapt more quickly to a foreign environment. More widespread underreporting of profits may also explain the low profitability of the Hong Kong and Taiwanese firms. A study by Kao, Lee, and Lin (1992) finds that underreporting of profit is quite common among Taiwanese firms in China. Transfer-pricing, another factor, is probably practiced by all foreign-invested firms.

The conclusions reached here based on CIER data are also broadly corroborated by a study on the operations of foreign-invested firms in Shanghai in 1997 by the Bureau of Industrial and Commercial Administration of the Shanghai Municipal Government, which concluded that "more than half" the overseas companies in Shanghai showed a loss in 1997.[13] However, a 1998 survey conducted by the Bureau of Taxation in China found that one-third of the foreign-invested firms were making profits, and two-thirds were incurring losses. The latter figures are likely biased because the tax collection organization itself conducted the survey:

Table 6-18

Estimated Rates of Return of U.S. Direct Investment Abroad, 1994–2002 (percent)

	All Countries	China
1994	11.26	2.66
1995	12.50	7.23
1996	11.77	14.73
1997	12.03	15.51
1998	9.06	5.23
1999	9.40	8.03
2000	10.16	10.87
2001	7.74	12.62
2002	8.15	14.08
Average	10.23	10.11

Source: U.S. Department of Commerce 2000c, 2003b.

respondents would have incentives to understate their profits for tax avoidance and evasion.[14]

With data collected by the Bureau of Economic Analysis of the U.S. Department of Commerce on income from direct investment abroad, an estimated rate of return on U.S. direct investment based on historical cost can be calculated (table 6-18). Table 6-18 shows that while the rate of return on U.S. direct investment in China has greater variability than all U.S. direct investment abroad as a whole, the average level has not been significantly lower. Over a nine-year period, 1994–2002, the average annual rate of return for U.S. direct investment in China was 10.11 percent, compared with almost 10.23 percent for all U.S. direct investment abroad. In 1995 the average rate of return on all U.S. direct investment in China was 7.23 percent, not inconsistent with the CIER survey finding of a median rate of return (especially taking into account the possibility of underreporting) of 0–3 percent. Many smaller ventures may not be profitable, but a few large ventures are profitable and raise the overall average rate of return.

Rates of return clearly vary significantly both across firms and over time. However, the variability appears true not only for U.S.-invested firms but also for other foreign-invested firms. The variability may be due in part to the number of years in operation. A U.S.-invested firm may be less profitable because it began operation in China recently. It may also be due in part to the nature of a specific industry. A firm may be engaged in a more capital-intensive industry and require a longer gestation period for profitability. A definitive answer awaits further research.

7

Chinese Investment
in the United States

Capital flowing into the People's Republic of China from foreign sources, including the United States, has attracted much attention from academic researchers as well as policymakers. The previous chapters assessed the trend, nature, and characteristics of such FDI into China. China's gradual emergence as a major capital exporter is far less known. As the Chinese economy and its international trade continue to grow, more Chinese enterprises have begun to operate globally. In 2002, China State Construction Engineering Corporation and China Harbor Engineering Company, both Chinese enterprises, were listed as the twenty-second and the forty-first largest international contractors in the world, with international revenues of $1.1 billion and $589 million, respectively.[1] In 2002, approved direct investment outflows from China, according to official Chinese statistics, amounted to $982.68 million. The cumulative amount of direct investment abroad from China was estimated to be $9.34 billion.[2]

Chinese enterprises invest overseas for reasons similar to those of U.S. corporations to invest in China: to gain more direct access to the U.S. and other markets and to secure needed resources. To acquire additional iron ore, China Metallurgical invested $180 million in the Channar iron mine in Australia. A developing economy such as China has another important reason for investment abroad: to try to obtain advanced technology. Shougang (Capital Steel Works), one of the largest Chinese steel-makers, acquired 70 percent of Masta Engineering, a U.S. manufacturer and designer of metallurgical equipment. The acquisition allowed Shougang to obtain access to the firm's technology. Partly as a

121

result of this acquisition, Shougang has been able to supply metallurgical equipment to India, Indonesia, Malaysia, and the Philippines.[3]

Among the destinations of China's foreign direct investment, Hong
Kong is clearly and overwhelmingly the most important.[4] By the end of
1994 the cumulative stock of China's direct investment in the nonmanufacturing sectors of Hong Kong was an estimated $12 billion (Hong Kong
Census and Statistics Department 1996b).[5] Although the bulk of Chinese
direct investment abroad is in Hong Kong, China's direct investment in the
United States has also been increasing.

How great is the extent of Chinese investments in the United States? In
terms of annual flows, according to U.S. government data, Chinese direct
investment in the United States is both small and volatile (see table 7-1). In
its recent peak year, 1994, Chinese direct investment inflow into the United
States amounted to $170 million, less than 0.4 percent of total FDI inflow
into the United States of $45 billion in that year.[6] U.S. government esti-
mates indicate that the Chinese direct investment position in the United
States has been growing steadily in terms of cumulative stocks. Although
capital inflow from China slowed significantly after the June 4, 1989, incident, it resumed its growth as the Chinese economy recovered in 1993. By
2002, China had a total direct investment (stock) position of $233 million
in the United States, which, however, represented only 0.02 percent of the
total inward FDI (stock) position in the United States. China's capital outflows may be significantly underestimated because a large proportion of the
outflows are channeled through Hong Kong–based Chinese enterprises.
Although we do not know the exact amount of such capital re-exports, we
can estimate the upper bound by examining Hong Kong's total FDI position
in the United States. In 2002 the stock of such foreign direct investment
amounted to $2.189 billion, approximately only 0.16 percent of the total
stock of FDI in the United States. The combined foreign direct investment
position of China and Hong Kong came to 0.18 percent of the total stock
of inward foreign direct investment in the United States, hardly a significant
share. By comparison, in 2002 Mexico had a foreign direct investment
stock of $7.857 billion in the United States, or 0.58 percent of the total
stock of direct investment in the United States.

Table 7-1 shows the extent and some features of Chinese and Hong Kong
direct investment in the United States, based on official U.S. government data.

TABLE 7-1

DIRECT INVESTMENT OF CHINA AND HONG KONG IN THE UNITED STATES, 1989–2002 (US$ million)

	Direct Investment Position (historical basis)		Capital Inflows		Income	
	China	Hong Kong	China	Hong Kong	China	Hong Kong
1989	87 (0.02%)	1,124 (0.30%)	98	388	−60	−15
1990	124 (0.03%)	1,511 (0.38%)	37	259	−20	−16
1991	192 (0.05%)	1,162 (0.28%)	11	50	2	−48
1992	167 (0.04%)	1,358 (0.32%)	−23	147	−2	−64
1993	109 (0.02%)	1,518 (0.32%)	−49	152	19	44
1994	244 (0.05%)	1,505 (0.31%)	170	404	61	51
1995	329 (0.06%)	1,511 (0.25%)	79	−134	59	20
1996	197 (0.03%)	1,711 (0.29%)	−129	57	69	82
1997	182 (0.03%)	1,656 (0.24%)	41	77	17	84
1998	251 (0.03%)	1,458 (0.19%)	77	145	59	64
1999	295 (0.03%)	885 (0.09%)	39	−256	41	125
2000	277 (0.02%)	1,493 (0.12%)	−6	669	−22	12
2001	363 (0.03%)	1,542 (0.11%)	80	50	−13	21
2002	233 (0.02%)	2,189 (0.16%)	−128	645	8	58

SOURCE: U.S. Department of Commerce 1994a, 1996a, 1996c, 1998b, 1999b, 2000a, 2003f; Bargas 1997b.

NOTE: Estimates are based on historical costs; capital flows are direct investment related flows; capital outflows are recorded as negative; income refers to direct investment income, net of U.S. and foreign withholding taxes. Figures in parentheses are percentages of the total FDI position in the United States.

Direct investment incomes in the United States for both China and Hong Kong were *negative* for quite a few years. (*Direct investment income* is the return on foreign direct investment in the United States. It consists of earnings and interest on intercompany debts.) China's direct investment earned positive returns for 1991, 1993–99, and 2002. But Hong Kong's direct investment experienced negative incomes for 1989–92, in part because neither the Chinese nor the Hong Kong enterprises had any superiority in technology or management know-how over their U.S. competitors. Typically, multinational firms enjoy economic rents away from their home countries because of some unique intangible asset such as technology and know-how, often embodied in patents or other forms of intangible capital.[7] That case clearly did not hold for most enterprises of China or Hong Kong. If those firms come to the United States to purchase technology, as in the case of the Chinese steelmaker Shougang, the returns may not show up until much later, when the acquired technology can be adequately internalized. Even then, income is likely to show up as income to the parent companies in China or Hong Kong, where the manufacturing bases are located and labor and other costs are lower. Some direct investment may also have been made to provide supporting services in the United States for the trading operations of Chinese and Hong Kong enterprises, in which case no a priori reason would expect them to show significant profits, especially given the higher corporate income tax rates in the United States compared with Hong Kong.[8]

For comparative purposes, we can also look at estimates made by the Chinese government. Official Chinese figures indicate that up to 2002, cumulative approved Chinese overseas direct investments amounted to $9.34 billion, of which direct investments to the United States amounted to $835 million, undertaken by some 703 Chinese enterprises.[9] The $835 million reported by the Chinese government is on an *approval* basis and is expected to be larger than the $233 million reported by the U.S. government, which is on an arrival or realized basis.

Significant illegal and officially unapproved and unreported capital outflows come from China. Some Chinese capital outflows eventually find their way back to China by masquerading as "foreign" direct investment to take advantage of favorable tax treatments accorded to foreign investments by the Chinese government.[10] Other illegal outflows reach Hong Kong. Still others may be invested in the United States. U.S. government records such capital

TABLE 7-2

FOREIGN OFFICIAL AND PRIVATE HOLDINGS OF U.S. TREASURY SECURITIES
BY COUNTRY AT YEAR-END, 1995–2002 (US$ billion)

	1995	1996	1997	1998	1999	2000	2001	2002	Rank in 2002
Japan	208.3	271.3	288.6	292.6	301.0	325.6	329.7	386.7	1
China	36.8	47.8	49.3	48.7	63.1	62.3	81.9	109.3	2
Hong Kong	17.4	23.2	36.0	46.0	40.9	39.8	49.5	51.6	3
Germany	59.5	77.2	96.8	279.2	58.9	50.7	50.3	48.4	4
United Kingdom	NA	NA	NA	NA	NA	36.5	7.6	47.5	5
Korea, Republic of	NA	NA	NA	18.4	23.0	29.7	33.3	45.0	6
Taiwan	29.3	37.0	34.8	33.6	42.7	34.5	37.0	37.4	7
Cayman Island	NA	NA	NA	NA	NA	8.0	19.4	31.6	8
Mexico	NA	NA	NA	NA	NA	15.6	19.8	24.0	9
Italy	NA	NA	NA	NA	NA	21.5	19.9	20.6	10
Total foreign holdings	880.0	1,097.7	1,252.0	1,318.8	1,080.4	1,026.1	1,039.7	1,214.2	

SOURCE: U.S. Department of Commerce 1998b, 1999b, 2000a, 2003a.

flows as inflows from China even though the Chinese government may not necessarily record them as outflows to the United States (or as outflows at all). U.S. government figures may more accurately reflect the true extent of Chinese capital outflows to the United States as well as the Chinese foreign direct investment position in the United States than the Chinese government figures.[11]

In addition to FDI, China holds a substantial amount of U.S. Treasury securities, primarily through the People's Bank of China (the central bank) and the four major commercial banks (all state-owned). On a current flow basis, the People's Bank of China is probably one of the top purchasers of U.S. Treasury securities among foreign central banks in recent years.

Table 7-2 shows a large increase in the foreign demand for U.S. Treasury securities, particularly by Western European countries, in both 1996 and 1997. Chinese holdings of U.S. Treasury securities have been growing quite substantially since 1998. As of year-end 2002, Japan and China were the two largest investors in U.S. Treasury securities. Part of the Hong Kong holdings of U.S. Treasury securities may also be ultimately attributable to China, since many Hong Kong enterprises are Chinese owned.

Both Chinese direct investment abroad and Chinese direct investment in the United States have been growing. Because they both started from a low base, by the end of 2002 the stock of Chinese direct investment in the United States came to $233 million, only 0.02 percent of the stock of total inward direct investment in the United States. Even with adding direct investment from Hong Kong, the total share of FDI in the United States attributed to China and Hong Kong combined would come to only 0.18 percent.

But China is the second largest investor in U.S. Treasury securities, with a total value of $109.3 billion as of year-end 2002. The bulk of it is held by the People's Bank of China, the central bank. If for any reason China needs to sell these securities (for example, to raise U.S. dollars to defend the renminbi), the liquidation of the securities, if not done in an orderly manner, could significantly affect the market for such securities. Depending on the conditions that underlie the market and the U.S. economy, such liquidation could lead to a higher rate of interest and a somewhat lower rate of economic growth for the United States.

8

Effects of U.S. Direct Investment and Implications for U.S. Policy

The previous chapters have documented and analyzed the nature, extent, and characteristics of U.S. direct investment in China. We have also contrasted various features of U.S.-invested firms with other foreign-invested enterprises (FIEs) operating in China. This chapter focuses on the effects of such U.S. direct investment outflows on both the United States and China, and the implications for U.S. policy. Specifically we highlight four sets of effects: the effects on U.S. employment (jobs), the effects on U.S.-China trade, the effects on technology transfer, and the effects on Chinese GDP and economic growth.

Effects on U.S. Employment

From the standpoint of the United States, one immediate concern about direct investment abroad (including direct investment in China) is the potential loss of jobs in the United States.[1] U.S. firms, attracted by low wage rates, could move their domestic production facilities to China and cause a first-round loss of jobs. Firms could then export finished goods back to the United States, and the lower-priced goods could compete with similar goods made by U.S. workers at *other* U.S. firms. Such increased competition might cause a second-round of job displacements in the United States.

Let us examine the above scenario. First, as chapter 2 discussed, low labor cost is only one of several reasons for U.S. firms to locate in China. Firms also want to penetrate the Chinese market, to take advantage of preferential tax and tariff treatments, and to tap natural resources. According to a 1990 survey of the U.S.-China Business Council, U.S. firms operating in China primarily want to sell in the Chinese domestic market. Taking advantage of the low wage rates in China is an important, but not primary, reason for U.S. direct investment (U.S.-China Business Council 1990).[2] Other surveys have found that "market size" and "tax incentive programs" are almost as important as "abundant labor supply" as motivation for direct investment in China (see chapter 2). In a more recent study, Fung, Iizaka, Lin, and Siu (2002) found that tax incentives, market size, and labor quality are the top three reasons for the location choices of U.S. direct investment in China. Labor cost is a factor but not among the most important determinants.

True, wage rates are low in China compared with those in the United States. Wage rates in China are low even compared with those in Mexico.[3] A Mexican worker earned an average monthly rate of $640 to $800 in 2000, about three to four times the 2000 average monthly wage rate of $186.10 in Shanghai, the location in China with the highest labor cost that year. However, even Mexican wage rates are at most only a fifth of those in the United States. If U.S. firms are motivated to set up production facilities abroad because of noncompetitively high U.S. wage rates, they can consider many potential locations, including Mexico or the Philippines. The existence of China as a low-wage location only marginally influences decisions of U.S. firms to locate at home or abroad—they can just as easily locate in places other than China.

Low-wage, low-skilled Chinese labor does not compete with U.S. labor. Those Chinese workers do jobs that no U.S. workers have done for decades. They produce products that no U.S. workers have produced since the 1960s. If any workers lose jobs, they would be workers in Hong Kong, South Korea, and Taiwan, rather than the United States. U.S. workers long ago stopped producing such light industrial manufactured goods as low-end garments, shoes, toys, and household electrical appliances, the bulk of exports of foreign-invested firms in China. A U.S. firm is more likely to have established a production facility in China to replace another overseas production facility than a production facility in the United States. More recently, many U.S. and foreign multinationals have set up some of their electronic components manufacturing plants in China. But as we have shown in previous chapters, the bulk of the U.S. direct investment abroad is still in other developed countries such as the European Union and Canada. Quantitatively, the share of U.S. direct investment in China is very small and thus the impact on the U.S. labor market should also be relatively minor.

Furthermore, according to data from surveys conducted by the Chung-Hua Institution for Economic Research in 1993 and 1995 (reported in chapter 6), direct investment by U.S. firms in China did *not* lead to plant closings at home. Most U.S. firms produced completely *different* products in China from what they produced in the United States. The findings are completely consistent with the argument that Chinese workers in U.S.-invested firms in China have not significantly been taking away jobs from U.S. workers. U.S. direct investment in China results in few first-round job losses. And even if some U.S. firms do move to China because of its low wage rates, the job losses in the longer run would be inevitable, as the high labor costs in the United States render it uncompetitive in certain low-skilled industries in the global environment. By moving their operations to China, U.S. firms could at least save some managerial, design, and marketing jobs in the United States.

Furthermore, as also reported in chapter 6, data from three CIER surveys show that U.S.-invested firms in China sold most of their products in the Chinese domestic market. In 1992, 1993, and 1995, respectively, U.S.-invested firms in China sold 69.5 percent, 82.5 percent, and 84.5 percent of their goods in China (CIER 1994, 1996). The proportion of the goods made by U.S.-invested firms in China shipped back to the United States for sale declined from 15.6 percent in 1992 to 9.6 percent in 1993 and to 8.4 percent in 1995.[4] Clearly, goods made by U.S.-invested firms in China do not compete with goods made by workers in the United States for the U.S. domestic market. The second-round job-loss effect of U.S. direct investment in China can also be expected to be quite small.

Even if U.S.-invested firms in China sell only in the Chinese domestic market, could some still have been made by U.S. workers and exported to China instead? Production in the United States, given the structure of U.S. costs, would have to remain basically competitive. But in that case a U.S. firm must have invested in China for different strategic reasons: for example, proximity to customers, transportation and warehouse cost savings, and tariff and quota jumping. The argument actually has some merit regarding the so-called tariff- (and quota-) jumping direct investment. If a U.S. firm invests and produces in China for the Chinese domestic market solely to circumvent the Chinese tariff and nontariff trade barriers, then absent the tariff and nontariff barriers, production in the United States is actually competitive.[5] Thus, with China in the World Trade Organization, the job displacement effect in the United States of U.S. direct investment in China became even smaller.

The evidence demonstrates the weakness of the case that U.S. direct investment in China results in significant loss of U.S. jobs. Moreover, on a net basis, there may well have been a gain in jobs. U.S. direct investment in China typically leads to increased demand (by firms operating in China) for U.S.-produced capital goods as well as U.S.-produced intermediate goods—such as components, parts, and services—not to mention managerial and other service jobs at the U.S. investing firms themselves. For example, a U.S. personal computer manufacturing operation in China might need to import microprocessors from Intel and to purchase software licenses from Microsoft.

Effects on U.S.-China Trade

U.S. direct investment in China can also have an important impact on U.S.-China trade and on U.S.-China *relations*. What are the effects of U.S. direct investment in China on U.S.-China trade? Does it increase or decrease exports from the United States to China? Does it increase Chinese exports to the United States?

First, U.S. direct investment in China can increase U.S. exports of both goods and services to China because U.S.-invested firms in China may have demands for U.S.-produced machinery and equipment, intermediate inputs—components, parts, and raw materials—and services. But U.S. direct investment can also decrease U.S. exports of both goods and services because of the potential for U.S.-invested firms in China to produce goods for the Chinese domestic market as well as other overseas markets that can otherwise be supplied directly from the United States. The available empirical evidence from the CIER surveys suggests that the U.S.-invested firms in China typically produce completely different products from their parents. Not much substitutability occurs between the outputs of U.S.-invested firms in China and the outputs of their parents in the United States. The U.S. direct investment in China would scarcely reduce exports. U.S. direct investment in

FIGURE 8-1

RELATIONSHIP BETWEEN U.S. FDI IN CHINA AND U.S.-CHINA TRADE, 1989–2002

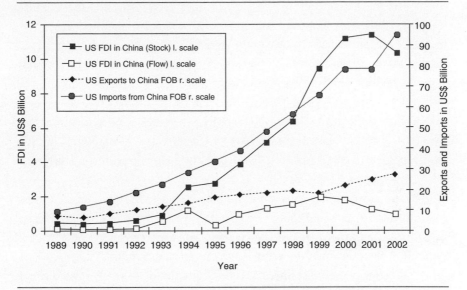

SOURCE: Authors' calculations, using data from table 5-1; PRC, General Administration of Customs, Economic Information and Agency 1995, 1996, 1997, 1998, 1999, 2000, 2001, 2002; U.S. Department of Commerce 2003h; PRC, HKSAR, Hong Kong Census and Statistics Department 1996a, 2000, 2001, 2002, 2003.

China can also increase U.S. imports of goods and services from China because of the possibility of U.S.-invested firms in China shipping their output (finished and semifinished goods, components, parts, and raw materials) to the United States for sale in the U.S. domestic market. The empirical evidence, again based on the CIER surveys, suggests that U.S.-invested firms typically ship a relatively small proportion of their output (less than 10 percent in 1993 and 1995) to the United States. Moreover, since the product lines of the U.S.-invested firms in China hardly overlap with their U.S. parents (see chapter 6), any increase in U.S. imports from China as a result of the U.S.-invested firms does not likely happen at the expense of domestic U.S. production. Instead, the U.S. imports from China probably substitute for U.S. imports from other developing countries.

Figure 8-1 plots the time-series of U.S. direct investment in China in both cumulative stock and annual flow (based on official U.S. data), U.S.

exports to China (including reexports through Hong Kong), and U.S. imports from China (again including reexports through Hong Kong) from 1989 to 2002. U.S. direct investment (and exports) to China declined in 1990 after the Tiananmen incident on June 4, 1989, and then grew explosively in 1993, only to slow again in 1995. Investment resumed its growth in 1996 and appeared to have stabilized at approximately $1.5 billion a year in the late 1990s. The U.S. FDI position (stock) has continued to rise steadily and reached $10.29 billion in 2002. With China's joining the WTO, U.S. direct investment may increase over the next few years. U.S. imports of goods from China grew rapidly during the 1990s, at an average of 21 percent. U.S. exports of goods to China grew at a slower, but still respectable, rate of 13 percent. However, the latter appeared to have stabilized in more recent years.

Can any growth in U.S.-China trade be attributed to U.S. direct investment in China? Although both U.S.-China trade (exports and imports) and U.S. direct investment in China have been growing during the 1990s, it is difficult to attribute any direct causality between trade and direct investment. Some evidence points to changes in U.S.-China trade positively related to the changes in the annual flow of U.S. direct investment to China (although the relationship is weaker for U.S. exports to China). Figure 8-2 plots the annual changes in U.S. exports to and imports from China, FOB, adjusted for reexports and reexport markups, against the change in the annual flow of U.S. direct investment to China, lagged one period, for 1991–2002. The annual changes in both exports and imports appear on average positively related to the annual change in U.S. direct investment in China. A definitive conclusion requires a longer sample period; other influential factors were at work (for example, a significant effective devaluation of the renminbi against the U.S. dollar between 1990 and 1994). But the results are consistent with the view that U.S. direct investment in China promotes U.S.-China trade.

Intrafirm Trade

One particularly important manifestation of increased U.S.-China trade resulting directly from U.S. direct investment in China is *intrafirm trade*;

FIGURE 8-2

RELATIONSHIP BETWEEN U.S. FDI POSITION (STOCK) IN CHINA AND U.S.-CHINA TRADE, 1991–2002

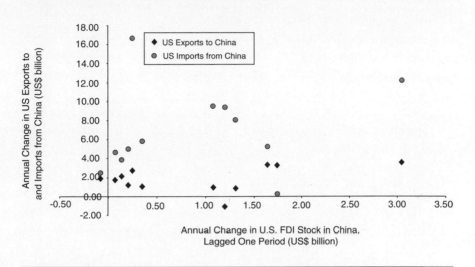

SOURCE: Authors' calculations, using data from table 5-1; U.S. Department of Commerce 2003h; PRC, HKSAR, various years.

that is, trade between U.S. parent companies (including their non-Chinese affiliates) and their affiliates in China. Intrafirm trade refers to trade between different units of one multinational corporation. Such trade obviously results from firms investing abroad. Through such trade U.S. firms can acquire cheaper inputs or resources from China. They can also take advantage of lower labor costs and globalize their supply chains by having their affiliates in China produce some stages of products and then shipping the finished or semifinished goods to the United States or elsewhere. U.S. affiliates in China can purchase machinery and equipment and intermediate goods from their parent companies. For an idea of the extent of such intrafirm trade, table 8-1 highlights U.S. intrafirm trade in goods with China, Hong Kong, and all countries in 1992 (a large share of the trade between the United States and China takes place via Hong Kong).

Table 8-1 shows that intrafirm exports accounted for 33.4 percent of U.S exports to all countries, while intrafirm imports made up 41.5 percent of U.S. imports. (In the value of imports and exports, the table includes

TABLE 8-1

U.S. INTRAFIRM TRADE IN GOODS WITH CHINA, HONG KONG, AND ALL COUNTRIES, 1992 (US$ million)

	China	Hong Kong	All Countries
Total exports	7,418	9,077	448,164
Intrafirm exports (total)	1,456 (19.6%)	3,358 (37.0%)	149,504 (33.4%)
By U.S. parent companies to their majority-owned affiliates located in the foreign country	148 (2.0%)	2,746 (30.3%)	100,737 (22.5%)
By foreign affiliates located in the U.S. to their foreign parent groups	1,308 (17.6%)	612 (6.7%)	48,767 (10.9%)
Total imports	25,728	9,793	532,665
Intrafirm imports (total)	a (0.01%–19.9%)	4,823 (49.2%)	221,059 (41.5%)
By U.S. parent companies from their majority-owned affiliates located in the foreign country	a (0.01%–19.9%)	3,481 (35.5%)	83,260 (15.6%)
By foreign affiliates located in the U.S. from their foreign parent groups	502 (2.0%)	1,342 (13.7%)	137,799 (25.9%)

SOURCE: Zeile 1997.

NOTE: Figures in parentheses are the respective percentages of total U.S. exports to China, Hong Kong, and all countries and total U.S. imports from China, Hong Kong, and all countries, based on official U.S. data. Reexports to and from China through Hong Kong are not taken into account.

a. The figures are suppressed to avoid disclosure of data of individual companies.

only goods—including raw materials, industrial supplies, semifinished products, and machinery—not services. The chapter discusses service trade later on.) The extent of intrafirm trade documents the important link between direct investment and trade for the United States. For purposes of comparison, we treat the U.S. intrafirm trade shares for all countries as the norm or the average.

For China, the absolute amount of intrafirm trade was not trivial. However, intrafirm exports made up only 19.6 percent of total U.S. exports to China and less than 20 percent of U.S. imports from China. In contrast, intrafirm trade was responsible for 37 percent of U.S. exports to Hong Kong and 49.2 percent of U.S. imports. In percentage terms, intrafirm trade was active—above average—for Hong Kong but significantly below average for China.

U.S. parent companies with plants overseas on average conducted 67.4 percent of intrafirm exports and 37.7 percent of intrafirm imports.[6] U.S. multinationals were primarily responsible for U.S. intrafirm exports, while foreign multinationals were primarily responsible for U.S. intrafirm imports. U.S. parent companies exporting to their affiliates in China accounted for only 2 percent of total U.S. exports to China, while 0.01–19.9 percent of total U.S. imports were accounted for by U.S. parent companies importing from their affiliates in China.[7] The low level of exports by U.S. parent companies to their affiliates in China is unusual and inconsistent with the normal pattern of U.S. intrafirm exports. An overwhelming proportion of intrafirm exports from the United States to China in 1992 occurred because of Chinese affiliates in the United States exporting to their Chinese parent companies, with a value of $1.308 billion, or a share of 90 percent of the total U.S. intrafirm exports to China.

The unusually low level of exports by U.S. parent companies to their affiliates in China can be partly attributed to the significant proportion of trade between China and the United States conducted through Hong Kong.[8] U.S. parent companies may first ship their machinery and equipment, components, parts, and semifinished and finished products to their affiliates (or other intermediaries) in Hong Kong.[9] The goods are then reexported to their affiliates in China. Total U.S. intrafirm exports to Hong Kong amounted to $3.358 billion in 1992. In sharp contrast to exports to China, U.S. parent companies carried out 81.8 percent of those intrafirm exports, a share much higher than the average of 67.4 percent for all countries.[10] The import side also had an unusually large share, 72.2 percent, of intrafirm imports from Hong Kong accounted for by U.S. parent companies.

That pattern of intrafirm trade among the United States, China, and Hong Kong created by U.S. direct investment may be partly related to the entrepôt function of Hong Kong. Hong Kong is well known as the gateway of China. U.S. parent companies that may want to ship goods ultimately to their affiliates in China may ship their goods first to their

Hong Kong affiliates, which then distribute the goods to China either through other Hong Kong–based traders or by themselves. And many foreign multinationals often choose Hong Kong as the regional headquarters (particularly for the Chinese market). According to a 1993 survey of 7,800 foreign companies operating in Hong Kong, 624 served as regional headquarters. The United States had the most regional headquarters located in Hong Kong, with 182, followed by Japan, with 88. The third, the United Kingdom, had 81 regional headquarters there (Fung 1997).

With China and Hong Kong considered one entity, U.S. parent companies in 1992 accounted for $2.894 billion, or 60.1 percent, of U.S. intrafirm exports (a combined value of $4.814 billion). The share is much closer to the norm of 67.4 percent for all countries. The suppression of detailed data—to avoid disclosure of data on individual companies—prevents the calculation of a precise figure. However, it is possible to estimate that U.S. firms accounted for 65.2–81.3 percent share of total U.S. intrafirm imports from China and Hong Kong in 1992.[11] Even the lower bound is considerably higher than the norm of 37.7 percent. If China and Hong Kong are considered a single market, the intrafirm trade between U.S. parent companies and their affiliates accounts for a high percentage, more than 65 percent, of the U.S. intrafirm exports to and imports from this market.

U.S. direct investment in China creates trade among units within the same U.S. multinational corporations across borders. The pattern of such intrafirm trade is unusual compared with the norm. U.S. parent companies trade intensively with Hong Kong affiliates but much less with their affiliates in China. Hong Kong is apparently used as an intermediary to conduct the triangular trade on an intrafirm basis, with goods first shipped to Hong Kong before they are reexported to either China or the United States, as well as to other final destinations. Unfortunately, we do not have data on the intrafirm trade between China and Hong Kong or on the role played by U.S. affiliates in both China and Hong Kong in this intrafirm trade.[12] Moreover, intrafirm trade can include trade among affiliates, not only between affiliates in Hong Kong and China but also between affiliates in third countries and affiliates in China and Hong Kong.

Trade in Services

A second related implication of U.S. direct investment in China is an increase in the cross-border sales and purchases of private services, including intrafirm trade in services among different units of a multinational corporation located in different countries as well as trade between unaffiliated parties. Private services include travel; passenger fares; other transportation (which includes freight and port services); royalties and license fees; activities in education, financial services, insurance, telecommunications; and business and technical services such as advertising, computer and data processing, and legal work. The purchases and sales occur through two channels. First, service trade occurs as cross-border trade between U.S. and Chinese residents, including intrafirm trade within a U.S. multinational corporation, that is, between the U.S. parent company and its affiliate in China. A second channel is through the sale of services by affiliates of U.S. multinationals. Sales abroad by foreign affiliates of U.S. parent companies are considered transactions between foreign residents: They are not recorded as international transactions per se. The services provided by a U.S.-affiliated professional firm (for example, accounting or legal) in China to Chinese or other clients are not considered a U.S. export of services. Only the U.S. direct investors' share of the profits earned in those sales are recorded as international transactions; the actual value of these sales is not (U.S. Department of Commerce 2003d). Official data on trade in services most likely understate significantly the gross value of trade in services between U.S. and Chinese nationals.

Table 8-2 highlights the extent of private service transactions between the United States and China, based on official U.S. data. U.S. exports of services to China consistently exceed imports of services from China. In 2002 the United States exported $6.1 billion worth of services to China, while it imported $4.1 billion of services from China, with a resulting surplus of $1.9 billion in favor of the United States. The service trade comes about partly because U.S.-invested firms in China need to purchase services such as accounting, consulting and legal services, and telecommunication services from the United States. The increased demand for service exports from U.S.-invested firms in China creates additional demands for jobs in the United States.

TABLE 8-2

PRIVATE SERVICE TRANSACTIONS BETWEEN THE UNITED STATES AND CHINA, 1992–2002 (US$ million)

	U.S. Exports to China	U.S. Imports from China
1992	1,569	1,054
1993	1,916	1,306
1994	2,050	1,476
1995	2,509	1,683
1996	3,166	1,937
1997	3,610	2,225
1998	3,957	2,302
1999	4,027	2,683
2000	5,199	3,257
2001	5,650	3,654
2002	6,073	4,136

SOURCE: U.S. Department of Commerce 2003d.

FIE Exports

As a third implication of FDI in China, foreign-invested enterprises, including U.S.-invested firms, supply a large proportion of Chinese exports.[13] Although the phenomenon is not unique to China, the magnitude is unusually large in China. Profits (including the returns to capital) from exports supplied by foreign-invested firms accrue to the foreign nationals and should be attributed as gains to the respective home countries of the foreign direct investors, not as gains to China.[14] Measures that affect trade flows and direct investment flows between the United States and China may cause a reduction of returns to foreign, including U.S., direct investors. Trade sanctions imposed on Chinese exports to the United States would also restrict exports by foreign-invested firms located in China.[15] U.S. import restrictions would reduce profits of not only Chinese producers and workers, but also U.S. and other foreign-invested firms. Policymakers may have valid reasons for pursuing such measures, but the consequences should be fully understood.

FIGURE 8-3

EXPORTS BY FIEs AND EXPORTS TO THE UNITED STATES AND THE WORLD, 1990–2002

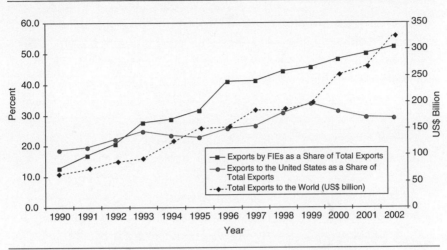

SOURCE: Authors' calculations, using data from table 8-3; PRC, General Administration of Customs, Economic Information and Agency 1995, 1996, 1997, 1998, 1999, 2000, 2001, 2002.

Figure 8-3 plots the shares of Chinese exports by foreign-invested firms, the shares of Chinese exports (including indirect exports)[16] to the United States, and total Chinese exports to the world. Between 1990 and 2002, Chinese exports rose from $62 billion to $326 billion, more than a fivefold increase. The share of exports supplied by foreign-invested firms rose dramatically—from 12.6 percent in 1990 to 52.2 percent in 2002. Foreign-invested firms supply half the Chinese exports and were responsible for most of the growth in exports in the 1990s. According to official Chinese data, the United States took in 21.5 percent of China's exports in 2002. If adjusted for the possible reexports of Chinese goods via Hong Kong, the total Chinese exports to the United States, direct and indirect combined, amounted to $94.8 billion in 2002, or 29.1 percent of total Chinese exports to the world. Between 1990 and 2001, the share of Chinese exports, direct and indirect combined, to the United States also grew, but more slowly, from 18.4 percent to 29.3 percent.

Precisely how much of Chinese exports to the United States do foreign-(including U.S.-) invested firms supply? Chinese customs statistics provide data on exports by foreign-invested firms but do not disaggregate such data by the ultimate destination. Thus there are no official published data on how much exports from China to the United States are carried out by foreign firms. One way to obtain an estimate specifically for the United States is to assume that the proportion of FIE exports destined for the United States is the same as the proportion of total exports destined for the United States. In 2002, foreign-invested firms in China exported $169.9 billion to the world. The share of Chinese exports to the United States, direct and indirect combined, is an estimated 29.1 percent. Using that percentage of total FIE exports, we estimate $49.5 billion (table 8-3, column 5) of total exports of foreign-invested firms in China going to the United States. Estimates for other years may be similarly derived.

Although the simple procedure provides a useful benchmark, it does not distinguish the motivation of foreign-invested firms operating in China. Hong Kong–invested firms may indeed have been established to take advantage of the low wage costs in China to manufacture there and then export the goods to their final overseas markets. As discussed in chapter 2 and chapter 6, the prime objective for U.S. firms in China is to penetrate the Chinese domestic market. (For a discussion of surveys about the motivation and characteristics of U.S. firms in China, see chapters 2 and 6.) Given the distance, even export-oriented U.S. direct investors might not plan to export back to the United States those goods produced in China. Producing goods in China to serve Asian markets makes sound business sense. If U.S. firms want cheap labor and proximity to their domestic market, Mexico may be a more appropriate choice. The percentage of goods exported by foreign-invested firms from China to the United States could differ substantially from the average exported by foreign-invested firms from China to all destinations.

To verify the robustness of those estimates, we turn to the CIER surveys, which indicate that foreign-invested firms exported 9.12 percent, 4.68 percent, and 7.44 percent of their products in 1992, 1993, and 1995, respectively, to the United States. Focusing on export markets alone (that is, omitting the value of goods sold in the Chinese domestic market), 19.21 percent, 11 percent, and 16.52 percent of the exports from the foreign-invested firms surveyed went to the United States in 1992, 1993, and 1995, respectively. Interpolating between 1993 and

TABLE 8-3

ESTIMATES OF EXPORTS (INCLUDING REEXPORTS THROUGH HONG KONG) BY FOREIGN-INVESTED FIRMS IN CHINA TO THE UNITED STATES, 1990–2002 (US$ million)

	Total Exports by Foreign-Invested Firms in China	Total Exports by FIEs/Total Exports (percent)	Total Adjusted Chinese Exports to the U.S./Total Exports (percent)	Estimated Exports to the U.S. by FIEs in China[a]	Alternative Estimated Exports to the U.S. by FIEs in China[b]
1990	7,800	12.6	18.4	1,438	NA
1991	12,100	16.8	19.5	2,355	NA
1992	17,400	20.5	22.0	3,821	7,250
1993	25,240	27.5	24.6	6,205	3,683
1994	34,723	28.7	23.5	8,144	6,308
1995	46,876	31.5	22.6	10,603	10,552
1996	61,506	40.7	25.6	15,756	14,720
1997	74,900	41.0	26.4	19,755	18,244
1998	80,962	44.0	30.6	24,796	19,813
1999	88,628	45.5	33.7	29,856	22,946
2000	119,441	47.9	31.3	37,385	30,744
2001	133,235	50.1	29.3	39,038	31,658
2002	169,936	52.2	29.1	49,495	40,445

SOURCE: Lardy 1994; PRC, General Administration of Customs, Economic Information and Agency 1995, 1996, 1997, 1998, 1999, 2000, 2001, 2002; CIER 1993, 1994, 1996; Fung and Lau 2000; and authors' calculations.

NOTE: The shares of adjusted Chinese exports destined for the United States in column 3 are calculated from the last column of table 4-3 in Fung and Lau 2000. They reflect adjustments for reexports and reexport markups. Figures reported in the tables may seem slightly off due to rounding of the calculated ratios.

a. Assuming the same share as total exports.

b. Using the CIER surveys.

1995 produces a figure of 13.76 percent for 1994. For years after 1995, we take the 1995 figure as the percentage of exports of foreign-invested firms in China destined for the United States. That assumption does pose two potential problems. First, the 16.5 percent represents only direct exports by foreign-invested firms in China to the United States and does not include indirect exports via Hong Kong. Unfortunately the CIER data, based on surveys of individual foreign-invested firms, do not contain information on reexports. (Often exporters themselves may not know the ultimate destinations of their goods.) Thus the 16.5 percent figure most likely represents only a lower bound. If one assumes that the proportion of direct to indirect exports for foreign-invested firms is the same for exports as a whole, then for 2001 the 16.5 percent would actually approach 23.8 percent. Similar adjustments can be made for other years. Second, figure 8-3 shows that the share of Chinese exports destined for the United States grew significantly during the 1990s. The share of exports by FIEs in China to the United States should also have been growing. A constant 16.5 percent, even adjusted by the ratio of total to direct exports, may underestimate the share of exports by FIEs to the United States after 1995. In any case, table 8-3 (column 6) also presents an alternative set of estimates.

It is remarkable (and reassuring) that the estimates obtained from the two different methods are almost identical for 1995, a year with actual survey data. The differences between the two sets of estimates between 1995 and 1997 are not pronounced, especially after taking into account that the alternative set of estimates may have a downward bias. However, the alternative set of estimates (column 6 of table 8-3) does not appear plausible before 1993 because it does not increase monotonically over time. Particularly disappointing are the alternative estimates for 1992 and 1993, years with actual survey data, which show a decline of FIE exports to the United States by 50 percent between 1992 and 1993 while both FIE exports to the world and adjusted total exports to the United States were rising. A possible sampling error in the CIER surveys of 1992 and 1993 may cause the problem. Between 1993 and 1997, the two sets of estimates appear to converge, with the alternative set of estimates systematically lower than the initial set of estimates except in 1995, when they are almost identical. After 1997 the alternative set of estimates appears to lag behind significantly. Because the FIE exports to the U.S. as a ratio of total FIE exports should also be rising over time, we used the first set of estimates (column 5 of table 8-3) exclusively here. In any case both sets of estimates highlight the phenomenon that foreign-, including U.S.-, invested firms generate a great percentage of Chinese exports to the United States and to the world.

Accounting gives no particular reason to separate out U.S. imports from China into imports from foreign-invested firms and imports from Chinese entities. Indeed no good economic reasons exist to focus on the bilateral trade balance in the context of the U.S.-China economic relationship. However, for political and other reasons, policymakers do pay unduly great attention to trade imbalances. In that context, to highlight the potentially different *economic welfare* characteristics of exports by foreign-invested firms and by Chinese firms, disaggregating Chinese exports to the United States in the above fashion may serve a useful purpose. One could ask who benefits the most from U.S.-China trade as well as its symmetric counterpart, who has the most to lose from a curtailment of U.S.-China trade. The source of Chinese exports to the United States makes a difference to the distribution of the gains of U.S.-China trade: Part of the gains may accrue to non-Chinese entities, some to the Chinese government, and some to individual Chinese citizens. By the same token a curtailment of U.S.-China trade—say, resulting from trade sanctions—may hurt other nationals in addition to Chinese enterprises and workers. Thus both Hong Kong and Taiwan have always supported the renewal of most-favored-nation (MFN) status for China (now known as normal-trade-relations status). As major direct investors in export-oriented enterprises in China, they have potentially the most to lose.

Processing and Assembly Exports

Another unique feature of Chinese exports to the world and to the United States is the large proportion of exports in the form of processing and assembly.[17] Foreign firms provide raw materials, components, and sometimes machinery, as well as designs to entities in China that in turn manufacture products with the imported inputs and reexport them to the foreign firms. Both the imported inputs and the finished outputs remain the property of the foreign firms.[18] While foreign-invested firms in China account for some processing and assembly, much of these activities, more than half by value, are actually contracted to Chinese firms, including state-owned enterprises. If the production process is contracted or sub-contracted to an entity that is fully Chinese, it is technically not related to foreign direct investment, since the foreign firm supposedly has no direct management control or ownership interest over the Chinese entity. But in practice foreign firms do exert de facto control over the subcontracted production of the products in some cases. The boundary between FDI and contracting or subcontracting is not so clear-cut in the Chinese case.[19]

In 2002, according to official Chinese data, Chinese exports in the form of processing and assembly amounted to $47.5 billion, or 14.6 percent of total Chinese exports. The amount of Chinese exports in the form of processing and assembly comprise: Chinese state-owned enterprises accounted for $28.3 billion; total of foreign-invested enterprises accounted for $16.6 billion (which included $1.9 billion from Sino-foreign contractual joint venture, $4.6 billion from Sino-foreign equity joint venture, and $10.1 billion from foreign-owned enterprises). Collective enterprises accounted for $2.2 billion, and other enterprises accounted for $0.4 billion. Including exports related to processing and assembly, exports from foreign-invested firms ran to $169.9 billion from China in that year. All exports accounted for by foreign-invested firms and by processing and assembly executed by Chinese firms came to $200.9 billion, or 61.7 percent of total Chinese exports. *More than half* of Chinese exports in 2002 concerned FDI: exports either of foreign-invested firms or processing and assembly.

The amount of processing and assembly exports shipped to the United States is unknown.[20] Official Chinese statistics do not provide such information. As with FIE exports, we can estimate yearly figures by assuming that the proportion of such exports destined for the United States is the same as the proportion of all Chinese exports ultimately destined for the United States.

Table 8-4, with the results of those calculations, estimates total processing and assembly exports from China to the United States in 2002 at $13.8 billion, or almost 14.6 percent of total Chinese exports to the United States including reexports via Hong Kong.[21] The estimated total exports from China to the United States accounted for by either foreign-invested firms or processing and assembly items was $58.5 billion in 2002. Since 1996, more than half of U.S. imports from China have been related to FDI in China, either from foreign-invested firms or processing and assembly activities. The feature distinguishes China from other Asian economies such as Japan and South Korea. Based on the extent of FDI in

China and the exports attributable to it, China may be a much more open economy than most of its neighbors, despite the continued existence of some trade barriers (see, for example, Lardy 1994).

As with exports related to foreign-invested firms, exports related to processing and assembly activities raise the issue of how much economic benefit China derives from exports to the United States. With foreign-invested firms, the issue is the amount of profit that accrues to foreign owners of capital in China. For exports associated with processing and assembly, the concern is likely to be the extent of value added in China. By definition under processing and assembly, inputs and raw materials are all imported, and the finished outputs are all exported. Since imported inputs and materials and the exported finished outputs belong solely to foreign firms, the value added by the processing entities in China is likely to be relatively small.

Information on value added related to processing and assembly activities is difficult to obtain. However, we can attempt to arrive at an estimate in two ways. First, while no explicit data exist on value added, official Chinese data do report the extent of imports associated with processing and assembly. *Chinese Customs Statistics* provides data on imports associated with processing and assembly as well as imports of equipment associated with processing and assembly (the former, imports associated with processing and assembly, excludes imports of equipment associated with processing and assembly). The former may be considered an estimate of the value of imports of intermediate inputs—components, parts, and raw materials—associated with processing and assembly. By subtracting the value of the imports associated with processing and assembly from the value of exports associated with processing and assembly, we obtain an estimate of the value added generated in China on account of processing and assembly activities.[22] If we assume that the value-added content of processing and assembly exports to the United States is the same as that of processing and assembly exports to the world, we can arrive at an estimate of the value added in China due to processing and assembly exports to the United States.

Alternatively, we can use assumptions or educated guesses on the extent of value added as a share of the value of Chinese processing and assembly exports to the United States. The available figures are based on reports from some Hong Kong academics and from discussions with some Hong Kong traders. Chinese firms that engage in processing and

TABLE 8-4

PROCESSING AND ASSEMBLY EXPORTS AND EXPORTS BY FOREIGN-INVESTED FIRMS FROM CHINA TO THE UNITED STATES, 1995–2002 (US$ billion)

	1995	1996	1997
Chinese exports to the world FOB	148.8	151.0	182.8
Estimated Chinese exports to the U.S. FOB adjusted for reexports and markups	33.7	38.7	48.2
Exports to the U.S./exports to the world	22.62%	25.62%	26.38%
Processing and assembly exports to the world FOB	20.7	24.2	29.5
Processing and assembly exports to the U.S. FOB	4.7	6.2	7.8
Processing and assembly exports by foreign-invested firms to the world FOB	2.9	4.5	6.1
Processing and assembly exports by non-FIEs to the world FOB	17.8	19.8	23.3
Processing and assembly exports by non-FIEs to the United States FOB	4.0	5.1	6.1
Exports by foreign-invested firms to the U.S. FOB	10.6	15.8	19.8
Chinese exports to the United States by foreign-invested firms or processing and assembly	14.6	20.8	25.9
Share of Chinese exports to the United. States accounted for by processing and assembly or by foreign-invested firms	43.46%	53.81%	53.73%

SOURCE: PRC, General Administration of Customs, Economic Information and Agency 1995, 1996,

assembly activities are often paid a processing fee. The processing fees received by the Chinese entities in these arrangements may average 10 percent of the value of the exports (see, for example, Ho 1993). The fees represent a lower bound on the value added in China on account of processing and assembly activities because they do not include direct costs of Chinese labor as well as returns to the capital and equipment provided by the foreign firms. Some traders in Hong Kong indicated in 1996 that the value added in processed exports was about 20 percent.[23] We use 20 percent as the basis for our alternative estimation.

1998	1999	2000	2001	2002
183.8	194.9	249.2	266.2	325.6
56.3	65.7	77.9	78.1	94.8
30.63%	33.69%	31.25%	29.35%	29.12%
30.7	35.8	41.1	42.2	47.5
9.4	12.0	12.8	12.4	13.8
7.2	10.4	13.1	14.3	16.6
23.5	25.4	28.0	27.9	30.9
7.2	8.6	8.8	8.2	9.0
24.8	29.9	37.4	39.0	49.5
32.0	38.4	46.2	47.2	58.5
56.84%	58.49%	59.31%	60.44%	61.71%

1997, 1998, 1999, 2000, 2001, 2002; Fung and Lau 2000; authors' calculations.

Table 8-5 presents the estimates obtained from both methods. The first method subtracts the value of imported raw materials and intermediate inputs associated with processing and assembly (row 2) from the value of processed exports (row 1). For 2002 the procedure estimates value added of $13.3 billion and a value added to gross value of exports ratio of 28 percent.[24] The second method takes 20 percent of the gross value of processed exports as the value added—for 2002 an alternative estimate of value added of $2.76 billion. The proportion of value added in processing and assembly exports has been rising; the 20 percent figure, while reliable in the mid-1990s, is most

TABLE 8-5

ESTIMATES OF VALUE ADDED OF CHINESE PROCESSING AND ASSEMBLY EXPORTS TO THE UNITED STATES, 1993–2002 (US$ billion)

	1993	1994	1995
Chinese processing and assembly exports to the world	16	18.2	20.7
Chinese processing and assembly imports from the world	13	15.1	16.2
Chinese value added as a proportion of Chinese processing and assembly exports to the world	18.8%	16.7%	21.7%
Chinese processing and assembly exports to the United States	3.9	4.3	4.7
Value added of Chinese processing and assembly exports to the United States	0.7	0.7	1.0
Value added as 20% of Chinese processing and assembly exports to the United States	0.8	0.9	0.9

SOURCE: PRC, General Administration of Customs, Economic Information and Agency 1993, 1994,

likely an underestimate today. Preferred estimates of value added from Chinese processing and assembly exports to the United States are the figures based on the reported values of processing and assembly exports and processing and assembly imported inputs (row 5). The 20 percent figure cited by Hong Kong traders in 1996 (presumably referring to practices in prior years) is quite close to our independently estimated figure of 21.7 percent for 1995 (row 3); the trend of our estimated proportion of value added in processing and assembly exports has been steadily upward, as expected.

The characteristics and magnitudes of trade generated by FDI and processing and assembly activities in China give some merit to disaggregating Chinese exports to the United States to distinguish exports by foreign-invested firms; exports by Chinese firms through processing and assembly activities, which are essentially also directed by foreign firms; and exports by Chinese firms. The first two types are related to FDI (including U.S.) activities in China. The Chinese domestic values added resulting from processing and assembly exports to the United States are relatively low but

1996	1997	1998	1999	2000	2001	2002
24.2	29.4	30.7	35.8	41.1	42.2	47.5
17.8	20.9	19.9	23.6	28.0	28.9	34.2
26.4%	28.9%	35.2%	34.1%	31.9%	31.5%	28.0%
6.2	7.7	9.3	12.1	12.9	12.4	13.8
1.6	2.2	3.3	4.12	4.12	3.91	3.86
1.2	1.5	1.9	2.4	2.6	2.5	2.8

1995, 1996, 1997, 1998, 1999, 2000, 2001, 2002; Fung and Lau 2000; authors' calculations.

rising over time. For 2002 Chinese domestic value added from processing and assembly activities may be estimated at 28 percent of the gross value of exports from such activities.[25]

Effects on Technology Transfer

A third implication of U.S. direct investment in China is technology transfer. U.S. multinationals, through their direct investment, machinery and equipment exports, and licensing activities, are agents of *technology transfer*. The United States may be concerned about slowly losing its technological advantage to a potential competitor. China wants to develop its economy in the high-technology information age. The United States, as the world leader in advanced technology in many industries, is a potentially important source of technology transfer for China. According to the CIER survey for 1995, 38 percent of U.S.-invested firms in China used technology provided by their parent companies (37.3 percent in the survey for

1993). Including technology provided by other U.S. firms, the share rose to 42 percent (38.7 percent for 1993).

The extent of technology transfer can be approximately measured by one category of service trade: the receipts and payments of royalties and license fees. According to the U.S. Department of Commerce (1996b, 1998d), royalties and license fees "cover transactions with foreign residents that involve patented or unpatented techniques, processes, formulas, and other tangible property rights used in the production of goods, as well as transactions involving copyrights, trademarks, franchises, broadcast rights and other intangible rights." The category covers the area loosely termed *technology transfer*. Although some critics of U.S. direct investment abroad (including investment in China) argue that technology transfer harms the U.S. economy, royalty and license fee payments show that U.S. firms do benefit directly in monetary terms. Because technology transfers by U.S. firms are private transactions, the firms must have found it profitable to sell their technologies. Selling technology can still harm the U.S. economy if positive externalities associated with such technology exist for the rest of the U.S. economy. Assessing the extent of such spillovers is difficult. Incomes from the transactions represent welfare gains to the U.S. economy. But the possible illegal appropriation and use of technology or trademarks should concern U.S. firms. In terms of intellectual property rights, the United States already has a Special 301 agreement with China, which helps to prevent some problems.[26] The U.S. executive branch is authorized to impose trade sanctions on a foreign country if that country violates the intellectual property rights of U.S. persons and companies. (For details of the section 301 trade law and the Special 301 trade law, see Finger and Fung 1994.) Table 8-6 presents data documenting the royalties and license fees transactions between the United States and China between 1992 and 2002.

Table 8-6 shows that in 2002 the United States had a net receipt of royalties and license fees from China of $723 million. U.S. parent companies received a large proportion of that figure from their affiliates ($497 million, or 69 percent), a direct result of direct investment in China. The major area of technology transfer between U.S. firms and unaffiliated parties operating in China, which resulted in royalties and fees amounting to $48 million in 2002, was industrial processing. Through U.S. direct investment, the technology transfers to China (but remains under control by affiliates of U.S. firms in

China) and in return generates monetary gains, albeit quite modest, for the U.S. economy. Royalties and license fees alone understate the extent of technology transfer as well as the returns to the technology transfer. In many U.S.-China joint ventures, the technology of the U.S. partner is explicitly recognized as part of its contribution to the equity capital of the joint venture. Reported royalties and license fees do not include the value of technology or the income attributable to the equity capital.

As a comparison, we examine information provided by the Chinese government on the extent of technology transfer between the United States and China. The term *technology transfer*, as used by the Chinese government, is not explicitly defined, and it is not clear how much of it is related to U.S. direct investment in China. Nonetheless, such data provide an additional source of useful information. In 1995 the introduction of U.S. technology into China reportedly amounted to $2.27 billion, an increase of 282 percent over the year before. In 1996 the amount was $2.13 billion. In 1998 it increased to $3 billion. Technology use includes complete electric power generation plants, security warning systems, complete chemical plants, telecommunication equipment, aircraft, and airport and subway construction (PRC, Economic Information and Agency 1997a, 2000a). From the official description, technology transfer according to the Chinese government clearly includes some purchases of services, some investment in plants and equipment, and some trade in goods. The data do not directly compare with those in table 8-6. With increased investment in China by U.S. high technology companies since China joined the WTO, it is expected that technology transfer from the United States to China should increase substantially.

Effects on Chinese GDP and Economic Growth

In addition to effects on U.S. employment, U.S.-China trade, and technology transfer, U.S. direct investment in China augments the capital stock in China, creates employment there, and increases Chinese GDP. But even FDI as a whole is not a large factor in aggregate investment in China, as discussed in chapter 1, and U.S. direct investment is only a fraction of total FDI in China.

TABLE 8-6

NET RECEIPTS OF ROYALTIES AND LICENSE FEES FROM CHINA BY THE UNITED STATES, 1992–2002 (US$ million)

	1992	1993	1994	1995
Total net receipts	72	111	64	113
Total net receipts between affiliated parties	35	a	23	54
By U.S. parents from affiliates in China	35	a	23	52
By Chinese affiliates located in the U.S. from Chinese parents in China	0	a	b	2
Total net receipts between unaffiliated parties	37	a	40	59
Industrial processing	35	59	26	31
Books, records, and tapes	1	1	1	1
Broadcasting and recording of live events	b	0	b	1
Franchise fees	0	b	3	4
Trademarks	NA	NA	3	8
General use computer software				
Other	1	a	9	14

SOURCE: U.S. Department of Commerce 1996e, 1998e, 1999g, 2000d, 2001a, 2002c, 2003e.

a. Figures have been suppressed to avoid disclosure of data of individual companies. For earlier years, trademarks are not listed as a separate item.

Table 8-7 presents estimates by the U.S. Department of Commerce on the extent of the direct contributions of U.S. direct investment on the GDPs of selected host countries. U.S. direct investment contributed 0.5 percent to China's GDP in 2001, less than the 0.9 percent for Japan and 1.0 percent for South Korea and more than the 0.4 percent for India. In contrast, in 2001 the gross product of U.S. direct investment accounted for 4.8 percent of Hong Kong's GDP, 5.7 percent of Malaysia's GDP, and 12 percent of Singapore's GDP. The order of magnitude of the contributions does not appear to change much over time. Contributions of U.S. direct investment on Chinese GDP showed an upward trend in the 1990s—but the initial base of U.S. direct investment was relatively low. In long-run equilibrium, the contribution of U.S. direct investment to

1996	1997	1998	1999	2000	2001	2002
153	250	318	409	501	571	723
90	165	212	310	346	401	497
87	164	211	308	346	400	497
3	1	1	1	b	1	b
63	85	106	100	155	170	226
43	52	47	32	44	43	48
1	1	b	2	3	4	5
1	1	1	2	4	3	1
5	5	5	5	4	a	3
7	6	5	10	17	9	20
		46	49	83	102	144
6	20	1	0	0	a	6

b. Less than $500,000.

Chinese GDP should not be significantly greater than its effect on Japanese GDP. Overall the direct contribution of U.S. direct investment to Chinese GDP continues at a rather modest rate. (This is comparable in order of magnitude to the value added attributable to Chinese processing and assembly exports to the United States.)

Although the direct contribution of U.S. direct investment to the Chinese GDP is small, its impact on the economic development of China can still be significant. In addition to its direct role in the transfer of technology and know-how, foreign (including U.S.) direct investment can be a major stimulus of innovations in the economy: It helps to bring in new concepts and ideas, new tools, and new ways of doing things; it opens up new markets, both domestic and foreign; it establishes new models and

TABLE 8-7

GROSS PRODUCT OF MAJORITY–U.S. OWNED FOREIGN AFFILIATES AS PERCENTAGE OF GDPS OF HOST COUNTRIES, SELECTED YEARS

	1982	1989	1994	1995	1996	1997	1998	1999	2000	2001
China	a	a	0.1	0.2	0.3	0.4	0.3	0.4	0.5	0.5
Hong Kong	3.1	5	3.7	4.1	4	4.1	4.5	5.1	5.2	4.8
India	0.1	0.1	0.1	0.1	0.1	0.2	0.1	0.2	0.4	0.4
Japan	0.4	0.5	0.5	0.5	0.6	0.6	0.6	0.7	0.8	0.9
Republic of Korea	0.3	0.3	0.4	0.4	0.5	0.5	0.5	0.8	1.0	1.0
Malaysia	6.3	4.6	5.1	4.9	4.8	5.0	4.2	6.0	5.8	5.7
Mexico	2.1	2.4	2.3	2.7	3.1	2.9	3.4	3.7	3.4	3.2
Singapore	7.3	8	8.1	8.8	7.5	9.7	9.2	11.7	14.3	12.0

SOURCE: Mataloni and Fahim-Nader 1996; U.S. Department of Commerce 1998f, 1999f, 2000b, 2002a, and 2003g.

NOTE: Figures for 1982 and 1994 exclude the gross products of majority–U.S. owned banking affiliates abroad.

a. Indicates less than 0.05 percent.

sets new standards of quality and service. It also provides training for Chinese workers and helps to upgrade the human capital. In a transition economy such as China, those spillover effects can be profound. FDI can create further demand for domestically produced intermediate inputs in the Chinese market and spur the further development of domestic industries through its supply of critical inputs. FDI, including that from the United States, can have an important *institution-building* effect. Contacts with foreign firms and the foreign market encourage domestic producers to learn to play by the rules of the market, not the rules of the command economy. FDI introduces competition in the Chinese market and forces domestic Chinese enterprises to emulate foreign-invested firms and become more efficient. To be competitive in a market economy, the Chinese firms must meet deadlines to deliver materials, inputs, or products; pay attention to the quality of their outputs; and honor commercial contracts. Without the constant challenges posed by the openness of the economy and by FDI, Chinese enterprises would be complacent and stagnant, the economy would turn inward, and competition would diminish.

Eventually, incentive to be efficient and innovative would disappear (Lau 1994; Fung 1997).

Implications for U.S. Policy

The first conclusion that we can draw about U.S. direct investment in China is that it is on a net basis beneficial for the U.S. economy. Our analysis shows that the effect on domestic U.S. employment may on balance be positive rather than negative. The effect on trade is positive—there is some evidence that U.S. exports to China are enhanced by increases in U.S. direct investment flows to China. Specific monetary gains result from the transfer of technology from the United States to China. In most instances U.S.-invested firms maintain control over such technology. U.S. policy should aim at facilitating U.S. direct investment. The government should have a policy goal of maintaining a level playing field in China for both domestic and foreign-, especially U.S.-, invested firms. It should demand national treatment for U.S. firms wherever possible. It should take measures to protect U.S. direct investment from unfair appropriation. An investment protection treaty with China and availability of Overseas Private Investment Corporation insurance to U.S. firms would help U.S. firms, as would a tax treaty with China to reduce or eliminate double taxation. Strengthening protection of intellectual property rights in China for U.S. firms must remain a high priority of the U.S. government.

Second, the large proportion of intrafirm trade generated by U.S. direct investment in China has substantive policy significance. The most important implication is that for both the United States and China any policy that may result in a disruption of trade between the economies may also disrupt the normal operations of U.S. and Chinese multinational corporations. A significant amount of trade between the United States and China is cross-border trade between different units of the same firm: If trade sanctions on China are contemplated, policymakers should take into account how they may restrict trade between U.S. parent companies and their affiliates. Similarly, a Chinese attempt to erect more trade barriers to pursue an industrial policy might disrupt the operations of U.S.

firms in China as well as Chinese firms in the United States. The incidence of restrictions on imports from China and exports to China by the
United States is likely to be borne not only by Chinese enterprises and
workers, but also substantially by foreign-, including U.S.-, invested firms
in China and by foreign and U.S. firms engaged in processing and assembly activities.

Finally, the value-added content of Chinese exports is relatively low,
even though it has risen in recent years. For processing and assembly
exports, value added in China may be estimated at approximately 28 percent of the gross value of exports. However, even of the 28 percent, a significant proportion (for example, returns to capital) actually accrues to
foreign nationals through their direct and indirect investments in China.
Not much is known about the value-added content of non–processing
and assembly exports, although anecdotal evidence suggests a value-
added content of 40 percent. In contrast, the value-added content of many
U.S. exports to China—for example, aircraft, semiconductors, timber, and
wheat—is quite high. All the considerations suggest a more detailed exam-
ination before drawing conclusions about the relative distribution of welfare gains from trade between China and its trading partners. In particular,
in a multilateral world one cannot assume that a country running a trade
surplus vis-à-vis another necessarily derives greater benefits from the trading relations in terms of income or employment generated for its citizens.

9

Conclusion

Previous chapters have examined and analyzed the trends, characteristics, and implications of the direct investment relationship between the United States and China. To gather as detailed information as possible about U.S. direct investment in China as well as Chinese investment in the United States, we have employed a variety of sources: official U.S. and Chinese government statistics; data from international organizations, including the World Bank, the International Monetary Fund, the World Trade Organization, the Asian Development Bank, and the United Nations Conference on Trade and Development (UNCTAD); official government and private-sector information from Hong Kong; and the results from three large-scale surveys of foreign-invested firms in China conducted by the Chung-Hua Institution for Economic Research, Taipei. The diversity of the sources has allowed us to conduct a comprehensive study on this important topic.

To summarize our findings, we answer the following series of questions on U.S. direct investment in China:

How Large Is U.S. Direct Investment in China?

In terms of annual flows, according to U.S. government data, U.S. direct investment in China is running at the average annual rate of $1.4 billion a year, barely 1 percent of the average annual U.S. direct investment outflow of approximately $127 billion.[1] In terms of cumulative stock, the share of U.S. direct investment in China is even smaller. In 2002 the U.S. direct investment position abroad (measured by historical cost) was $1.52 trillion, while such investment in China amounted to $10.3 billion, or only 0.68 percent.

According to Chinese government data, the average annual inflow of U.S. direct investment into China is approximately $3.69 billion a year, 8.97 percent of the average total annual inflow of FDI of approximately $41.2 billion. In 2002 the United States was the second largest direct investor in China, behind Hong Kong.

Although U.S. direct investment in China is quantitatively rather small, it does have important implications. The investment significantly affects the amount of trade between the two countries and introduces subtle complications in the formulation of trade policies toward each other. Current U.S. direct investment in China affects the future ability of U.S. firms to sell in the rapidly growing Chinese domestic market. Finally, U.S. investment also affects the long-term growth prospects of the Chinese economy.

How Large Is Chinese Direct Investment in the United States?

Chinese direct investment in the United States is both small and volatile. In its recent peak year, 1994, Chinese direct investment inflow into the United States amounted to $170 million, less than 0.4 percent of the total FDI inflow into the United States of $45 billion.[2] In terms of cumulative stock, Chinese direct investment in the United States is also small. In 2002 China had a direct investment position (measured by historical cost) of only $233 million in the United States, approximately one-fiftieth of the U.S. direct investment position in China. The amount represented only 0.02 percent of the total FDI position in the United States. Even if Hong Kong direct investment in the United States were included as Chinese direct investment, the combined direct investment from China and Hong Kong would amount to only 0.18 percent of the total foreign direct investment position in the United States.

Why Do U.S. Firms Invest in China?

U.S. firms invest in China primarily to establish a beachhead to penetrate the large and rapidly growing Chinese domestic market. In 1995, U.S.-invested firms in China sold 84.5 percent of their output to customers in

China and exported only 8.4 percent of their outputs back to the United States. The concentration of most U.S. direct investment in regions where per-capita incomes, retail sales, and wage rates are relatively high by Chinese standards suggests that the focus of U.S. direct investment is the potential size of the local markets rather than the level of the local wage rates. Other reasons cited for investment include the abundant labor supply, preferential tax and tariff treatment given to foreign direct investors, avoidance of transport costs and tariff and nontariff barriers to trade, exploitation of China's natural resources, and establishment of a low-cost production base to supply Asian and other markets.

Where Do U.S. Firms Locate?

In 2002 the top five regions in China for the location of U.S. direct investment in terms of the total value of contracted investment were, in descending order, Jiangsu, Shandong, Liaoning, Guangdong, and Shanghai. Those coastal regions boast relatively high per-capita incomes, retail sales of consumer goods, and average monthly wage rates. The five regions alone, of a total of thirty-one such regions, accounted for more than half (68.3 percent) of U.S. contracted direct investment in China in that year.

What Modes Do U.S. Firms Select?

Excluding joint development (discussed separately below), the three most important modes of U.S. direct investment in China are the equity joint venture, the contractual joint venture, and the wholly foreign-owned enterprise. In an equity-joint venture, both the U.S. and the Chinese partners contribute capital to the venture, with profits distributed accordingly. In a contractual joint venture, the arrangements are flexible, with the specific agreements on capital contributions (including contributions in kind) and profit distribution embodied in the specific contracts. A wholly foreign-owned enterprise is owned and controlled solely by the U.S. direct investor; there is no Chinese partner. In the early 1990s, more than 80 percent of U.S.-invested firms (excluding those engaged in joint development) were in equity joint ventures, slightly more than 10 percent were wholly foreign-owned enterprises, and approximately 5 percent were in contractual joint ventures. The stock of U.S. investments reflected those figures: almost three-quarters in equity joint ventures, a quarter in contractual joint ventures, and slightly more than 2 percent in wholly foreign-owned enterprises.[3] However, the wholly foreign-owned enterprise has been gaining in popularity among U.S.- and other foreign-invested firms.

A joint development venture is typically set up between a Chinese corporation or a ministry and a foreign partner to develop and explore natural resources such as coal, oil, and natural gas. Although in general this mode of FDI is not an important form of FDI in China, some U.S. direct investment in China—for example, the petroleum industry—finds it fairly significant.

In What Sectors Do U.S. Firms Invest?

Based on U.S. government statistics, the bulk of U.S. direct investment in China occurs in the manufacturing sector. In 2002, 59.9 percent of the total cumulative stock of U.S. direct investment, valued at historical cost, was in manufacturing, and 20 percent in mining and utilities. Among the manufacturing industries, electronic and other electrical equipment accounted for almost 25 percent. That sector has been the manufacturing industry with the most U.S. direct investment since 1995. Among the service industries, wholesale trade claimed the highest share of investment, with about 5 percent in 2002.

Does U.S. Direct Investment in China Cause a Loss of Jobs in the United States?

Most output produced by U.S.-invested firms in China was sold in the Chinese domestic market (85 percent in 1995). Surveys in 1993 and 1995 indicate that more than 80 percent of the U.S. firms investing in China did not shut down their plants at home. At least 35 percent of the surveyed U.S. firms reported an increase of their domestic investment. U.S. direct investment in China increases the export demand for U.S. capital goods, intermediate goods, and services. In 1995, U.S.-invested firms in China imported more than one-third of their principal equipment, measured by value, from home, and more than 42 percent of U.S.-invested firms relied on either their parent companies (38 percent) or other firms (4 percent) at home as their primary source of technology. More than 90 percent of U.S.-invested firms produced goods not directly competitive with those produced by their parent companies; two-thirds of the U.S.-invested firms in China produced products either totally different from or of lower grade than the products produced by their parent companies (see chapter 6). In general, U.S. direct investment in China does not compete with domestic producers. On a net basis it is likely to be job enhancing, and not job displacing, in the United States.

Most light industrial products exported to the United States from China, such as garments, shoes, and toys, generate low-wage, low-skilled jobs, which the United States lost three or even four decades ago, first to Japan, then to Hong Kong, then to Taiwan, and then to Southeast Asian countries such as Indonesia, Malaysia, Philippines, and Thailand. The jobs that the Chinese workers have today are most likely to have been lost by workers in Hong Kong and Taiwan. China has gradually climbed up the technology ladder and has begun to produce high-tech items such as notebook computers, hard disc-drives and computer chips. Nonetheless, China is still manufacturing items from the low-technology spectrum of the electronics industry. It may be competing directly with Southeast Asian countries such as Malaysia, but it is far from directly competing with the United States.

How Does U.S. Direct Investment
Affect Trade between the Two Countries?

As mentioned, U.S. direct investment in China increases the demand for U.S. capital goods, intermediate goods, services, and technology. In particular, it increases intrafirm trade between different units of the same U.S. multinational corporations. In 1992, intrafirm exports from the United States to China amounted to $1.456 billion, or almost 20 percent of total U.S. exports to China in that year. U.S. direct investment also increases trade in services between the two countries. In 2002, U.S. exports of services to China amounted to $6.073 billion. The United States has consistently run a surplus vis-à-vis China in trade in services.

Moreover, U.S.- and other foreign-invested firms in China are responsible for a large fraction of exports from China. In 2002, foreign-, including U.S.-, invested firms in China produced 52.2 percent of Chinese exports. Foreign-invested firms in China produced a similar percentage of Chinese exports to the United States. Exports generated by foreign-invested firms have different economic welfare properties: The profits from such exports accrue in part to the foreign owners of those firms, not to the host country.

A large fraction of Chinese exports are related to processing and assembly activities. Since 1996 more than half of Chinese exports have been generated either by foreign-invested firms or through processing and assembly activities. Such exports from China are in part responsible for consumer goods in the industrialized economies, including the United States, remaining inexpensive; if the imported Chinese goods were supplied by their traditional domestic producers, prices would have been much higher.

However, by most indications, the value-added content in China associated with processing and assembly activities is relatively low. The value-added content of such exports is approximately one-third of the gross value of such exports.

Do U.S. Firms Make Profits in China?

Obtaining reliable data concerning the profits of foreign-invested firms in China (or for that matter in most other developing countries) can be difficult because multinational corporations often use transfer pricing to shift profits among their various affiliates to minimize their global tax burden. According to survey data collected by the Chung-Hua Institution of Economic Research, in 1995 12.5 percent of U.S. firms had a rate of return on their invested capital (at historical cost) of 15 percent or more; another 15.3 percent had a rate of return of 8–15 percent; 16.7 percent of the firms had a rate of 3–8 percent; and 11.1 percent had a rate of 3 percent or less. Of the rest, 1.4 percent broke even, and 43.1 percent reported losses.

The CIER survey shows that in 1993 more than 80 percent of the U.S.-invested firms planned to increase their production the following year and more than 25 percent planned to increase their investment in China. Those plans would appear to indicate that some U.S.-invested firms must have been making profits. At a minimum they must have been optimistic about the prospects of profits in the Chinese market.

From data collected by the Bureau of Economic Analysis of the U.S. Department of Commerce, the average annual rate of return for all U.S. direct investment in China between 1994 and 2002 may be an estimated 10.11 percent, compared with almost 10.23 percent for all U.S. direct investment abroad. But in 2002, the estimated rate of return of U.S. direct investment in China was 14.08 percent, compared with 8.15 percent for U.S. direct investment in all countries.

Such reported profits do not include the returns to technology transfers from the United States to China in the form of net payments of royalties and fees from Chinese firms to U.S. firms. In 2002 the total net receipts by U.S. firms associated with such transfers amounted to $723 million.

Does U.S. Direct Investment Affect Economic Growth in China?

The U.S. government has estimated that outputs of U.S.-invested firms in China collectively accounted for 0.5 percent of the Chinese GDP in 2000. The effect is small, but not insignificant, especially considering that U.S. direct investment is only a very small fraction, approximately 1 percent, of the annual gross domestic investment (domestic and foreign) in China. Qualitatively, however, U.S. direct investment should have a large long-term impact on the Chinese economy. Technologically the United States is the most advanced country in the world. To modernize, China needs to import advanced technology from the United States. Direct investment is the appropriate vehicle for the transfer of technology, with U.S.-invested firms maintaining control of and directly benefiting from their proprietary technologies and know-how. U.S. and other foreign direct investors are more advanced in management techniques, corporate governance, and market institutions. Their presence in China will accelerate the transformation of Chinese enterprises as well as the process of Chinese transition to a market economy. In the long run, the presence of U.S. and other foreign direct investment will significantly enhance the efficiency and the productivity of the Chinese economy.

The investment ties between the United States and China generate significant and growing mutual economic benefits to both countries on an overall basis. They should be further encouraged. The United States and China are economically complementary. The two countries seldom compete in the same world markets. China cannot produce what the United States exports. The United States long ago generally stopped producing what China exports. China needs U.S. capital goods and technology, and the United States needs a reliable source of low-cost yet high-quality consumer goods. The two countries can provide markets for each other. U.S. firms invest in China fundamentally to implement a strategy for acquiring potential market shares in goods, services, and technology. U.S. direct investment in China is basically good for both the United States and China and is likely to increase trade between the two countries in both the short and the long run.

Notes

Chapter 1
Introduction

1. China Population Information and Research Center 2003.
2. See the discussion below.
3. See Kahn 2003.
4. Ibid.
5. China was the eleventh largest exporter in 1998. If Chinese reexports through Hong Kong were taken into account, China would have surpassed Belgium-Luxembourg in the world ranking of exporters in 1999.
6. The fundamental benefit of trade is the enlarged consumption possibilities for the trading partners. A subtler question is the quantity of value-added actually generated in each country with a given volume of exports to the other country. See Chen, Cheng, Fung, and Lau 2000.
7. For a discussion of various government policies of China, Hong Kong, and Taiwan, see Lau 1997. For an in-depth analysis of the sources of growth in the East Asian newly industrialized economies, see Kim and Lau 1994.

Chapter 2
Reasons for U.S. Direct Investment in China

1. The survey was intended as a comparative study of foreign firms in China and was not confined to U.S. firms. The sample of all foreign firms surveyed was large—more than a thousand firms. For more details, see chapters 5 and 6.
2. Strictly speaking, the survey is for Japanese firms investing in the manufacturing sector of both China and Hong Kong. Since by 1999 there were relatively few manufacturing activities within Hong Kong, much of the survey applies to China.
3. For details, see Ministry of Economy, Trade and Industry 2001.
4. See http://www1.chinadaily.com.cn/news/2002-09-24/87404.html.
5. For details, see Kahn 2003.

Chapter 5
General Characteristics of U.S. Direct Investment

1. The percentage is obtained by dividing the official U.S. direct investment outflow to China figure by the official Chinese total realized foreign direct investment inflow figure.

2. The relationship between the direct investment position and the direct investment outflow does not imply that one can simply add the current year's direct investment outflow to the previous year's direct investment position to obtain the current year's direct investment position. One also has to make relevant adjustments with respect to withdrawals and write-offs, which the table does not reflect.

3. Foreign direct investment in China from other countries such as Japan also declined. But Japan recovered from its decline much more quickly than did the United States.

4. Data on contracted U.S. direct investment in China for 1997 are also available in PRC, Economic Information and Agency 1999b. However, for unknown reasons, information on U.S. direct investment in two important regions (Liaoning and Jilin) is missing. Moreover, the almanac has several serious misprints. Thus we do not use the data for 1997 in our analysis but include them in table 5-11.

5. If we do not include JDs, used primarily in large-scale natural resource development projects, the distribution by mode would have been EJVs, 43 percent; CJVs, 45 percent; and WFOs, 12 percent.

6. See "The Economic and Trade Relations between China and the United States in 1995," in PRC, Economic Information and Agency 1997b.

Chapter 6
Comparison of Foreign Direct Investment

1. CIER commissioned two other surveys. The first, conducted in 1995, was based on the sample of 1,427 firms in the 1994 survey, focused on labor-management relations of the Taiwanese firms. The second, conducted in 1997, focused on foreign-invested firms in the service industry. This study does not use the results of the two surveys.

2. Tables 4-3 and 4-4 report the incidence of joint ventures. CIER (1994) reported that between 1979 and 1993, only 1 percent of the foreign-invested firms were in the form of a joint development.

3. Table 5-8 reports those figures. They are percentages of the total number of firms surveyed and not given in terms of the shares of the aggregate total value of direct investment.

4. In terms of values, the top three destinations of U.S. direct investment in 1995 were Jiangsu, Guangdong, and Shanghai, with Shandong fourth. Tables 5-4 and 5-5 report the figures and ranking.

5. The figures refer to the number of firms and are not given in terms of values. Table 5-9 presents values of U.S. direct investment in various industries.

6. The underlying sample of foreign-invested firms surveyed in 1994 and 1996 (for the years 1993 and 1995) were essentially identical. The differences in the survey results are due to differential rates of attrition and nonresponse.

7. It would have been preferable to use weights based on total sales of the firms. Unfortunately, the quality of the sales data from the surveys was unreliable (too many nonresponses as well as implausible responses) and cannot be readily adjusted. Thus total investment weights are used.

8. See, for example, *Economist* 1998. Dorgan (1999) reported that relatively few U.S. companies are realizing profits or even a return on their investments in China.

9. For example, Volkswagen announced plans to double its already considerable investment in China within the succeeding five years (Johnson 1999). Even though precise figures were not given, the company mentioned excellent profits.

10. For 1993, the comparable figures were 53 percent, 7.5 percent, and 39.5 percent, respectively. See Chung-Hua Institution for Economic Research 1994, 226.

11. The figures are broadly consistent with the results of a survey done by Tenbridge in 1999 and reported in *Economist* (1999, 72), that "60 percent of the multinationals that had arrived in China after 1993 had achieved positive cashflow."

12. Although profit figures are not generally available, anecdotal evidence suggests that some U.S. multinational corporations have been quite successful in China. Procter & Gamble reported that its sales in China rose from $50 million in 1994 to $1 billion in 1999 (Johnson 1999). The firm continued to increase its direct investment in China.

13. *Agence France-Presse* 1998.

14. Reported in Chen 1999, 14.

Chapter 7
Chinese Investment in the United States

1. For details, see PRC, Asia Economic Information and Consultancy Ltd. 2003.

2. Zhan (1995) reported that the average Chinese FDI outflow per year was $2.4 billion, larger than the average annual outflows from the whole region of Latin America and the Caribbean for the same period. For additional statistics on the capital outflows of China, see United Nations Conference on Trade and Development 1996.

3. See Zhan 1995; Wilson 1996. Some Chinese investment abroad, including investments in the United States, may also represent illegal capital transfers from China. For a discussion, see Fung and Lau 1996.

4. For a detailed analysis of the extent, motives, and impact of Chinese investments in Hong Kong, see Fung 1997.

5. This is measured at historical costs. Moreover, at the end of 1994, the total value of net assets attributable to China's direct investment in the nonmanufacturing sectors of Hong Kong came to $16.9 billion (see Hong Kong Census and Statistics Department 1996b). The difference between the stock of direct investment from China and the total value of net assets attributable to China's direct investment is that the latter also includes third-party loans.

6. In 1994, total FDI inflow into the United States was $45.095 billion. See U.S. Department of Commerce 1998a.

7. Indeed, exploiting a superior intangible asset is often the most important reason why firms become multinationals. For a detailed discussion and a survey of recent work on multinational corporations, see Markusen 1995.

8. Another possible explanation is that Chinese and Hong Kong enterprises, like multinational firms of other countries, allocate and report their incomes in different countries to maximize their global, after-tax, profits. They may understate their profits in the United States through such methods as transfer-pricing and book their profits in Hong Kong and other jurisdictions with lower corporate income tax rates than the United States. Thus they will show little or no profit in the United States for their direct investments.

9. See PRC, Asia Economic Information and Consultancy Ltd. 2003.

10. See chapter 4 for a discussion of the extent of such capital round-tripping.

11. Differences in the definitions of foreign direct investment occur in different countries. Unfortunately the term "approved overseas investments" as used in the almanac was not explicitly defined.

Chapter 8
Effects of U.S. Direct Investment and Implications for U.S. Policy

1. A recent study on the impact of U.S. multinationals on U.S. jobs concluded that substitution between labor employed by parents in the United States and their affiliates abroad is rather low. For details, see Brainard and Riker 1997.

2. Theories concerning the reasons for FDI can fall into two types: (1) the proximity-concentration hypothesis, which states that companies trade off between more proximity to their customers and concentrated production that can result in economies of scale; and (2) the factor-proportion hypothesis, which argues that firms move abroad because of differences in factor prices caused by differences in factor endowments. For more details, see Brainard 1997 and Markusen 1995.

3. Strictly speaking, we should be comparing unit labor costs across countries, but given the general unreliability of labor productivity measures in China and other developing economies, we simply assume that China's labor productivity is at least comparable to those of other countries at a similar stage of economic development.

The assumption is generally consistent with anecdotal evidence. Moreover, the fact that a significant proportion of the goods made by foreign-invested firms in China is also exported implies that firms located in China can be cost-competitive in the world market (at least for exported goods made by Chinese workers).

4. Loosely speaking, this is consistent with information provided by Zeile (1997) indicating that U.S. parent companies importing from their affiliates in China accounted for 0.01–19.9 percent of U.S. total imports from China, according to U.S. Department of Commerce figures.

5. However, table 2-1 shows that less than 5 percent of the U.S.-invested firms considered tariff and quota jumping as an important reason to invest in China.

6. The table does not show the percentages. The shares are calculated by using figures from the column labeled *all countries*. For example, within total intrafirm exports of $149.504 billion, U.S. parent companies conducted $100.737 billion, or a share of 67.4 percent.

7. The wide range results because the detailed data have been suppressed to avoid disclosure of data on individual companies.

8. For an in-depth analysis of the issue of Hong Kong reexports, see Fung and Lau 1998, 2001; Fung 1998; and Feenstra, Woo, and Yao 1997.

9. For a detailed discussion of how U.S. and Japanese semiconductors are first shipped to Hong Kong before they are reexported to China, see Howell, Nuechterlein, and Hester 1995.

10. The 81.8 percent was calculated by dividing the amount of U.S.–Hong Kong intrafirm exports accounted for by U.S. parent companies ($2.746 billion) by the total U.S.–Hong Kong intrafirm exports ($3.358 billion). The table does not show the figure 81.8 percent.

11. The lower and upper bounds may be computed by assuming that the share of total U.S. imports from China accounted for by imports from Chinese affiliates of U.S. parent companies is alternately 0.01 percent or 17.9 percent, with a share of U.S. intrafirm imports from China in total U.S. imports from China of 2.01–19.9 percent.

12. Intrafirm trade also raises the issue of transfer pricing, quite common among multinational corporations and also in trade, including reexporting, between China and Hong Kong.

13. Not all those exports are ultimately destined for the home countries of the respective foreign direct investors.

14. Strictly speaking, except in cases involving wholly foreign-owned enterprises, a part of the profits also accrues to Chinese residents who are partners in joint ventures.

15. Unless sanctions could be selectively applied to various types of producers in China, trade restrictions would impede imports from both Chinese and U.S. firms. Operationally it may be difficult to sort out the true nature of the various types of exports.

16. As discussed in Sung 1991; Lardy 1994; Naughton 1996; Feenstra, Woo, and Yao 1997; and Fung and Lau 1997, 1998, and 2000, a significant portion of Chinese exports is first sent to Hong Kong and then reexported to other markets such as the United States (those may be referred to as *indirect exports*).

17. In general, however, Slaughter (1995) found that U.S. multinationals did not outsource to a great extent, at least in the 1980s: as with Brainard (1997), home and foreign production workers were found to be weak substitutes. Feenstra and Hanson (1995) conversely argue that outsourcing can be an important factor in contributing to wage inequality in the United States.

18. Explanations of the meaning of *processing and assembly* can be found in the explanatory notes of various issues of *China's Customs Statistics*.

19. Lardy (1994) discusses the general industrial processing trade of China. Here we highlight the aspect of trade specifically in the context of the U.S.-China trade imbalance. We also provide some estimates of the extent of such form of trade between the United States and China.

20. Because Chinese firms carry on a large fraction of exports associated with processing and assembly, the use of CIER surveys, which indicate only where foreign-invested firms sell their products, would be inappropriate.

21. See the entries on the second row and the last column of table 8-4. Total processed exports to the world are given in *China's Customs Statistics*. We multiply those exports by the estimated shares of exports that go to the United States to obtain estimates of processed exports to the United States.

22. First, the value added generated in China is not equivalent to the value added generated by Chinese entities, as the machinery and equipment are owned by foreign firms and the returns to such capital should be attributed to the foreign firms. Second, not all value added is generated by the processing and assembly contractors and subcontractors in China, as they may have purchased, especially in recent years, some intermediate inputs in China. Nevertheless, such purchases still generate value added in China.

23. For example, William Fung, the managing director of Li & Fung, one of the largest trading firms in Hong Kong, indicated in a speech in 1996 at the University of Hong Kong that the average value added of processing and assembly in China is about 20 percent (Fung 1996).

24. According to *China's Customs Statistics*, in 2002 the value of exports associated with processing and assembly was $47.5 billion and the value of imports associated with processing and assembly was $34.2 billion, with a resulting Chinese value added of $13.3 billion. The U.S. share of China's export market was 29.1 percent. We attribute 29.1 percent of the value added to processing and assembly exports to the United States, with a resulting value of $3.86 billion in 2002. The 28 percent value-added ratio seems, however, to differ considerably from the widely held view that the import content of Chinese light industrial exports is approximately 62 percent.

25. To put the number in perspective, consider the export of $1 billion of wheat from the United States to China, then almost 100 percent of the gross value of the wheat exports is U.S. domestic value added resulting from the wheat exports (unless significant imported inputs—for example, imported insecticides or chemical fertilizer—are used in the production of wheat).

26. An important remaining problem of Chinese violations of intellectual property rights is the actual implementation and the enforcement of the relevant Chinese laws as well as the Sino-U.S. Special 301 agreement. One issue about enforcement seems to be that local and provincial governments are less vigilant than the central government in cracking down on various piracy activities.

Chapter 9
Conclusion

1. Total U.S. FDI outflows for 1996–2002 were, respectively, $84.426 billion, $95.769 billion, $131.004 billion, $209.392 billion, $142.627 billion, $103.767 billion, and $119.742 billion. See U.S. Department of Commerce 2003b. The average of the seven years is $126.675 billion.

2. In 1994, total FDI inflow into the United States was $45.095 billion. See U.S. Department of Commerce 1998b.

3. The proportion of the value of the stock of U.S. direct investment in the form of wholly U.S.-owned enterprises, derived from the CIER surveys, is significantly underestimated because of nonresponses from large U.S.-invested enterprises.

References

Aerospace Industries Association of America (AIA). 2001. Statement by John W. Douglass, president and chief executive officer, Aerospace Industries Association of America, Inc., before the U.S.-China Security Review Commission. Mimeographed. Washington, D.C.: AIA.

Agence France-Presse. 1998. More Than Half of the Foreign Firms Show Losses. Shanghai, December 2.

American Electronics Association (AeA). 2001. High-Tech Industry Applauds the Conclusion of Negotiation on Terms for China's Entry into the World Trade Organization. Mimeographed. San Jose, Calif.: AeA.

Asian Development Bank. 1996. *Asian Development Outlook: 1996 and 1997.* New York: Oxford University Press.

———. 1997. *Asian Development Outlook: 1997 and 1998.* New York: Oxford University Press.

———. 1999. *Asian Development Outlook: 1999.* New York: Oxford University Press.

———. 2001. *Asian Development Outlook: 2001.* New York: Oxford University Press.

———. 2002. *Asian Development Outlook: 2002.* New York: Oxford University Press.

———. 2003. *Asian Development Outlook: 2003.* New York: Oxford University Press.

Bargas, Sylvia E. 1997a. Direct Investment Positions for 1996: Country and Industry Detail. *Survey of Current Business* 77 (7) (July): 34–55.

———. 1997b. The Foreign Direct Investment Position in the United States on a Historical-Cost Basis: Country and Industry Detail for 1995 and Changes in Geographic Composition since 1982. In *Foreign Direct Investment in the United States: An Update,* 17–26. Washington, D.C.: U.S. Department of Commerce, Economics and Statistics Administration.

———. 2000. Direct Investment Positions for 1999: Country and Industrial Detail. *Survey of Current Business* 80 (7) (July): 57–68.

Brainard, S. Lael. 1997. An Empirical Assessment of the Proximity-Concentration Trade-off between Multinational Sales and Trade. *American Economic Review* 87 (4) (September): 520–44.

Brainard, S. Lael, and David A. Riker. 1997. Are U.S. Multinationals Exporting U.S. Jobs? NBER Working Paper 5958. Cambridge, Mass.: National Bureau of Economic Research.

Brecher, R., and C. Gelb. 1997. Joining the World's Trading Club. *China Business Review* 24 (3) (May–June): 14–21.

Chen, S.K. 1999. Taxes and Reported Profits. *Commercial Times*, Taipei. January 1.

Chen, Xikang, Leonard K. Cheng, K. C. Fung, and Lawrence J. Lau. 2000. Domestic Value-Added Induced by Exports: The Case of China. Mimeographed research report. Stanford: Stanford University, Asia/Pacific Research Center.

Cheng, Leonard K. 1995. Foreign Direct Investment in China. Mimeographed. Hong Kong: Hong Kong University of Science and Technology, Department of Economics.

China Population Information and Research Center. 2003. Population in China. Available at http://www.cpirc.org.cn.

Chung-Hua Institution for Economic Research (CIER). 1993. *A Comparative Study of Foreign Investment in Mainland China* (in Chinese). Taipei: CIER.

———. 1994. *A Comparative Study of Foreign Investment in Mainland China* (in Chinese). Taipei: CIER.

———. 1996. *A Comparative Study of Foreign Investment in Mainland China* (in Chinese). Taipei: CIER.

———. 1999. *A Comparative Study of Foreign Investment in Mainland China* (in Chinese). Taipei: CIER.

Corne, Peter Howard. 1997. *Foreign Investment in China: The Administrative Legal System*. Hong Kong: Hong Kong University Press.

Dorgan, Michael. 1999. Beijing's Bait and Switch: Billions Spent in Futile Attempt At Toehold, Report Finds. *San Jose Mercury News*. March 3.

Economist. 1998. Daimler-Benz: Stalling in China. April 18.

———.1999. Infatuation's End. September 25.

Feenstra, Robert, and Gordon Hanson. 1995. Foreign Investment, Outsourcing, and Relative Wages. NBER Working Paper 5121. Cambridge, Mass.: National Bureau of Economic Research.

Feenstra, Robert, Wing T. Woo, and Shunli Yao. 1997. Evaluating the U.S.-China Trade Balance: The Role of Hong Kong. Mimeographed working paper. Davis: University of California at Davis, Department of Economics.

Finger, J. Michael, and K. C. Fung. 1994. Can Competition Policy Control "301"? *Aussenwirtschaft* 49 (6): 379–416.

Fortune. 1996. Five Hundred Largest U.S. Corporations. April.

———. 1997. Five Hundred Largest U.S. Corporations. April.

———. 1998. Five Hundred Largest U.S. Corporations. April.

———. 1999. Five Hundred Largest U.S. Corporations. April.

———. 2000. Five Hundred Largest U.S. Corporations. April.

———. 2001. Five Hundred Largest U.S. Corporations. April.

———. 2002. Five Hundred Largest U.S. Corporations. April.

Fung, K. C. 1996. Mainland Chinese Investment in Hong Kong: How Much, Why, and So What? *Journal of Asian Business* 12 (2): 21–39.

———. 1997. *Trade and Investment: Mainland China, Hong Kong and Taiwan.* Hong Kong: City University of Hong Kong Press.

———. 1998. Accounting for Chinese Trade: Some National and Regional Considerations. In *Geography and Ownership as a Basis for Economic Accounting,* ed. Robert Baldwin, R. Lipsey, and J.D. Richardson, 173–200. Chicago: University of Chicago Press.

Fung, K. C., and Lawrence J. Lau. 1996. The China-United States Bilateral Trade Balance: How Big Is It Really? Occasional paper. Stanford: Stanford University, Asia/Pacific Research Center, Institute for International Studies, April.

———. 1997. Foreign Economic Relations. In *China Review 1997,* ed. Maurice Brosseau, Hsin-Chin Kuan, and Y. Y. Kueh, 209–34. Hong Kong: Chinese University Press.

———. 1998. The China-United States Bilateral Trade Balance: How Big Is It Really? *Pacific Economic Review* 3 (1) (February): 33–47.

———. 2000. New Estimates of the United States-China Bilateral Trade Balances. Stanford: Stanford University, Asia/Pacific Research Center, Institute for International Studies.

———. 2001. New Estimates of the United States-China Bilateral Trade Balances. *Journal of the Japanese and International Economies* 15:102–130.

Fung, K.C., Hitomi Iizaka, Chelsea Lin, and Alan Siu. 2002. An Econometric Estimation of Locational Choices of Foreign Direct Investment: The Case of Hong Kong and U.S. Firms in China. Paper presented at an international conference in honor of Gregory Chow. City University of Hong Kong, June 14–16.

Ho, Yin-Ping. 1993. China's Foreign Trade and the Reform of the Foreign Trade System. In *China Review 1993,* ed. Joseph Cheng Yu-Shek and Maurice Brosseau, pp. 17.1–17.41. Hong Kong: Chinese University Press.

Howell, Thomas R., Jeffrey D. Nuechterlein, and Susan B. Hester. 1995. *Semiconductors in China: Defining American Interests.* San Jose: Dewey Ballantine.

Hsueh, Tien-tung, and Tun-oy Woo. 1991. The Changing Pattern of Hong Kong-China Economic Relations since 1979: Issues and Consequences. In *Industrial and Trade Development in Hong Kong,* ed. Edward K. Y. Chen, Mee-Kau Nyaw, and Teresa Y. C. Wong. Hong Kong: University of Hong Kong Press, Centre of Asian Studies, Occasional Papers and Monographs.

Inside China Today. 1998. Study Shows 50% of Foreign Ventures Report Losses. December 2.

Jiang, Xiaojuan. 2000. Foreign Direct Investment (FDI) in China: General Situation and Prospects. China Development Forum Background Material 6. Beijing: People's Republic of China, State Council, Development Research Center.

Johnson, Ian. 1999. VW to Double China Investment to Upgrade Plants, Unveil 2 Cars. *Asian Wall Street Journal.* October 1.

Kahn, Joseph. 2003. Made in China, Bought in China: Multinationals Succeed, Two Decades Later. *New York Times*. January 5.

Kao, Charles, Joseph C. Lee, and Steven Lin. 1992. *An Empirical Study of Taiwan Investment in Mainland China* (in Chinese). Taipei: Commonwealth Publishing Company.

Kim, Jong-Il, and Lawrence J. Lau. 1994. The Sources of Economic Growth of the East Asian Newly Industrialized Countries. *Journal of the Japanese and International Economies* 8 (3) (September): 235–71.

Kuzmik, J. T. 1992. Technology Transfer: A Vital Element in Foreign Investment. *Asian Law and Practice* 33 (2) (March): 33–36.

Lardy, Nicholas. 1994. *China in the World Economy*. Washington, D.C.: Institute for International Economics.

Lau, Lawrence J. 1994. China in the Twenty-First Century. In *Asian Capital Markets: Strategic Investing in Asia*, ed. Lilia C. Clemente and Roberto S. Mariano, 63–68. New York: Asian Securities Industry Institute.

———. 1995. The Economy of the PRC: Analysis and Forecasts. In *Studies by the Salomon Brothers Panel of PRC Experts*. Hong Kong: Salomon Brothers, Asia-Pacific Equity Research.

———. 1997. The Role of Government in Economic Development: Some Observations from the Experience of China, Hong Kong and Taiwan. In *The Role of Government in East Asian Economic Development: Comparative Institutional Analysis,* ed. Masahiko Aoki, H. K Kim, and M. Okuno-Fujiwara, 41–73. Oxford: Clarendon Press.

Lau, Lawrence J., and Jung-Soo Park. 1995. Is There a Next Mexico in East Asia? Working paper. Stanford: Stanford University, Department of Economics.

Lee, Joseph. 1996. The Integration of Labor Markets in South China Growth Triangle. In *The Emergence of South China Growth Triangle*, ed. Joseph Lee, 253–86. Taipei: Chung-Hua Institution for Economic Research.

Markusen, James. 1995. The Boundaries of Multinational Enterprises and the Theory of International Trade. *Journal of Economic Perspectives* 9 (2) (Spring): 169–89.

Mataloni, Raymond J., Jr. 1998. U.S. Multinational Companies: Operations in 1996. *Survey of Current Business* 78 (9) (September): 47–73.

———. 1999. U.S. Multinational Companies: Operations in 1997. *Survey of Current Business* 79 (7) (July): 8–35.

———. 2000. U.S. Multinational Companies: Operations in 1998. *Survey of Current Business* 80 (7) (July): 26–45.

Mataloni, Raymond J., Jr., and Mahnaz Fahim-Nader. 1996. Operations of U.S. Multinational Companies: Preliminary Results from the 1994 Benchmark Survey. *Survey of Current Business* 76 (12) (December): 11–37.

Melloan, George. 1997. China Spawns Legal Reforms. *Wall Street Journal (Europe)*. July 29.

Melvin, S., and K. Sylvester. 1997. Shipping Out. *China Business Review* 24 (3) (May–June): 30–34.

Ministry of Economy, Trade and Industry (METI). 2001. *Wagakuni Kigyou no Kaigai Jigyou Katsudou* 29. Tokyo.

Naughton, Barry. 1996. China's Emergence and Prospects as a Trading Nation. *Brookings Papers on Economic Activity* 25 (2): 273–344.

Ouyang, Zhongmou. 1997. Present Situation and Future Development of the Chinese Electronics Industry. Mimeographed (in Chinese).

People's Republic of China (PRC). Asia Economic Information and Consultancy Ltd. 2002. *Yearbook of China's Foreign Economic Relations and Trade.* Beijing: PRC.

———. Asia Economic Information and Consultancy Ltd. 2003. *Yearbook of China's Foreign Economic Relations and Trade.* Beijing: PRC.

———. Economic Information and Agency. 1993. *Almanac of China's Foreign Economic Relations and Trade.* Hong Kong: China Economics Publishing House.

———. Economic Information and Agency. 1994. *Almanac of China's Foreign Economic Relations and Trade.* Hong Kong: China Economics Publishing House.

———. Economic Information and Agency. 1995. *Almanac of China's Foreign Economic Relations and Trade.* Hong Kong: China Economics Publishing House.

———. Economic Information and Agency. 1996. *Almanac of China's Foreign Economic Relations and Trade.* Hong Kong: China Economics Publishing House.

———. Economic Information and Agency. 1997a. *Almanac of China's Foreign Economic Relations and Trade.* Hong Kong: China Economics Publishing House.

———. Economic Information and Agency. 1997b. *Yearbook of China's Foreign Economic Relations and Trade.* Beijing: PRC.

———. Economic Information and Agency. 1998a. *Almanac of China's Foreign Economic Relations and Trade.* Hong Kong: China Economics Publishing House.

———. Economic Information and Agency. 1998b. *Yearbook of China's Foreign Economic Relations and Trade.* Beijing: PRC.

———. Economic Information and Agency. 1999a. *Almanac of China's Foreign Economic Relations and Trade.* Hong Kong: China Economics Publishing House.

———. Economic Information and Agency. 1999b. *Yearbook of China's Foreign Economic Relations and Trade.* Beijing: PRC.

———. Economic Information and Agency. 2000a. *Almanac of China's Foreign Economic Relations and Trade.* Hong Kong: China Economics Publishing House.

———. Economic Information and Agency. 2000b. *Yearbook of China's Foreign Economic Relations and Trade.* Beijing: PRC.

———. Economic Information and Agency. 2001a. *Almanac of China's Foreign Economic Relations and Trade.* Hong Kong: China Economics Publishing House.

———. Economic Information and Agency. 2001b. *Yearbook of China's Foreign Economic Relations and Trade.* Beijing: PRC.

————. Economic Information and Agency. 2002. *Almanac of China's Foreign Economic Relations and Trade*. Hong Kong: China Economics Publishing House.

————. General Administration of Customs, Economic Information and Agency. 1990. *China's Customs Statistics*. Hong Kong.

————. General Administration of Customs, Economic Information and Agency. 1991. *China's Customs Statistics*. Hong Kong.

————. General Administration of Customs, Economic Information and Agency. 1992. *China's Customs Statistics*. Hong Kong.

————. General Administration of Customs, Economic Information and Agency. 1993. *China's Customs Statistics*. Hong Kong.

————. General Administration of Customs, Economic Information and Agency. 1994. *China's Customs Statistics*. Hong Kong.

————. General Administration of Customs, Economic Information and Agency. 1995. *China's Customs Statistics*. Hong Kong.

————. General Administration of Customs, Economic Information and Agency. 1996. *China's Customs Statistics*. Hong Kong.

————. General Administration of Customs, Economic Information and Agency. 1997. *China's Customs Statistics*. Hong Kong.

————. General Administration of Customs, Economic Information and Agency. 1998. *China's Customs Statistics*. Hong Kong.

————. General Administration of Customs, Economic Information and Agency. 1999. *China's Customs Statistics*. Hong Kong.

————. General Administration of Customs, Economic Information and Agency. 2000. *China's Customs Statistics*. Hong Kong.

————. General Administration of Customs, Economic Information and Agency. 2001. *China's Customs Statistics*. Hong Kong.

————. General Administration of Customs, Economic Information and Agency. 2002. *China's Customs Statistics*. Hong Kong.

————. General Administration of Customs, Economic Information and Agency. 2003. *China's Customs Statistics*. Hong Kong.

————. Hong Kong Special Administrative Region (HKSAR). Hong Kong Census and Statistics Department. 1996a. Analysis of Hong Kong's Retained Imports, 1989–1994. *Hong Kong Monthly Digest of Statistics*. February.

————. HKSAR. Hong Kong Census and Statistics Department. 1996b. *External Investments in Hong Kong's Non-Manufacturing Sectors, 1993 & 1994*. Hong Kong.

————. HKSAR. Hong Kong Census and Statistics Department. 2000. Analysis of Hong Kong's Retained Imports, 1990–1999. *Hong Kong Monthly Digest of Statistics*. December.

————. HKSAR. Hong Kong Census and Statistics Department. 2001. Trade Analysis Section.

————. HKSAR. Hong Kong Census and Statistics Department. 2002. Trade Analysis Section.

————. HKSAR. Hong Kong Census and Statistics Department. 2003. Trade Analysis Section.

————. National Bureau of Statistics. 1996a. *China's Regional Economy: A Profile of Seventeen Years of Reform and Opening-Up*. Beijing: PRC.

————. National Bureau of Statistics. 1996b. *China Statistical Yearbook*. Beijing: China Statistical Publishing House.

————. National Bureau of Statistics. 1997. *China Statistical Yearbook*. Beijing: China Statistical Publishing House.

————. National Bureau of Statistics. 1998. *China Statistical Yearbook*. Beijing: China Statistical Publishing House.

————. National Bureau of Statistics. 1999. *China Statistical Yearbook*. Beijing: PRC.

————. National Bureau of Statistics. 2000. *China Statistical Yearbook*. Beijing: China Statistics Press.

————. National Bureau of Statistics. 2001. *China Statistical Yearbook*. Beijing: China Statistics Press.

————. National Bureau of Statistics. 2002. *China Statistical Yearbook*. Beijing: China Statistics Press.

————. National Bureau of Statistics. 2003. *China Statistical Yearbook*. Beijing: China Statistics Press.

Sachs, Jeffrey, and Wing T. Woo. 1997. Understanding China's Economic Performance. Mimeographed. Harvard University and University of California, Davis.

Scholl, Russell B. 1997. The International Investment Position of the United States in 1996. *Survey of Current Business* 77 (7) (July): 24–33.

Shih, T. L. 1989. The PRC's Hong Kong-based Conglomerates and Their Role in National Development. In *Global Business: Asia-Pacific Dimension,* ed. Erdener Kaynak and Kam-Hon Lee, chap. 17, 368–87. London: Routledge.

Silver, K. 1997. Removing the Rose-Colored Lenses. *China Business Review* 24 (3) (May–June): 10–13.

Slaughter, Matthew. 1995. Multinational Corporations, Outsourcing and American Wage Divergence. NBER Working Paper 5253. Cambridge, Mass.: National Bureau of Economic Research.

Sung, Yun-Wing. 1991. *The China-Hong Kong Connection: The Key to China's Open-Door Policy*. Cambridge: Cambridge University Press.

United Nations Conference on Trade and Development. 1996. *World Investment Report 1996*. New York: UN.

U.S.-China Business Council. 1990. *Special Report on U.S. Investment in China*. Washington, D.C.: U.S.-CBC.

U.S. Department of Commerce. Bureau of Economic Analysis. 1994a. Foreign Direct Investment in the United States: Details for Historical-Cost Positions and Related Capital and Income Flows, 1993. *Survey of Current Business.* August.

———. Bureau of Economic Analysis. 1994b. U.S. Direct Investment Abroad: Detail for Historical-Cost Position and Related Capital and Income Flows, 1993. *Survey of Current Business.* August.

———. Bureau of Economic Analysis. 1995. U.S. Direct Investment Position Abroad: Detail for Historical-Cost Position and Related Capital and Income Flows, 1994. *Survey of Current Business.* August.

———. Bureau of Economic Analysis. 1996a. Foreign Direct Investment in the United States: Detail for Historical-Cost Position and Related Capital and Income Flows, 1995. *Survey of Current Business.* September.

———. Bureau of Economic Analysis. 1996b. Operations of U.S. Multinational Companies: Preliminary Results from the 1994 Benchmark Survey. *Survey of Current Business.* December.

———. Bureau of Economic Analysis. 1996c. U.S. Direct Investment Abroad: Detail for Historical-Cost Position and Related Capital and Income Flows, 1993. *Survey of Current Business.* September

———. Bureau of Economic Analysis. 1996d. U.S. Direct Investment Position Abroad: Detail for Historical-Cost Position and Related Capital and Income Flows, 1995. *Survey of Current Business.* September.

———. Bureau of Economic Analysis. 1996e. U.S. International Sales and Purchases of Private Services: U.S. Cross-Border Transactions in 1995 and Sales by Affiliates in 1994. *Survey of Current Business.* November.

———. Bureau of Economic Analysis. 1997a. U.S. Direct Investment Abroad: 1994 Benchmark Survey, Preliminary Results. *Survey of Current Business.* January.

———. Bureau of Economic Analysis. 1997b. U.S. Direct Investment Abroad: Detail for Historical-Cost Position and Related Capital and Income Flows, 1997. *Survey of Current Business.* September.

———. Bureau of Economic Analysis. 1998a. Foreign Direct Investment in the United States: Detail for Historical-Cost Position and Related Capital and Income Flows, 1997. *Survey of Current Business.* September.

———. Bureau of Economic Analysis. 1998b. The International Investment Position of the United States. *Survey of Current Business.* July.

———. Bureau of Economic Analysis. 1998c. U.S. Direct Investment Abroad: Detail for Historical-Cost Position and Related Capital and Income Flows, 1997. *Survey of Current Business.* September.

———. Bureau of Economic Analysis. 1998d. U.S. Direct Investment Abroad: Detail for Historical-Cost Position and Related Capital and Income Flows, 1997. *Survey of Current Business.* October.

———. Bureau of Economic Analysis. 1998e. U.S. International Sales and Purchases of Private Services: U.S. Cross-Border Transactions in 1997 and Sales by Affiliates in 1996. *Survey of Current Business.* October.

————. Bureau of Economic Analysis. 1998f. U.S. Multinational Companies: Operations in 1996. *Survey of Current Business*. September

————. Bureau of Economic Analysis. 1999a. Foreign Direct Investment in the United States: Detail for Historical-Cost Position and Related Capital and Income Flows, 1998. *Survey of Current Business*. September.

————. Bureau of Economic Analysis. 1999b. The International Investment Position of the United States. *Survey of Current Business*. July.

————. Bureau of Economic Analysis. 1999c. U.S. Direct Investment Abroad: Detail for Historical-Cost Position and Related Capital and Income Flows, 1998. *Survey of Current Business*. September.

————. Bureau of Economic Analysis. 1999d. U.S. International Sales and Purchases of Private Services: U.S. Cross-Border Transactions in 1997 and Sales by Affiliates in 1998. *Survey of Current Business*. October.

————. Bureau of Economic Analysis. 1999e. U.S. International Services: Cross-Border Trade in 1998 and Sales through Affiliates in 1997. *Survey of Current Business*. October.

————. Bureau of Economic Analysis. 1999f. U.S. Multinational Companies: Operations in 1997. *Survey of Current Business*. September.

————. Bureau of Economic Analysis. 1999g. U.S. International Services: Royalties and License Fees. *Survey of Current Business*. October.

————. Bureau of Economic Analysis. 2000a. The International Investment Position of the United States. *Survey of Current Business*. July

————. Bureau of Economic Analysis. 2000b. U.S. Multinational Companies: Operations in 1998. *Survey of Current Business*. July.

————. Bureau of Economic Analysis. 2000c. U.S. Direct Investment Abroad: Country Detail for Selected Items. *Survey of Current Business*. September.

————. Bureau of Economic Analysis. 2000d. U.S. International Services: Royalties and License Fees. *Survey of Current Business*. October.

————. Bureau of Economic Analysis. 2001a. U.S. Direct Investment Abroad: Detail for Historical-Cost Position and Related Capital and Income Flows, 2000. *Survey of Current Business*, September.

————. Bureau of Economic Analysis. 2001b. U.S. International Services: Royalties and License Fees. *Survey of Current Business*. November.

————. Bureau of Economic Analysis. 2002a. Operations of U.S. Multinational Companies: Gross Product of Majority-Owned Nonbank Foreign Affiliates as a Percentage of the Gross Domestic Product of Selected Host Countries, 1989, 1994, and 1999. *Survey of Current Business*. March.

————. Bureau of Economic Analysis. 2002b. U.S. International Services: Cross-Border Trade in 2001 and Sales through Affiliates in 2000. *Survey of Current Business*. October.

————. Bureau of Economic Analysis. 2002c. U.S. International Services: Royalties and License Fees. *Survey of Current Business*. October.

————. Bureau of Economic Analysis. 2003a. The International Investment Position of the United States of Yearend 2003: Foreign Official and Private Holdings of U.S. Treasury Securities by Selected Countries at Yearend. *Survey of Current Business.* July.

————. Bureau of Economic Analysis. 2003b. U.S. Direct Investment Abroad: Country Detail for Selected Items. *Survey of Current Business.* September.

————. Bureau of Economic Analysis. 2003c. U.S. Direct Investment Abroad: U.S. Direct Investment Position Abroad on a Historical-Cost Basis. *Survey of Current Business.* September.

————. Bureau of Economic Analysis. 2003d. U.S. International Services: Private Services Trade by Area and Country, 1992–2002. *Survey of Current Business.* October.

————. Bureau of Economic Analysis. 2003e. U.S. International Services: Royalties and License Fees. *Survey of Current Business.* October.

————. Bureau of Economic Analysis. 2003f. Foreign Direct Investment in the United States: Country Details for Selected Items. *Survey of Current Business.* September.

————. Bureau of Economic Analysis. 2003g. U.S. Multinational Companies: Operations in 2001: Gross Product of Majority-Owned Nonbank Foreign Affiliates as a Percentage of the Gross Domestic Product of Selected Host Countries, 1994, 1999, 2000, and 2001. *Survey of Current Business.* November.

————. Bureau of Economic Analysis. 2003h. U.S. International Transactions, First Quarter 2003: U.S. Trade. *Survey of Current Business.* July.

Wallace, Cynthia. 1990. *Foreign Direct Investment in the 1990s.* Boston: Martinus Nijhoff.

Wilson, D. 1996. China Goes Transnational. *Hong Kong Business* 15 (171) (December): 6–8.

World Bank. 1993. *China Updating Economic Memorandum: Managing Rapid Growth and Transition.* Washington, D.C.: World Bank.

————. 1998. *World Development Report 1998/99: Knowledge for Development.* New York: Oxford University Press.

World Trade Organization (WTO). 2002. *Annual Report, 2002.* Geneva: WTO.

————. 2003. *Annual Report, 2003.* Geneva: WTO.

Zeile, William J. 1997. U.S. Intra-firm Trade in Goods. *Survey of Current Business* 77 (2) (February): 23–37.

Zhan, J. X. 1995. Transnationalization and Outward Investment: The Case of Chinese Firms. *Transnational Corporations* 4 (3) (December): 67–100.

Zheng, Henry R. 1993. The Special Economic Zones and Coastal Cities. In *Doing Business in China,* ed. W. P. Streng and A. D. Wilcox, pt. 5, chap. 20, pp. 25–40. New York: Matthew Bender.

Index

A. T. Kearny, 13

Access to domestic markets, *see* Domestic Chinese market

AeA (American Electronics Association), 18

Aerospace industry, FDI growth in, 20

Aerospace Industry Association (AIA), 20

Age of equipment, cross-country analysis of, 100, 101–3

Agricultural sector, 9, 32–33

AIA (Aerospace Industry Association), 20

American Electronics Association (AeA), 18

Ameritech, investment levels, 78

Anheuser-Busch, investment levels, 79, 81, 82

Apparel industry, 96

Arbitration clauses in FDI contracts, 40–41

ASEAN, realized investment flows, 88–89

Asian markets, as target for FIE-sponsored exports, 140

Autonomy of operations and advantages of WFOs, 26

Avon Products, investment levels, 78

Banking sector, 10, 35, 105–7, 125–26

Beijing Coca-Cola Bottling Co., Ltd., investment levels, 80

Bell Atlantic, investment levels, 78, 79

Black & Decker, 83, 108

Capital

comparison of foreign types, 55–58

equity capital outflows from U.S. to China, 60

illegal transfer of Chinese, 16, 45–46, 62–63, 86

return on capital for FDI firms, 117–20

royalty and license fee contribution to U.S. firms, 151

working capital sources for FDI firms, 104–7

Capital accounts, nonconvertibility of, 34

Capital Steel Works (Shougang), 121–22

Catalogue for the Guidance of Foreign Investment Industries, 32

Cell phone market in China, 3, 13–14

CEs (collective enterprises), 91–92, 92–93, 144

Cheap light manufactured goods, 128, 129, 161

China Harbor Engineering Company, 121

About the Authors

K. C. Fung is a professor of economics and cofounder of the Santa Cruz Center for International Economics at the University of California–Santa Cruz. He served as a senior economist on the White House Council of Economic Advisers during the George H. W. Bush and Clinton administrations. He has been a consultant for the World Bank, the World Trade Organization, and the Asian Development Bank Institute, and a U.S. delegate to the Organisation for Economic Co-operation and Development. Mr. Fung has also taught at Stanford University, Mount Holyoke College, and the University of Hong Kong. He is currently the North American Editor of *Pacific Economic Review*.

Lawrence J. Lau is the vice chancellor of the Chinese University of Hong Kong. He is also the Kwoh-Ting Li Professor of Economic Development in the Economics Department at Stanford University, where he has served as the director of both the Asia-Pacific Research Center and the Stanford Institute for Economic Policy Research. Mr. Lau is a fellow of the Econometric Society, a member of Academia Sinica, and has been a John Simon Guggenheim Memorial Foundation Fellow, a fellow of the Center for Advanced Study in the Behavioral Sciences, and an overseas fellow of Churchill College, Cambridge. He has published more than one hundred and sixty articles in professional publications. He developed one of the first econometric models of China in 1966 and has continued to revise and update his model ever since. He has served as a consultant for the World Bank, the Asian Development Bank, the Rand Corporation, and the United Nations Development Programme.

Joseph S. Lee is the dean of the School of Management at National Central University in Taiwan. In 1992, he was appointed the vice president of the Chung-Hua Institution for Economic Research in Taipei. In 1997, he became the director of the Research Center for Taiwan Economic Development. He has also held the positions of professor and director of the Institute of Human Resource Management at the same university. Mr. Lee currently serves on the editorial boards of several professional journals.

George L. Priest
John M. Olin Professor of Law and
Economics
Yale Law School

Jeremy Rabkin
Professor of Government
Cornell University

Murray L. Weidenbaum
Mallinckrodt Distinguished
University Professor
Washington University

Richard J. Zeckhauser
Frank Plumpton Ramsey Professor
of Political Economy
Kennedy School of Government
Harvard University

Research Staff

Gautam Adhikari
Visiting Fellow

Joseph Antos
Wilson H. Taylor Scholar in Health
Care and Retirement Policy

Leon Aron
Resident Scholar

Claude E. Barfield
Resident Scholar; Director, Science
and Technology Policy Studies

Roger Bate
Visiting Fellow

Walter Berns
Resident Scholar

Douglas J. Besharov
Joseph J. and Violet Jacobs
Scholar in Social Welfare Studies

Karlyn H. Bowman
Resident Fellow

John E. Calfee
Resident Scholar

Charles W. Calomiris
Arthur F. Burns Scholar in
Economics

Liz Cheney
Visiting Fellow

Veronique de Rugy
Research Fellow

Thomas Donnelly
Resident Fellow

Nicholas Eberstadt
Henry Wendt Scholar in Political
Economy

Eric M. Engen
Resident Scholar

Mark Falcoff
Resident Scholar Emeritus

J. Michael Finger
Resident Scholar

Gerald R. Ford
Distinguished Fellow

John C. Fortier
Research Fellow

David Frum
Resident Fellow

Ted Gayer
Visiting Scholar

Reuel Marc Gerecht
Resident Fellow

Newt Gingrich
Senior Fellow

Jack Goldsmith
Visiting Scholar

Robert A. Goldwin
Resident Scholar

Scott Gottlieb
Resident Fellow

Michael S. Greve
John G. Searle Scholar

Robert W. Hahn
Resident Scholar; Director,
AEI-Brookings Joint Center
for Regulatory Studies

Kevin A. Hassett
Resident Scholar; Director,
Economic Policy Studies

Steven F. Hayward
F. K. Weyerhaeuser Fellow

Robert B. Helms
Resident Scholar; Director,
Health Policy Studies

Frederick M. Hess
Resident Scholar; Director,
Education Policy Studies

R. Glenn Hubbard
Visiting Scholar

Leon R. Kass
Hertog Fellow

Herbert G. Klein
National Fellow

Jeane J. Kirkpatrick
Senior Fellow

Marvin H. Kosters
Resident Scholar

Irving Kristol
Senior Fellow

Randall S. Kroszner
Visiting Scholar

Desmond Lachman
Resident Fellow

Michael A. Ledeen
Freedom Scholar

James R. Lilley
Senior Fellow

Lawrence B. Lindsey
Visiting Scholar

John R. Lott Jr.
Resident Scholar

John H. Makin
Resident Scholar; Director,
Fiscal Policy Studies

Allan H. Meltzer
Visiting Scholar

Joshua Muravchik
Resident Scholar

Charles Murray
W. H. Brady Scholar

Michael Novak
George Frederick Jewett Scholar
in Religion, Philosophy, and Public
Policy; Director, Social and Political
Studies

Norman J. Ornstein
Resident Scholar

Richard Perle
Resident Fellow

Alex J. Pollock
Resident Fellow

Sarath Rajapatirana
Visiting Scholar

Michael Rubin
Resident Scholar

Sally Satel
Resident Scholar

William Schneider
Resident Fellow

Daniel Shaviro
Visiting Scholar

Joel Schwartz
Visiting Scholar

J. Gregory Sidak
Resident Scholar

Radek Sikorski
Resident Fellow; Executive
Director, New Atlantic Initiative

Christina Hoff Sommers
Resident Scholar

Fred Thompson
Visiting Fellow

Peter J. Wallison
Resident Fellow

Scott Wallsten
Resident Scholar

Ben J. Wattenberg
Senior Fellow

John Yoo
Visiting Fellow

Karl Zinsmeister
J. B. Fuqua Fellow; Editor,
The American Enterprise